Gilles Deleuze's
Logic of Sense

For the Russell cousin series

Mathilde

Fenn

Théodore

Rebecca

Xavier

Delphine

Africa

Valentin

Nathan

Declan

Alice

Luca

Gilles Deleuze's
Logic of Sense
A Critical Introduction and Guide

JAMES WILLIAMS

Edinburgh University Press

© James Williams, 2008

Edinburgh University Press Ltd
22 George Square, Edinburgh

Reprinted 2009

Typeset in 11/13pt Monotype Baskerville
by Servis Filmsetting Ltd, Manchester, and
printed and bound in Great Britain by
CPI Antony Rowe, Chippenham, Wilts

A CIP record for this book is available from the British Library

ISBN 978 0 7486 2610 6 (hardback)
ISBN 978 0 7486 2611 3 (paperback)

The right of James Williams
to be identified as author of this work
has been asserted in accordance with
the Copyright, Designs and Patents Act 1988

Contents

Contents

Preface

Deleuze's *Logic of Sense* is, like most of his works, a notoriously difficult book. It is also largely neglected by commentators, who often argue that it is somewhat of an impasse in the Deleuze corpus, the work of a structuralist Deleuze, still under the influence of Lacan and psychoanalysis, two unfortunate aspects which his meeting with Guattari enabled him to get rid of – the real Deleuze, before and after *Logic of Sense*, the vitalist Deleuze, herald of the Bergsonian virtual, of difference, becomings and haecceities, is not found in *Logic of Sense*, an accident in a distinguished philosophical career.

James Williams's book is a welcome answer to this unjust critical *doxa*. By engaging in a close reading of the intricacies of this complex book, which he unravels with admirable lucidity and considerable pedagogic flair, he reconstructs a fascinating, and still urgently needed, philosophical project, and puts up a spirited defence of the concepts that Deleuze develops in this book, and almost nowhere else in his works: series, sense, events, etc.

James Williams has an amazing talent for extracting simple and important questions out of an apparently abstruse argument: he does so at regular intervals, so that the reader has the comforting conviction (which, thanks to Williams is not sheer illusion) to grasp Deleuze's argument as it unfolds and to share in his intelligence.

Now that the quasi-totality of Deleuze's work has been translated and that we may understand the complexity in the development of his thought, the time has come to do justice to the important step in this development that *Logic of Sense* embodies. James Williams's book, therefore, is not only welcome: it is necessary. It will be essential reading for whoever wants to master Deleuze's philosophical project.

Jean-Jacques Lecercle

Acknowledgements

I am grateful to the British Academy for a grant supporting my research on Deleuze, Péguy and the event in Orléans in January to June 2007. Dundee University supported this book through research leave and support for my postgraduates, notably through successive PhD scholarship schemes, alongside grants from the Arts and Humanities Research Council and the Overseas Research Students Award Scheme. The School of Humanities provided essential conference travel grants. This work benefited greatly from research with my current PhD students working on Deleuze across many fields (Yannis Chatzantonis, Tim Flanagan, Jenny Kermally, Fabio Presutti, Brian Smith and Dominic Smith). Their research took mine in unexpected directions and I hope to have helped their theses as much as they did my book. I have run undergraduate projects and dissertations on Deleuze for many years now; each of these projects has shown me new reaches for Deleuze's thought and novel problems and criticisms to be addressed. I am in debt to every student for the risks taken and the successes achieved in those projects. My work on *Logic of Sense* owes much to the research and support of many colleagues working in fine art, politics, education, design, nursing, medicine, languages, philosophy, literature, sociology, geography, architecture and history (and many other areas). It would be invidious to single out a subset of this group of friends, but I thank them all for the challenges they have drawn up and the ideas they have developed. If there are still academics out there working under the delusion that creative critical thinking has not taken a new and important turn, all they need to know is that somewhere near them there is sure to be a novel series of Deleuzian events underway:

Acknowledgements

conservatives and lovers of fixed identities beware. In Appendix IV of *Logic of Sense*, Deleuze speaks of the encounter with other individuals as the expression of a possible world we do not have access to except through their sensations and sense. As always this process is dual, and any potential owes everything to communicating emotions – Claire.

Note on references

In the text, references to *Logic of Sense* and *Logique du sens* are given in the following form (LoS, English page reference, French page reference). All dates for Deleuze's works given in the text refer to the original edition; translation dates and details are provided in the Bibliography.

1

Introduction to the logic of sense

EVENT AND STRUCTURE

First published in 1969, Gilles Deleuze's *Logic of Sense* is about the relations of events to series. It is a book on the cusp between structuralism and poststructuralism because it seeks to combine a concern with structures and series with a philosophy of events. Structuralism can be seen as searching for fixed patterns of relations that allow us to identify and explain different related things, for example repeated configurations in social practices within a culture or across different cultures. Events introduce change and differences within those structures, thus the event of a variation in a social practice draws a society out of line with known and expected patterns; it introduces difference and novelty. 'Series' is the key concept for understanding the scope and function of Deleuze's philosophical move. For him, an event runs through series in structures, transforming them and altering relations of sense along the series. According to this view an event, such as the beginning of a book, is never an absolutely new start, it is rather a change in waves resonating through series. This event is never simply an occurrence for the mind of a conscious human being. It is rather a set of multiple interactions running through bodies, ideal structures (such as languages or moral codes) and virtual structures (such as relations of emotional investment considered in abstraction from the bodies that carry them – changes in the ratios of the intensities of fear and attraction in a new relationship, for instance).

Deleuzian events must not therefore be confused with completely new occurrences, like an entirely new beginning or an absolute

1

historical break. Nor must they be confused with completely new entities, such as something hitherto unseen or the arrival of something considered unthinkable. Though we may speak of these things, they are not the event proper. *As an event, a beginning must be understood as a novel selection in ongoing and continually altering series.* Examples of events could be a set of animals altering course due to climatic change, or politically disinterested citizens woken from apathy by events, or the slow silting of a river strangling a port and its estuary into decay. In each of these cases there is a change that includes many continuing series of processes; the event has an impact thanks to its capacity to run along many different strands. In order to think through these complex relations, Deleuze uses the resources from his many early studies in the history of philosophy (on Hume, Nietzsche, Kant and Bergson) and from his own original philosophy that gives priority to difference over identity and to repetitions of variations over sameness. Deleuze's work on sense responds to the problems set by the questions 'What happens to these series, when an event resonates through them?' and 'How must these series be structured in order to allow for events and yet also for the continuity and connectedness of all series?'

According to Deleuze, an event is a two-sided selection, something that runs through a series but that is also transformed by it. Here, two-sidedness or resonance means an interaction where the event is played out in the series but also where the series carry and transform the event. Series are not inert and passive receivers of an excitation, like a chain of marbles transferring movement to one another or a patch of mud impacted by a hard projectile. They transform themselves with the event that has selected them, like an emulsion where two substances that cannot be blended form a temporary novel mix while drawing energy from an external excitation. If we see events as essentially involving an unchanging force or object and a malleable recipient, we misunderstand the importance of series as ongoing variations. According to this philosophy, each marble is altering and the hardness of any external projectile is only relative, it too is bending, though imperceptibly from some points of view. *No event is one-sided and no event is limited since they take place in infinite and multiple series that only exist as continuing mutual variations.*

For Deleuze, these ongoing transformations are non-linear through time and discontinuous through well-ordered spaces. This means that the relations cannot be plotted on a timeline that goes continuously from past to future, nor located as points in a continuous and well-ordered space. This explains the extent of innovative work done on time and the surprising elision of references to standard spaces in *Logic of Sense* in favour of novel work on thought as topological and diagrammatic. In order to free his concept of the series from a mapping on to linear timelines, where series would become time-sequences, Deleuze splits time according to two new concepts, Aiôn and Chronos, both of which resist linearity and continuity in time (though a different use of continuity is very important for him). So series must not be confused with sequences, that is they cannot be subjected to a prior ordering (first, second, third). In order to render well-ordered space secondary to series, Deleuze also removes references to space as a prior receptacle for series and for events. Spaces are constituted by series and events – rather than containing them (this claim is developed to its full potential, much later, in Deleuze and Guattari's *A Thousand Plateaus* through the concepts of territorialisation and deterritorialisation, and stratified and smooth space).

For instance, if viewed according to Deleuze's study of the two-way relation of structures to events, the evolution of species and alterations in individuals due to climate change must be accompanied by changes in sense. To use one of his favoured terms for sense, different associated 'pure differences' or values, such as 'to consume – good' and 'to diminish in number – bad', alter in intensity, in their potential for significance, as their relations alter when they are expressed in the species and environmental variations. My use of the term 'value' is explanatory here and throughout this book: we can think of sense as introducing value or meaning into a neutral system. We must not, though, think that 'value' can be restricted to any given set of values, a 'good' set or a set of 'goods'. Nor must we think that Deleuze's 'sense' is a form of linguistic meaning. It is closer to significance rather than meaning, that is to the way in which meaning matters or makes things matter. This difference is tricky to convey and explains Deleuze's innovative terminology, because he wants to expand linguistic meaning and significance to include changes in the relations of value-terms we associate with events. So my use of value should be quickly overtaken by a broader meaning of pure differences as any variation independent of identified varying objects (for example, as captured by the infinitives 'to consume', 'to diminish', 'to shrink').

When citizens resist and modify the political turmoil that envelops them they change its value and themselves. Neither an estuary nor a port are submissive recipients of changes in river flows, they exploit new opportunities and struggle against the silting of their ongoing life-forms, thereby implying different senses and values in the changes in flow. These 'pure variations' of sense in two-way processes are the hardest aspect of the series and event relation to understand. In terms of the estuary example, they mean that the actual physical processes have effects beyond their physical environment by changing relations between values (sense). This underpins the capacity of variations to have an impact way beyond their immediate context. It also implies that physical changes – Deleuze calls them actualisations and differenciations – must be seen as incomplete without their effect on pure differences. Metaphorically, we can say that sense flows through actual things; it is changed when they change, but it changes all actual things when it varies. The extinction of a species is a neutral event if considered without values or sense; the sense of the extinction therefore brings something essential to the physical process by allowing it to be differentiated – *not an indifferent extinction, but this significant one, here, reverberating forward and back in time.* However, the values themselves change in terms of their interconnections each time they are expressed in a given actualisation. For example, when sea minks actually become extinct, the sense associated with wearing their fur and the sense associated with all hunting change in terms of their internal relations: things that once were easily thinkable and bearable become much harder. Indeed, the sense of what was once done also changes (steps on the way to the disaster are revealed as such) as does the sense of what will yet come (changes in sense accompanying an extinction condition what can be thought in future). This is one way to understand Deleuze's innovations in the philosophy of time in terms of paradoxical relations between two times, Aiôn and Chronos: he needs a time for sense to move through and a time for actual occurrences, but he also needs these to be in contact without reducing their difference.

The components of sense – the pure variations – do not change in themselves. The intensity of their multiple relations does. There is always a 'to hunt' as a component of sense, but its relations to other verbs 'to wear', 'to eat', 'to take pleasure' alter with actual extinctions or abundance. This explains his apparently contradictory statements about sense, that it changes and does not, or that it is pure and yet in contact with actual things, or that sense is everywhere yet also different from actual things. Intensities of relations change in the realm of sense, but the relations themselves are eternal. Series of actual things are incomplete without variations in the intensity of sense, and, as a varying realm, sense is incomplete

4

without actual changes. Much of the technical work in *Logic of Sense* is designed to allow these statements to work, for example in allowing for different forms of causality that do not flatten sense and actual things onto each other according to a single uniform causal law. One of the most important sources of this technical work is the book Deleuze published around the same time, *Expressionism in Philosophy,* an intricate study of Spinoza's achievements in maintaining complex relations between substance, attributes and forms without eliminating their differences.

Deleuze's *Logic of Sense* is about the relation of this many-sided view of reality to life understood as a collection of interconnected worlds constituted by series, themselves determined by individual selections. An event and the way it is replayed select a many-sided world in contact with many others. This does not mean that the book is about choice or about consequences. On the contrary, Deleuze's philosophy is perhaps the most important non-reductive contemporary work opposed to the modern foundations of free choices and their judgement through actual or predicted consequences. Selection means the emergence of transformed and connected series, not the deliberate choice of one series or another. This emergence it itself always open to new evaluations and dependent on individual perspectives – no consequential judgement has the last word on it. Deleuzian selection is not a free choice, it is a two-way individuating path running through series. This may well involve choices, but they will not be a pure or independent foundation for the path. It may well also involve consequential judgements, but again, these will neither provide the final justification nor explanation for the paths.

Multiple interconnected series surround selections and, when considered as a complete set, these constitute an undetermined chaos. This explains the necessity of individuating selection in providing a relative order over a grounding chaos. The event, understood as a selection in series, is therefore also two-sided in terms of determinacy and chaos: it highlights a zone, but it also spreads what happens at that zone along all other series and back again, granting a form of determinacy against an accompanying chaotic background. (This explains Deleuze's frequent references to chaos and to a chaotic cosmos, a 'chaosmos', for example, with Félix Guattari in *What Is Philosophy?*) It also explains the odd claims about multiple connected worlds rather than a single one, since different events and individuating selections determine different worlds related through sense (which can perform this relation without making all the worlds the same, due to its separateness, as described above). When members of a species alter course their movement impacts on a world; habitats are consumed and food chains disturbed. 'To consume' and 'to disturb' are two pure variations, in the usage developed by Deleuze. They are 'sense' expressed as a value or emotion and extended beyond a given location. This sense is akin to an affect or mood that can invest very distant and apparently distinct phenomena with a similar sense – an unshakeable feeling of pointlessness or enthusiasm spreading far from an initial occurrence, for example. So though the focus on those members at that point is a contingent selection of an event, the determinations that follow through all other series have necessary characteristics. Deleuze's book investigates these characteristics and their necessity as properties of the reverberation of intense events, selections and valuations through structures of relations. That's why it is *logic* of sense.

Here, 'logic' does not have its familiar meaning of a deductive system in a formal language, because the series that Deleuze describes are not formal and fixed but rather fluid and changing. His search is for the relatively stable structural patterns that will allow us to work with the effects of events as they run through all structures. One of the more stable rules that he charts is that these effects are resistant to repeatable deductions. *Events do not flow through series with the repeatable certainty of formal logical inference.* A good way of understanding why this is the case can be found in the accompanying chaos cited above: when an event occurs it must do so in relation to something incalculable, a chaos that alters the effect. Any necessity explained by Deleuze is therefore not one of secure deductive outcomes but of characteristics governing the effects of events. We cannot be sure of the outcomes of events, but we can describe where and how they have reverberated. However, even this description must take account of the unrepeatable quality of events in relation to series. It is only by taking events and series up creatively in novel situations that we can relate them to other occurrences. This explains Deleuze's constant insistence on the importance of creativity, for example, in *Difference and Repetition* and *What Is Philosophy?* The logic of sense can neither deduce nor promise outcomes.

Deleuze's *Logic of Sense* is wide-ranging, since it charts many different effects in many different connected fields. It is also conceptually innovative and rich, and hence complex, because he has sought to provide names and descriptions of underlying processes that are very rarely the focus of our attention. This is due to the historical dominance in philosophy of fixed rules for formal languages rather than of changing patterns across series. We therefore tend to look for valid and timeless arguments, rather than for ever-changing and contingent patterns. (It is worth noting that Deleuze does not think that, despite all its empiricism, science is immune from this search for permanence or from the dominance of fixed logical and deductive systems.) These factors make the book hard to approach on a first reading and I give detailed solutions to this difficulty in the next section. At this stage, it is important to stress that its difficulty and originality stem from the novelty of the task. It is as if Deleuze had set the challenge of answering a practical and edifying question such as 'What practical remedies can we deduce from the manner fear and hatred flow through the populations of these actual nations?' rather than a theoretical question like 'What are the valid logical steps that lead to true conclusions about fear?' The first question is experimental and messy, whereas the second is more clear-cut and independent of experience. The first question commits learning to an ongoing transforming process whereas the latter provides firm blocks of knowledge and capacities. This distinction is reflected in Deleuze's work through its many observed fields and in its multiple and complex essays on descriptions and patterns. It is also reflected in his book's resistance to a closed logical consistency, which it replaces by a series of problematic paradoxes connected by partial and differently problematic responses. The book is designed to puzzle and to unsettle at the same time as it explains and resolves. As such, it prefigures Deleuze's later works with Félix Guattari and their wide-ranging social and political pragmatic descriptions, allied to series of theoretical innovations: *Anti-Oedipus* (1972), *Kafka: Toward a Minor Literature* (1975), *A Thousand Plateaus* (1980) and *What Is Philosophy?* (1991).

LIFE AND MORALS

In Deleuze's account of series and events, life is *only* constituted by series and events, that is by wave-like alterations running through series of relations. To occur at all any event highlights some changing relations and makes others dimmer. This stress on distinctness *and* obscurity, against the Cartesian clarity and distinctness, is a recurrent theme of Deleuze's work. 'Distinct and obscure' comes from *Difference and Repetition* (1969); related forms include 'figure and diagram', from his work on Francis Bacon, *The Logic of Sensation* (1981), or 'tree and rhizome' from *A Thousand Plateaus*. The inseparability of distinctness and obscurity in series leads to a focus on

7

connections and shifts in emphasis, rather than to clear analytical distinctions. Selections and events are not cuts and abstractions. Instead, they must be cuts, connections, shadings and highlights, where none of these terms is separable from the others. In the philosophy put forward in *Logic of Sense*, any analytical cut, any final distinction, any absolute difference between terms must be an incomplete approach to life, that is an approach fated to miss more subtle and significant differences in emphasis and intensity. *No living problem is clear-cut and no strict distinction ever really solves a problem in life.*

This leads to another way of understanding Deleuze's new definition of 'sense' and the connections drawn through the thirty-four series of *Logic of Sense*. Sense is the marker of increases and decreases of intensity, the *rise in the strength* of thirst driving a Northern drift, or *the increases or decreases* in desires accompanying physical and environmental attunement and discord, or *the choking* of the flow of water, *the stifling* of trade and the accompanying *amplification* of misery as a once great city slowly dies. The sense of such events lies then not in objective series, but in the changing flows that invest them with value. Deleuze often describes pure differences or sense through infinitives such as the 'to diminish' I used in the previous section. As sense, these infinitives must also be understood as involving relations of intensity with other pure differences: the intensity of 'to diminish' changing in relation to 'to rise'. This shift to sense as disembodied and as situated on a virtual 'surface' as opposed to the 'depth' of objects, to use two key terms from the book, should not be seen as a flight to abstraction and a lack of care for the physical incisions and punctures that accompany pain and generate desire. Both such forms of abstraction would contradict the connections his philosophy depends upon. For Deleuze, life is depth *and* surface; it is value *and* its actualisation in physical series. Yet, equally, the essential role given to depth should not be seen as leading to an essential role for objects; these only carry a slight role within varying series. It is the series of variations across objects that matters; objects only play a role as tokens for kinds of variations. The object allows the series to be identified, in the meaning of approached initially, but the puncturing or wounding of depth is carried by value, as a variation along the series, and not as frozen state of objective matter.

Logic of Sense is therefore a book about two sides of events captured in the distinction made between surface and depth. One of the important recurrent patterns that the book describes is a difference drawn between these terms, or between the expression of

events in bodies and their expression in values, themselves understood through Deleuze's new concept of sense. An event sets off 'parallel' and interconnected processes through surface series and
depth series, for example through an ascription of surface-value (*the
intensities of 'to fear', 'to flee' and 'to hate' are increasing in unison*) alongside effects in depth-bodies (*under threat of war the nation came under
the grip of fear, lost its tolerance and its capacity for empathy waned*). This
concern with the relations of surface and depth in the context of
events gives the book an important attention to how life should be
lived when events strike. Where humans are implicated, this can be
read, cautiously, as lending a moral dimension to the book. This is
not in the often specialist and isolated form of modern moral and
ethical debate around paradigmatic questions in moral philosophy,
such as 'Is euthanasia wrong?' or 'Are correctable imbalances in
wealth morally justified?' Instead, another key aspect of Deleuze's
philosophy directs his moral enquiry: practical answers in response
to events follow from the philosophical roles of selection and of the
interconnection of series. A moral attitude must be a creative selection and interaction with an event, that is an individual combination
of activity and passivity that responds to and triggers other series. It
asks localised questions such as 'Should we select euthanasia here?'
and then only answers temporarily through actions against a background of ever wider circles of problems that it does not pretend to
solve, but rather moves on creatively.

Given Deleuze's commitment to the connection of series, each
'moral' selection must have unlimited effects and causes in the series
it interacts with. So there are no pre-set boundaries for a selection,
both in terms of what leads to it and in terms of what follows. This
explains why a piecemeal and general approach to moral questions
fits poorly with Deleuzian thought, since both the cutting away from
a wider set of considerations and the move to a widely applicable
level of generality deny the prior conditions for his understanding
of events and selections. Had we a taste for labels, we should call his
combination of connection and selection 'problem-based moral
holism'. However, such categorising expressions run counter to
Deleuze's philosophy, by creating distinct groups that fail to fully
reflect what they are supposed to contain. Problems are the prior
ground in Deleuze's approach; they are driven by tensions between
connection and individuation, and between events and series.
Individuation is the selection that allows distinctness to appear in
the series. It can be compared to the way events require an individual perspective (as conveyed by the preliminary moral question

'What does it mean for me and for them?') but only if we remember that neither selection nor events have a necessary human focus for Deleuze. Individuation is a process of determination in series in relation to events and to a chaotic background; it must not be confused with the decisions of individuals.

Problems are a counter-intuitive ground for Deleuze's philosophy, since they determine an uncertainty or lack of grounding that is itself determined according to the relation between an individual path and its events. We therefore have an ever-shifting ground rather than a solid foundation. This thought avoids finding general solutions to common moral questions followed by a softening of that generality in particular applications. Instead, his moral philosophy focuses on individuating responses to problems, themselves determined by events. These responses are then situated in, and must necessarily take account of, many other series and individuations. The key contrast is between a prior abstraction and a prior selection, where the former depends on the legitimacy of its claims to validly represent common questions and solutions, and the latter depends on being able to hold together individuation and common effects without reducing them to one another. It is therefore important to note that 'effect' and 'cause' are given new and wide-ranging definitions, as well as parallel innovative terms, in *Logic of Sense*. It is even more important to note that 'individual' here has nothing to do with an individual subject or actor, but describes the way a selection picks out an individual path through multiple series; it is a process, an individuation, rather than an identified originator, a subject and self.

A version of Deleuze's life (or moral) problem is then: *How is life to be lived here (on this individuating path through series) with these relations of surface and depth, and these events?* This is a moral concern with balances of ongoing struggles and cooperations, desires and repulsions, injuries and benefits, in an individually selected and event-driven context. It stresses individuating paths through shared situations, where no single rule can govern, but where each path is implicated in all others. Thus the traditional 'either individual, or collective' opposition is not valid for understanding what Deleuze means by individuation. An individuation is necessarily collective and implicates all series, but in an individual way. A collective is necessarily a collective of interacting individuations rather than their reduction to a collection of members brought under a universal rule, or sharing universal properties, or belonging to the same class. Deleuze's life problems are then responded to, among others, by

plant mutations, human decisions, geological shifts and animal evolutions, where the isolation of any one of these as the privileged
source of either the problem or the solution is necessarily mistaken
about the nature of the interconnected relations of events, series,
individuals and structural patterns. This is why it can be called a
moral holism – kept from a universalising reductionism by the individuation of problems. This work on questions of life and events
explains the amount of work on the Stoics in *Logic of Sense*, in terms
of the importance of events to moral attitudes and in terms of the
situation of such attitudes within wider theories of nature. However,
in reading his work on Stoicism, it is crucial not to settle with the misleading image of the philosophies of, say, Chrysippus or Marcus
Aurelius as leading to a resignation to events. On the contrary,
Deleuze's view of Stoicism is rather that we should (and living things
do) replay events such that we neither deny them nor, though, deny
the truths they hold for us.

Deleuze returns to the Stoics in order to trace relations of
dependency between accounts of nature, moral recommendations
and individuating responses to events. His view of life and of moral
problems stresses that none of these can be treated as prior to or
independent of the others. Individuating selections are necessary,
but they take place in shared natural patterns. Individual paths
within natural patterns respond to events that they neither control
nor escape – in any domain. This is a view of life that refuses causal
and statistical determination, *and* human freedom. It replaces them
with four interlocked conditions for the relation between series and
events:

1. The determination of series through problematic structural patterns.
2. The openness of series through the selection of individuating
   paths.
3. The determination of series by events that exceed their patterns.
4. The individuating selection of paths through a creative doubling
   or counter-actualisation of events.

These conditions can seem quite abstract and philosophically daunt-
ing, so here is a more approachable, though less precise version:

1. Life is determined by structural patterns running through series.
2. Individuating paths are not fully determined by those patterns
   and the patterns are incomplete and hollow when not determined by individuating paths.

11

3. Individuating paths are determined by events.
4. This determination is a two-way process where the sense of the event only emerges as the individuating path replays the event by acting it out anew.

What follows is a version applied to Deleuze's concern with events as wounds (a concern he shares with the Stoics). This must be treated with caution since wounds and injuries lead us very quickly into a model of events that he wants to resist (that is, a wound as represented in an individual human consciousness that then tries to cure itself). It is safer to think of a wound, in Deleuze's meaning, as a deep-seated factor that makes a given individual path different in positive and negative ways. A wound is then a rare event and a form of destiny, rather than the many injuries that assail a life without determining it (including deadly ones). If events are wounds, then:

1. How wounds run through nature is subject to problematic patterns.
2. These patterns only explain the general 'how' of a wound and not the 'why' of a wound (its significance) or its 'where from' and 'where to' (its destiny).
3. The 'why', 'where from' and 'where to' only appear when the wound is an event in an individuating path.
4. In order to be an event a wound must be worked through creatively in an individuating path, that is change and be changed by the path.

Finally, we could tentatively translate these conditions into a more traditional set of guiding moral questions for responding to a given situation. These have to be questions rather than imperatives in order to avoid contradicting the problematic structure of Deleuze's thought. A precept, command or imperative would give the philosophy an unproblematic heart at odds with his commitment to experimentation in response to problematic events. When struck by a moral challenge, a challenge about how to live, we might ask:

1. How does a problematic series of emotional, ideal and physical tensions determine this situation?
2. How is the situation still open to reinvigorating change?
3. Which events trigger sense or value here?
4. How shall these events be replayed?

These questions must not be seen as addressed to a particular human being or even type of consciousness. When foxes or seagulls adapt to city life, they are responding to questions and to problems. Nor must the questions be taken as allowing for a sufficient comprehension. The Deleuzian view of problems and his definition of the event is that they must be in part imperceptible and in part resistant to perfect or complete solutions, whether cognitive or not.

The combination of these conditions explains some of the most moving passages of *Logic of Sense* in their insistence on the necessity of events and on the potential they offer for open and reviving transformations. This is because the commitment to structural patterns allows Deleuze to remain within a natural and immanent philosophy, with no otherworldly sources, mysticism or consolations. Things are naturally determined. However, the commitment to sense avoids the reductive aspects of such natural explanations, because things are also individuated. Yet they are not individual through dependence on human freedom or godly intervention, but through the way events determine different individuals and the way different individuals replay their determining events, against any notion of pure freedom. Here, too, there is space for a resistance to a full and closed determination because the event only makes sense when it is affirmed and transformed. Deleuze's logic articulates the competing demands of pattern, individuation, destiny and openness through an affirmation of the event:

> Either morality is senseless, or it means this and nothing more: not to be unworthy of what happens to us. To grasp what happens to us as unjust and unmerited (it is always someone's fault) is, on the contrary, what makes our wounds repugnant – this is resentment in person, resentment against the event.
>
> (LoS, 149, 174–5)

The event is only affirmed when it is not denied or blamed on external necessity or on free acts. To be worthy of the event is therefore to work with it, in Deleuze's words, to redouble or 'counteractualise' it, not through any negation but by replaying it differently in all series.

READING LOGIC OF SENSE

Logic of Sense is difficult. The book has an intricate and experimental style, it is conceptually rich and unusual, and it contains radical and revolutionary ideas. So why bother? There are two strong reasons for persisting with the book despite its resistance to new readers, whether they are well-versed in philosophy or not, Deleuze experts or not. First, *Logic of Sense* plays a crucial role in bridging between Deleuze's most philosophically important single-authored text, *Difference and Repetition*, and his later contributions to a very wide set of fields (cinema, literature, philosophy, politics, political science, cultural criticism, sociology, aesthetics and art, to name a few). The book is therefore crucial in connecting his metaphysics and his ontology of difference and repetition to their later practical developments – including the reassessment of the concept of practice itself. Second, *Logic of Sense* is one of the main books for understanding Deleuze's philosophy in three central areas: moral philosophy, philosophy of language and what is sometimes known as philosophy of mind, but here must be called philosophy of thought and of the unconscious (the two cannot be treated separately in his work). In these areas, Deleuze's philosophy is as original as it is significant and provides a carefully reasoned foil to some of the dominant strands of contemporary theory.

There is also, though, a less 'central' reason to read Deleuze's book, yet perhaps a more meaningful one. *Logic of Sense* is artistic and humorous. This may seem a very strange assertion to make about a complex work of philosophy, and even more strange when we casually open it looking for one-liners or romantic poetry, but if we approach the book without taking account of the roles played by humour and aesthetic innovation in the writing and claims of the book, then we will have missed crucial aspects of its content and rewarding aspects of its style. Construction and gaiety (and also pathos) can greatly aid a reading of *Logic of Sense* by underpinning reading strategies informed by a set of apparently more lofty concerns. Put simply, the style and humour of the book are inherent in its philosophical message. Or, more strongly, *Logic of Sense* asserts that it is only with humour and creative experimentation that its deepest insights can be conveyed. It is a book to skip and stumble through rather than methodically plod or grind. Deleuze's surprising discussion of Lewis Carroll and his detailed study of *Alice's Adventures in Wonderland* are therefore not only designed to illustrate some of the kinds of series and events that are helpful in understanding his version of the logic of sense. The discussions reflect the importance of humour and paradoxical series in freeing sense from its most common contexts and meanings. *Logic of Sense* needs the resources of humorous 'nonsense' and puzzlingly interlocked series to break the barriers raised by serious expectations. A grave reading that fails to reflect the book's playfulness could easily founder, either on a superior but foolish dismissal or in disappointed frustration. The following points give an outline of different reading strategies that may be helpful in an approach to Deleuze's book in terms of its original form.

Order and series

The use of series as opposed to chapters in *Logic of Sense* is significant. In most books, the order of the chapters is important and resistant to jumbling or to skipping. This is not the case for series, since these are designed to operate in different orders and as independent blocks or connected chains. Though the series follow on from one another in some key ways, and though in some sense all the series are connected, they also operate independently of the order they are presented in. The connections between series are not order-dependent. It is therefore perfectly legitimate to open the book pretty much where it suits the reader's motivations and then to follow a pattern through the book that reflects different desires and capacities. More importantly, this means that a strategy of 'if stuck skip' will reap much better dividends than 'pummel away until tears of frustration flow'. Keep reading and skipping until something catches. When it does, the hook will always lead to further connections and there will be less risk of error and certainly more fun than in a last chance power read from beginning to end. Note also that if the catch is a question or problem that recurs through the book, then the reading will have discovered a key lesson of the logic of sense: series are set in motion by a problematic element ('a mobile empty place') that runs through them. This mobile factor will be discussed at length through this book. At this stage, all that needs to be stressed is that readers can bring their own elements to Deleuze's series in order to move among them.

Series within series

The point about the order and disorder between members of series is also true for the ordering inside any given member, which is itself also a series. Leibniz's very beautiful statement about monads is useful for understanding this internal complexity: 'Every portion of matter can be thought of as a garden full of plants, or as a pond full of fish. But every branch of the plant, every part of the animal, and every drop of its vital fluids, is another such garden, or another such pond' (Leibniz, 1998: 68). Deleuze writes so that all his series of concepts and arguments can be found in each of the others, though more or less explicitly, that is more or less distinctly. He is putting forward a philosophy of radical connection, but opposing a definition of connection as necessarily well-ordered and external, that is as ordered by reference to an external source such as a rule, a set of laws or a type. In his *Difference and Repetition* and later texts such as *The Fold: Leibniz and the Baroque* (1988), Deleuze describes his internal connection as the folding of ideas and things within one another. This is a useful account of the processes at work within *Logic of Sense*, since many folds provide paths through the series. Thanks to the helpful index in the English edition and through the series titles and extensive subtitles, readers can traverse the book by following concepts, themes and ideas as they unfold in different series. It is noteworthy that this reading strategy mimics the roles of individuation, event and series in the main thesis of the text. The reader's desires and associated motivations are the event that connects the series of the book with external series, thereby drawing out a path through the texts, this path is then an individuation that cannot be exactly the same as any other reading, but interferes and intersects with others. It is not a contradiction, here, to affirm this plurality of readings through an overall commentary; I am suggesting ways into Deleuze's text and not a final law or interpretation.

Like Leibniz's pond, series are always series of series within other series; all connect internally and with different degrees of development and distinctness. This means that two apparently opposed reading strategies work well together. It is fine to omit, but so long as at a certain point a section of text is studied in fine detail with a critical and creative approach. So the section that is read does not matter from the point of view of *Logic of Sense*, but it is important from the point of view of the reader. This is what is meant by creative and critical: start with a section of text that is of interest through other sources and questions that you are more familiar with; subject the text to critical and creative study, in the sense of setting the new connections outside the book to work; raise objections to Deleuze's arguments, yet also seek to provide illuminating contacts. This combination of creativity and critique allows for a reading that avoids two very common pitfalls. It is a mistake – yet very easy – to dismiss his work for 'obvious' lack of clarity or contradiction. I will show through this book that there are always counters to such dismissals, not least in a thorough critique of the role of the concept of contradiction in philosophy. This is not to say that Deleuze is always right, quite the contrary. All great philosophies are open to critique and out of tune with many contemporary ways of living, but the reasons they are wrong or absurdly dissonant are never simple or crude, because philosophy, with all its internal paradoxes and conflicts, is at stake in constituting and in challenging that supposedly external simplicity.

The other common mistake runs counter to the first. It is to treat Deleuze's work as law, as a sacred philosopher's stone that can be set alongside any other source and suddenly turn it into shining truth. This approach can only do harm both to Deleuze's work, by hiding its inherent flaws and problems, and to the external subject, by pretending that its inherent historical problems and difficulties can be resolved at a stroke, once we look at them through the right Deleuzian lens. This approach to Deleuze is mere wishful thinking and conceals repressive political desires behind a dissenting fad. Critique applied to even our most heartfelt beliefs is the only true dissent. *Logic of Sense* teaches the opposite to an uncritical approach; thought is about shared problems that overlap but cannot be reduced to one another. A prior concern needs to be brought to the book but with passion, scepticism and creativity. For these reasons it is perhaps not the first book by Deleuze to read, but equally, the deeper an engagement with his thought or with problems that he thinks through, the more likely that a close study of *Logic of Sense* will be required and rewarding.

Humour

Series 19 of *Logic of Sense* argues for the importance of humour in thought and life, not as an add-on, as some kind of desirable but inessential quality, but as a central aspect of philosophical teaching and learning. What role does humour play in learning? How does it work? Deleuze's argument is that some things can only be learnt with humour because they are resistant to rational demonstration and to forms of propositional understanding (the communication of a meaning and of a state of affairs, for example). Humour helps us to sense that meaning is not the point of certain forms of communication and that reason has limits that do not define a boundary with nonsense or absurdity, but with a different kind of sense allied to 'non-sense' and to paradox. In order to show this, humour cannot simply appeal to rational demonstration and to straightforward meaning. Instead, it combines physical actions with puzzlement and emotional change alongside a showing of the failure of reason and of transparent meaning. Deleuze takes instances from the Stoics and from Buddhist teaching to illustrate his point. When a pupil asks a master a difficult question, the answer takes some rational components and meanings from the question, but sets them in a comical and baffling situation: 'When Plato gives "featherless biped" as the signified of man, Diogenes the Cynic answers by throwing a plucked cockerel' (LoS, 135, 159). The bafflement, physical aspect, disquiet and laughter are essential to the lesson: they encourage the pupils to look for their own responses; they teach them that the question was in some ways unanswerable and fell beside the problem; they introduce a strong discomfort; and they trigger a life-affirming physical and emotional reaction.

Humour matters because we have to feel that some of the expectations of the question were mistaken, not in a way that could be corrected or refined, but in a more persistent manner: it was the wrong kind of question to ask and the wrong kind of answer to expect. This feeling is positive; it does not simply indicate that no answer is possible, rather, it gives physical clues to follow and, through laughter or sobs or both, it generates the desire and energy required for the task. This explains the necessity of the physical element of humour, though this could well be the literary expression of a physical moment rather than the moment itself. There has to be a physical – a bodily – moment to add to a purely intellectual one for the following reasons:

1. to show that there is something more than rational deductions and intellectual understanding;
2. to show that this something more is a material event;
3. to associate this material inscription with an emotional one;
4. to generate an affirmative charge that runs through each replaying of the initial event.

These reasons also explain Deleuze's suspicion of philosophical irony when compared to humour. Irony can lead to the same critique of reason, but it does not have the fully affirmative power of humour, replacing it instead with the danger of a nihilistic cynicism. Deleuze's view is that the ironist has nowhere to go when compared to the comedian, because the former closes down new possibilities while negating old ones.

According to Deleuze, in *Logic of Sense*, irony is a valuable but closed and tragic intellectual art, whereas humour is an open and affirmative physical one. The openness is afforded by a refusal to separate sense from nonsense, whereas irony deploys the promise of a higher sense against a failed lower one. Affirmation in humour is achieved by avoiding the security of self-identity and the power of representation – the self-aware swagger and descriptive verve of the ironic stance – in favour of mobile and disjointed series, synthesised briefly when a point runs through them:

> The tragic and the ironic give way to a new value, that of humour. For if irony is the co-extensiveness of being with the individual, or of the I with

representation, humour is the co-extensiveness of sense with nonsense; humour is the art of surfaces or doubles, of nomad singularities and of an always displaced aleatory point.

(LoS, 141, 166)

Irony displaces once, but humour and Deleuze's writing perform ongoing and multiple displacements. They refuse the final tragic resting place of irony, tragic because it settles on the breaking promise of the wholeness of existence, of nature or of a self-knowing 'I'. This explains the value given to nomadic movement in the above passage and, indeed, in many of Deleuze's works (in *A Thousand Plateaus*, for example). It also explains the importance of surfaces and doubles in their resistance to straightforward meaning and identity. Their duplicitous and veiling qualities are not to be viewed as negative deceptions, but as productive reflections of the mobility of reality.

Deleuze's written works replicate his spoken humour and other vocal differences in tone and presentation. There are many valuable sources for tracing his spoken interventions, notably the written record of his lectures and seminars on the excellent web-deleuze.com resource, the recordings of his seminars and his *Abécédaire* television programme. If a slow interpretation is not working, *Logic of Sense* can be enjoyed as if read by Deleuze or by an actor, that is with differences in emotional tone, with the fading in and out of a voice, periods of clarity but also moments of confusion and inattention. It is written in a style to be taken emotionally, and with puzzlement and amusement, as well as with seriousness and enquiring thought. We can experiment with our versions of Deleuze's or the book's voice and laugh. Its images and references should not only be decrypted and interpreted but sensed and lived through. They should be allowed to disturb, to shock, to sadden and to amuse. For example, here is the last line of series 20 from *Logic of Sense*: 'Starting from a pure event, mimes direct and double actualisation, they measure out mixtures thanks to an instant without mixture, and stop them from overflowing' (LoS, 147, 173). The line *means* that after events occur we have to be like actors or mimes who replay the event in the series it has occurred in. It means that we have to transform the event in same way as an actor transforming a part, or a mime transforming a show in line with audience laughter and participation (*the fear and thrill of standing close to the stage*). According to Deleuze, the event causes physical mixtures, that is it sets off clashes, punctures and wounds. This is what is meant by the depth aspect of the event, but this meaning is incomplete if we do not add

19

an individuating *sense* of the event. In order to express this physical aspect of the event adequately another element must be introduced: the value or sense associated with the event, or why it matters to the reader and mime, that is how it agitates them. These effects are not what any sentence represents in terms of knowledge and understanding, but rather how it *creates a felt sense* through the individual associations of values, images, phantasms and feelings that make an event bearable, or, more precisely, bearable because it is affirmed and transformed. So Deleuze's sentence must be made to do more than what it means. It must be set in motion: we have to be mimes when we read him.

Multidimensional sentences

The above sentence on the mime should then be read with an image of Marcel Marceau, or perhaps beyond Marceau and on to his inspirations in Keaton, Chaplin, Laurel and Hardy, or to new and as yet unexplored comic inventions (thereby connecting to Deleuze's work on film in *Cinema 1* and *Cinema 2*, 1983, 1985, but also to the concept of the productive phantasm that he develops in *Logic of Sense*). Which image or phantasm to follow must be an individual matter, but that there should be a further prompt and a sensual and bodily transfer is essential. Deleuze's style therefore demands a creative experimentation aided by the multidimensional quality of his style. Each sentence is a mixture of philosophical demonstrations and conceptual innovations, with literary and artistic references, with accessible images, with terms from many other disciplines (mathematics, psychoanalysis, literature, structuralism, . . .), with condensed physical metaphors and extremely varied analogies. It is a rich and chaotic style. Deleuze's multidimensional sentences should not be approached for a single meaning or single content, but for a multiple mixture of modes, meanings, physical hooks and emotional connections. For example, here is the first line of the first series of *Logic of Sense*: '*Alice* and *Through the Looking-Glass* involve a category of very special things, events, pure events' (LoS, 1, 9). The sentence has many functions. It starts the book with a puzzle ranging across very different subjects. (Why Alice? Why here? Why events? How can they be pure?) The sentence also has a strong referring function but again with strange juxtapositions (to *Alice's Adventures in Wonderland* and *Through the Looking Glass* but also to philosophical and everyday conceptions of the event). More discretely, the sentence shows Deleuze's humourous use of an assertively descriptive style. He seems to state unequivocally 'This is what *Alice* is about', but how could Deleuze of all people say exactly what a thing is about without allowing for other interpretations? The sentences of *Logic of Sense* often seem to dictate a certain description, but this is only an appearance; the descriptive style is in fact a suspension and should be read as a question, or smiling provocation, rather than the final word on a state of affairs. So the opening sentence means just what it says, but as a process it goes beyond and undermines that meaning. This is because Deleuze holds that every expression is a drama or dramatisation, not only a transfer of meaning but its re-enactment. For a reading to benefit from the power of his work, it needs to follow his lines of enquiry and connections, his questions and problems, rather than just what a sentence means, because sense according to Deleuze is not in what is said, but in what readers allow it to trigger.

PRELIMINARY CRITICAL QUESTIONS

Logic of Sense and Deleuze's philosophy are not only about maximising connections, they are also about the search for coherence across those connections. His commitment to multiplicity and his critique of any grounding role given to formal logic in philosophy (in *Logic of Sense* and then much later with Félix Guattari in *What Is Philosophy?*) could lead to the conclusion that his philosophy eschews consistency in favour of a productive but ultimately incoherent jumble. This is false and leads to a distorting picture of Deleuze's life-work, for example, in terms of his own critical readings of other philosophers through the detection of hidden and inconsistent presuppositions and exclusions in their work (Kant's dependence on a restrictive model of recognition as charted in *Difference and Repetition*, for instance). Deleuze's interpretations are always thorough, seek out the strongest version of a position and attempt to transform a philosophy through surprising links and contrasts. This combination of rigour and inventiveness is also a feature of *Logic of Sense* and comes to the aid of readers and critics alike. Deleuze is a traditional philosopher, in the sense of a powerful innovator and a peerless reader of the history of philosophy, but he is also an outstanding engineer of consistent systems resistant to straightforward flaws. He reserves an important place for paradox in his philosophy, but that place is carefully designed and backed by arguments that justify both its function and limits. An approach to *Logic of Sense* can therefore benefit from an awareness of the types of critical question that Deleuze is responding to through the book, if not overtly, then through his lines of argument.

How can there be the logic of sense without a prior understanding of the logic to be applied and a reference to an agreed form of logic?

In order to answer this question, it is worth making some general but relevant remarks on the translation of Deleuze's book. First, the English translation of *Logique du sens* gives the title as *The Logic of Sense*. I have preferred *Logic of Sense* because the French title is ambiguous about whether we should take it to be a logic (*une logique*) or the logic (*la logique*). Deleuze's philosophy of events does not allow for an external way of determining a final account of things, sometimes called a 'transcendent' or 'meta' position, the last word hovering outside a realm but legislating upon it. Instead, even his metaphysics and certainly his logic has to be considered as a speculative selection occurring in the middle of things. He is proposing *a* logic with a very individual take on things and topics (the works of Scott F. Fitzgerald alongside those of Antonin Artaud, for example). Brian Massumi, the translator of *Mille plateaux*, the later book with Félix Guattari, chooses to resolve the French ambiguity due to the lack of 'these' or 'the' thousand plateaus, between members of a set and the totality, by opting for *A Thousand Plateaus*. In my view a similar approach is justified for *Logic of Sense*, not only for the philosophical reason that there cannot be a sole logic of sense, but also because a reading that approaches the work as '*The*' *Logic of Sense* risks missing an experimental variety of interpretations, ideas, topics and concepts that supports a more creative and loose reading, that is one that constructs its version of the logic of sense taking account of Deleuze's speculative moves. This does not mean that that the current translation of the book is poor. Quite the contrary, Constantin Boundas, Mark Lester and Charles Stivale, the editor and translators, have done an excellent job at an extremely hard task. Nonetheless, Deleuze is giving us *a* logic of sense. But what kind of logic is that?

While *Logic of Sense* is conceptually rigorous and carefully argued, it is not producing a logic that can be separated from the notion of sense; as I have already noted, it is not about a formal logical system. So a reader brought to search for 'the logic' risks disappointment, confusion or a mistaken criticism of the book. This search for a different logic within sense redefined does not mean that the book is illogical or poorly and irrationally argued. It means that its traditional logical steps are not sufficient aspects of its argument; neither can they be easily disentangled, though many will be explained here. Deleuze is explicitly reacting to the limitations imposed by dependencies on logics from earlier philosophies, not only in purely formal models but, for example, in Hegelian logic. This latter logic is described by one of Deleuze's teachers at the Sorbonne, Jean Hyppolite, whose books on Hegel and translation of Hegel's *Phenomenology of Spirit* also insist on the importance of a logic of sense and perhaps inspire a different usage of the phrase 'logic of sense' in Deleuze. There are passages in Hyppolite's *Logic and Existence* (*Logique et existence*, 1952) with similar moves to Deleuze's with respect to sense and logic. Deleuze reviewed Hyppolite's book in 1954 praising its ontological focus on sense. Existence is sense and not to be confused with meaning for humans or with the sense of a deeper essence: 'Being, according to Hyppolite, is not *essence*, but *sense*. To say that this world is sufficient is not only to say that it is sufficient for *us*, but that it is sufficient unto itself, and that it refers to being not as the essence beyond the appearance, not as a second world which would be the intelligible world, but as the sense of this world' (Deleuze, 'Review of Jean Hyppolite, Logique et existence', p. 1). The world or Being is essentially sense, but not only sense *for us*, that is, not linguistic meaning with a set of preset grammatical and logical rules. To be is to matter, to be intensely significant, emotionally significant and existentially determined, prior to the rules that govern social communication and argument. The logic of sense is then not the logic of a language. It is a description of the structures that appear when being is understood as the encounter of events and series.

Deleuze often used his early reviews in his later books. In the case of the Hyppolite review, the careful study of his teacher's work is important for understanding some of the motivations behind *Logic of Sense*, not least why Deleuze chose this title when more accurately descriptive headings like 'Series and Event' or 'Language, Thought and Event' seem more appropriate to the book's material. Content is not what Deleuze is aiming at in choosing his title; instead, he is trying to express one of the central problems at work in the book: how can there be a logic of sense redefined? This problem is captured in Deleuze's early criticism of the limitation imposed by Hyppolite's and Hegel's assertion that the highest logical form is contradiction:

> Can we not construct an ontology of difference which would not have to go up to contradiction, because contradiction would be less than difference and not more? Is not contradiction itself only the phenomenal and anthropological aspect of difference? Hyppolite says that an ontology of pure difference would return us to a purely external and formal

reflection, and would prove in the final analysis to be an ontology of essence. However, the same question could be posed otherwise: is it the same thing to say that Being expresses itself and that it contradicts itself? If it is true that the second and third parts of Hyppolite's book ground a theory of contradiction in Being, where contradiction itself is the absolute of difference, in contrast, in the first part (theory of language) and the allusions throughout the book (to forgetting, to remembering, to lost sense), does not Hyppolite ground a theory of expression where difference is expression itself, and contradiction its merely phenomenal aspect?

(Deleuze, 'Review of Jean Hyppolite, Logique et existence', p. 1)

For Deleuze, logical contradiction comes after a concept of difference, itself paired with variations in repetitions, because contradiction cannot account for difference understood in terms of sense. Against Hyppolite, he affirms that an ontology of pure difference is the only one suited to sense. This explains why Hyppolite's book fails to reconcile the priority it gives to contradiction with its studies of language, forgetting, remembering and loss of sense. To be able to give these processes their due, Hyppolite would have to reinstate pure difference at the expense of contradiction. One of the key sets of cases in *Logic of Sense* concerns contradictions and paradoxes: Deleuze shows how these can make sense despite their logical invalidity (for example, as we shall see in the next chapter, he asserts that Alice is becoming bigger and becoming smaller simultaneously).

The answer to the question about the necessity of a prior understanding of logic is then that Deleuze does not think that it can be prior to sense. Logic is instead a secondary form that accounts for the structures that sense takes place in but only as a 'merely phenomenal aspect'. *Logic of Sense* is therefore an expression of how sense works rather than a straightforward account of a necessary logical structure. It is also a work that proceeds through paradoxes rather than deductions, that is Deleuze extends fields and series into one another through the way they respond to shared paradoxes. *A paradox is then a sign of a disjunction in a given series or structure and a genetic connection to others – paradoxes generate series by introducing connecting forks.* In reading the book, we should not look for necessary inferences, but for speculative proposals about the paradoxical connections of sense, event, logic and series as interlinked processes. This can seem very strange indeed, almost perverse, until we understand that Deleuze is not advocating paradoxes or nonsense for their own sake, but for their role in thought. Moreover, as I shall show in Chapter 5 on thought and the unconscious, thought must be perverse for Deleuze; it must be capable of a flexibility denying proper meanings and functions and recreating others that lay dormant within apparent propriety and blameless convention. Paradoxes matter because they reveal limits within systems and require passages beyond internal rules of validity and consistency. Thought moves on and connects through paradox and Deleuze therefore ascribes a genetic role for it: paradox bears its solutions while affirming their temporary and unsatisfactory nature.

What is a series? How can series communicate?

The first of these questions is not a typically Deleuzian question, since he thinks that philosophy should work with questions based on process (how? why? who?) rather than on identity (what?). However, once translated into a form more amenable to study in terms of processes, the problem of the determinacy of series, rather than of their recognition, becomes a critical one. This problem can be understood if we think of a sandy beach: is the beach basically one series of grains of sand (as a necessary condition for many sub-series)? Is there a limit on the form or number of possible series (in terms of the nature and number of grains of sand, for example)? How can we decide on potential series (can we trace anything we like)? Are series determined strictly within the beach, or do they require an external catalyst (the way the retreating tide leaves gullies and ridges, for example)? Or are there really no series at all (merely sets or groups)? Could we have the series without the beach (or is the boundary a necessary condition)? Does it make sense to speak of the series independent of a viewing consciousness that picks them out (the way our eyes or toes pick out a path in the wet sand)? In other words, are series really prior to other things and, if they are, how do series work in relation to one another and to events?

Many of the technical terms in *Logic of Sense* respond to this kind of question. They do so because Deleuze wants to avoid a set of answers running counter to his primary affirmation (*Life is series individuated by events and their re-enactment*). This affirmation is the source of many of his difficulties. For example, if the grains of sand are necessary for series and impose limits on them, then series are no longer primary, grains are (or, taking more philosophical instances, atoms or monads are). This is why there is a long discussion of atomism in the context of Stoicism in *Logic of Sense* and in its important appendix on Plato and Lucretius. For Deleuze series are not essentially series of objects or substances, they are variations independent of objects and not limited by them. The variation comes first, not the varied object or connected substance. Or, on a different tack, if a viewing and organising consciousness is essential for setting up the series, if the series are *for* that consciousness, then this latter becomes primary and the focus should turn to the intentionality that stands in relation to series (that which intends towards them and thereby determines them, while being determined in return). This explains why *Logic of Sense* contains Deleuze's longest and most significant engagement with phenomenology and Husserl. Series are independent of human observers or any kind of encompassing consciousness, intentionality or representing faculty. Or, in a further critical vein, are there not rules for what constitutes a proper series of grains, words, things, even variations? Are those rules not then prior to series and determining of what can be a valid series and what cannot? Deleuze is opposed to such rules or laws, hence his critique of logical validity and grammatical rules; for him, series are not defined by a logical function or a grammatical definition. They are processes to be observed, or better, lived through. We may deduce patterns and structures in them and thereby explain certain conditions under which series appear, but these are secondary to series as something sensed and expressed. Logic and grammar always come after; they follow change and events rather than dictate them.

Logic of Sense is therefore an answer to the question: 'How are series determined with no external reference point?' But this question brings in another problem that sets the critical questions in motion anew. Doesn't Deleuze speak of series, structures *and events*? Are events external to series? Then what are events, if not events *for* a form of consciousness and events *in* objective situations? Why refer to events at all, can't we make do with facts? Something is or is not the case; what do we add when we say that the something is an event if not a redundant term that we have a quaint attachment to due to prior ignorance? An event, then, would happen to something or to someone and be caused by someone or something, or it would be a dispensable term to be replaced by matters of fact, or maybe, given that there are only facts, our talk of events happening to people is merely retained as a shorthand for lists of facts. Deleuze's answer to these questions depends on three crucial and ubiquitous conditions in his account of the logic of sense:

1. Series are brought together through a process of disjunctive synthesis.
2. Sense and expression can never be reduced to one another.
3. There is a reciprocal determination of sense and expression.

Put simply, the first condition means that a series is synthesised or brought together only as a series of differences, that is a series is not a synthesis because it brings together the same things, but because it introduces a novel variation. So, if each of the following 'A's is taken to be exactly the same, this is not a synthesis of a series: A A A A A A . . ., whereas this is a synthesis despite its variations: A A′ A″ A‴ . . . A disjunctive synthesis is not a reduction through abstraction but a transforming addition that connects by creating differences. Events are such disjunctive syntheses. The second condition then adds that the syntheses take place on two irreducible sides of reality: on sense and expression; virtual and actual; surface and depth. So any process, or disjunctive synthesis, is dual: parallel but asymmetrical syntheses spread out on either side for any event and for any series. Though the sides are irreducible to one another, they cannot be separated, because for a series to be determined it must depend on the reciprocal determination of each of its sides – determination and difference always come from the other side. There is no determined sense without its expression and no determined expression without its sense. *What is a series, then? It is a disjunctive synthesis running in different ways across two interdependent but irreducible sides of reality.* But then what allows for this synthesis? What carries it? Deleuze's important and innovative answer is that synthesis is carried by mobile factors running along the series. I will show in the following chapter on language how these mobile factors are either empty places or elements without a place – thereby avoiding the critique that these synthesising factors introduce an external identity into the concept of disjunctive synthesis. A way of understanding this synthetic power of empty and placeless factors is to consider the role of questioning or puzzlement in an emerging series: the question and the puzzle such as 'Where should it go?' or 'Where has it gone?' achieve the synthesis before a common element is identified. This in turn shows Deleuze's humour and acuity in choosing Alice as one of his main prompts:

> 'What size do you want to be?' it asked.
> 'Oh, I'm not particular as to size,' Alice hastily replied; 'only one doesn't like changing so often, you know.'
>
> (Carroll, 2003a: Chapter V)

2

Language and event

EVENTS AS EFFECTS

How must language be constructed in order to explain its relation to events? This question underpins the opening series of *Logic of Sense*. It has two important consequences and a decisive presupposition: there are events and these demand an innovative approach to language. The first consequence is that Deleuze's work on language is critical in a very precise way because it seeks to extend traditional approaches to language by showing that they are not adequate to events. This demonstration depends on the formulation of paradoxes in the traditional views, which is another of the reasons for the choice of a logician's works, Lewis Carroll/Charles Dodgson's *Alice in Wonderland* and *Through the Looking Glass* as partners for Deleuze's discussion of language in the opening series of his book. For instance, Alice's changes in size and shape, described in the first series, provide Deleuze with an opportunity to explain how any such change involves all others. Alice does not grow bigger without growing smaller simultaneously. A translation into another claim allows us to understand this strange assertion: Alice is becoming smaller with respect to the bigger Alice who is growing away from her; but she is becoming bigger with respect to the Alice she is growing away from. *Assuming that you are growing in some direction – look back along the timeline and watch yourself receding and becoming smaller, as you become bigger; now look forward and watch yourself become bigger, as you become smaller.*

For Deleuze, the selection of one or other direction in time, and hence one or other change, is a contingent and false abstraction.

28

Events are not restricted and detached in this way, because they happen prior to directions in time and come to form them. His arguments depend on extending the reference point in the present from a punctual Alice, that is an Alice at one point referred to a bigger Alice at another point. Instead, Alice is never at a point, at an instant called the 'present' Alice, for example. Even in the present she is a stretch forward and back in time, becoming bigger and smaller and many other things. Among others, parents will recognise Deleuze's arguments and their relation to powerful emotions in the tensions collected in seeing a child grow up, between the sense of loss at the younger child growing smaller, and receding, and the sense of joy at the older version of the same child growing up and shedding its younger self. *The fear and joy as we open the old photograph folder.* Of course, a reversal of these perspectives works equally well and with wider application, though perhaps also more poignantly. As children, we live with parents growing older and younger at the same time: younger with respect to the older self they are becoming; older in relation to the younger figure they leave behind. The knot of emotions betrays the many dimensions of becoming, never a single direction in time, or a single movement, or one alteration, but all of them at different degrees of intensity, selected and expressed by our emotions and the ways we replay complex events. Holding a photograph of a child we can draw out its becoming smaller ('she still had her child's smile then') or we can shape its becoming bigger ('he's growing into his grandfather's grin'). In Deleuze's reality, the two apparently mutually exclusive directions belong together, which is why the emotions are not exclusive but inhere in one another – the bittersweet quality of emotions.

Paradoxes, such as Alice's growing bigger while growing smaller, demand extensions to what we understand language to be. These additions are not designed to solve the paradoxes; instead, paradoxes are signs indicating and generating the necessity of complementary but irreducibly different aspects of language in relation to events. The second consequence of his investigations into events is therefore that Deleuze does not view language as separate from events, as if it were designed to comment on events and judge them rather than participate in them. He is not trying to construct a new technical language, for example one that is able to maintain validity in formal arguments or one appropriate for a set of specific tasks such as well-defined kinds of communication or understanding. The search for adequacy is much bolder than that. It is to construct language so that events, and thought in line with events, are not excluded by the form of what we take language to be. It is a philosophy of language, events and thought as working together, rather than as they ought to work for other purposes or as we might want them to work. Under no circumstances should this be taken to mean that Deleuze's philosophy is opposed to the use of language as a communication tool or as a support for understanding. Rather, it means that such functions should not be seen as the only proper role of language, or goal for language, or sufficient basis for explaining the relation of language to events. Like his intuition that treating a change in abstraction from others is a false restriction, he counsels that any formal language or technical one is only ever a cut in a wider language that cannot be captured in formal rules or practical and empirical guidelines.

This relation between language and event is stated at the outset of *Logic of Sense*'s 'third series: of the proposition'. Like all the series, the third series begins in the middle of things as if it were taking up an ongoing and well-specified line of argument. Except that no such reference point can be found. Deleuze is exploiting the expectation caused by the feeling of a clear continuity to challenge the reader to construct that connection on the grounds of puzzlement or confusion. We turn back a few pages, turn forward a few, reread the initial sentence, we utter a grunt of incomprehension and frustration, but then plough on, trying to reconstruct sense and connections. He is therefore forcing the reader to think creatively and constructively in exactly the way recommended in his charting of the Stoic or Buddhist master in the nineteenth series, or in his defence of nonsense (and of non sense) in the eleventh. Deleuze returns to the effect of cuts on expectations, in much later books, in his discussion of montage in film-editing in his *Cinema 1* and *Cinema 2*. An edit can create movement and time images – put simply, images accompanied by sensations of differences constituting novel spaces and times – that provide gaps or fill them in unexpected ways in order to jolt thinking out of its usual patterns steeped in common sense and good sense. Film can create new movements and new times that break with our expectations in terms of 'ordinary' space and time; in turn, these are accompanied by new thoughts and ways of thinking. This observation on cinema is already there, in Deleuze's writing style, in *Logic of Sense*. The book's series cut to one another and cut within one another. But this is more than a matter of style. The claims about becoming in many different and apparently opposed directions, developed in *Logic of Sense*, are the conditions for the power of cuts to create movement and time images in *Cinema 1 and 2*.

In the third series of *Logic of Sense*, this experience of novel times and movements is achieved by referring at the outset to a clear referent with very few prior textual clues as to what the referent might be. The opening lines direct us to 'these' events-effects, but the closing lines of the preceding series offer little guidance as to what 'these' might be:

> Between these events-effects and language, or even the possibility of language, there is an essential relation. It is the characteristic of events to be expressed or expressible, uttered or utterable, in propositions which are at least possible. But there are many relations in a proposition, so which is the best suited to surface effects, to events?

> (LoS, 12, 22)

The reference to 'these' events-effects is in fact very wide and leads to many other series. Rather than link directly to an earlier series, the third one explains the relation of language to events-effects. An 'event-effect' is not what we might usually take to be an event, something that happens to something else, like the spilling of a cup of coffee, the rising of a street demonstration or the bursting of rain clouds over parched land. Deleuze's events are much more than an actual thing 'happening' in a limited space and time. This 'standard' sense of an event is frequently indicated by a gerund, a verb taken as a noun to indicate a process-like event that occurs somewhere and to something, the *spilling* of the coffee, the *raising* of the barricades or the *eroding* of the topsoil, for example. Instead, for him, an event is the effect of actual changes on a very different realm of sense. This effect is in principle unbounded and not situated in any actual space and time (sense must be associated with his concept of the virtual as developed in *Difference and Repetition*; in the vocabulary of that book, sense corresponds to the multiplicity of virtual Ideas *and* to the intensities that are expressed in virtual Ideas and in their actualisations). The effect even extends beyond the realm of sense and back into actual events because it is allied to a necessary 'counter-actualisation' or re-enactment of the initial effects in the actual realm, where counter-actualisation means playing out the event in the realm of sense in a different way. This can seem utterly baffling and unnecessarily complicated, but it follows from a distinction drawn between what happens in an actual event and its significance, or a distinction between the gerund of the verb associated with a spatio-temporal location (the spilling of C at place A at time t) and its value (the wider significance of the spilling).

For example, in a blazing rage so typical of your character, you spill a cup of coffee over a gift of reconciliation just handed to you by a lover. *Coffee all over the starfish, maple syrup and jam.* The actual event is a set of facts and the spilling seems to occur between them and to include them: the spilling between the facts 'No coffee on gift at space A at time 1' and 'Coffee on gift at space A at time 2'. These facts, and the things that change between them, can themselves be viewed in chains of further causes and effects: for example, the cause 'My anger at time 0' or 'This change in neuronal patterns at time 0' and the effect 'Gift torn to shreds and burned at time 3' or 'These violent muscular spasms at time 3'. It is debatable, and has long been debated in analytic philosophy of events, whether we even need to refer to the event of the spilling beyond the facts at all, because the notion of the spilling does not seem to add anything concrete to the given facts. (What is the spilling other than a set of facts?) This, however, is not Deleuze's objection, since he wants to take the notion of event even further away from a purely factual treatment. His definition of the event turns towards different and even less 'concrete' effects of changes in actual matters of fact, to the point where we could say that he is seeking the 'ideal' effects of what analytic philosophy calls events, or where we could translate his concepts of surface and depth into 'ideal event' (surface) and facts about changes associated with actual events (depth). The extension into surface and into differential changes in actual states will be one locus for his resistance to crude forms of fact-based naturalism in philosophy. It could be argued that if there is simplicity it is in Deleuze's approach eschewing the richness and subtlety of modern scientific discoveries, but this would not be his point at all, since it is rather an extension to this richness that is at stake. He is not anti-science, but opposed to an often concealed philosophical restriction of thought under the banner of a defence of fact-based science.

Deleuze's move away from the matters of fact we usually take for concreteness is captured in the following intuitions. If we focus on the image of the coffee spilling and the distress on the face of the loved one, then the purely factual effects seem to the supplemented by much greater significance than the facts could ever capture. This is something we might find out if we shouted 'It's only a stupid gift, you're being overemotional: your 5-hydroxytryptamine must be down. We can always buy a new one.' This excess is also expressed in what he would call a sign: a carrier of intensity that transmits a change in sense through a change in an actual moment (for example, in the dreadful hiatus following the spilling, or in the film-maker's 'unnaturally' long freeze-frame of the lover's face just before it cracks, or in the painter's evocation of the instability of numbing shock and inner turmoil in rendering movement through the contradictions of immobile lines and restless shades of colour, or in the video artist's repeated short loop of truncated facial shock and half-uttered moan). The important notion of sign is somewhat underplayed in *Logic of Sense*, but sign and sense can be reconnected through a paired reading with his work on Proust (*Proust and Signs*, 1964, 1970). Deleuze is interested in a different and seemingly more abstract concreteness than purely material facts, something like a significant emotion, or a reserve of emotional energy, or a shifting field of values, disturbed and communicated by events and by signs such as an olfactory trigger in Proust, a close-up of Greta Garbo, the shading of a cheek in Rembrandt, or your heart's overlong contraction and the squeeze it puts on the world when a lover's yelp is captured and matched to the wrong face. In some ways, this is indeed the same intuition as the one motivating the analytic extension of fact into event, but it is taken much further into forms of significance resistant to fact-based and meaning-based analysis.

Deleuze defines this fact-resistant significance as sense, where sense must be understood as variations in the intensity of relations of infinitives, rather than a state or altering states described by gerunds. The event is more than a 'spilling'; it is a change in a series of relations between 'to spill', 'to anger', 'to separate', 'to despair' as an effect of an actual change. So, in the example, sense is a change in the intense relations of the infinitives 'to anger', 'to hate' and 'to love' – and many others – against a chaotic background of all infinitives as expressed in a life. There is a reversal in the usual order of events here. Instead of a spilling happening to something, the spilling that happens to something finds its sense in the effect it has on a series of abstracted verbs. This relation between the event and infinitives is the basis for Deleuze's claim, in the twenty-sixth series 'of language', that events make language possible, because the event is 'enveloped' in verbs (LoS, 182, 213). The bodily side of the event, its mix of passions and actions, expresses series of movements captured in the infinitives. Without this expression the infinitives would be abstract and lacking determined relations to one another. Equally, though, without the expression of infinitives the event would lack significance and sense, because it would not express an alteration in relations between values or infinitives expressed and expressible in other events. Thus the connection of actual events is achieved through the changes of relations between infinitives, but these relations are only ever determined at all, that is rise out of a chaotic mass, through the events that capture them and express them: 'Because it is not true that the verb represents an action; it expresses an event, which is completely different. Neither is it true that language develops from primary roots; it is organised around forming elements determining it as a whole' (LoS, 184, 215).

The difference between the gerund and the infinitive is at the heart of the difference between the analytic approach, for instance in the works of Davidson, Thomson or Bennett (my use of the 'analytic' approach is only shorthand for a rich and varied set of arguments put forward by many thinkers), and Deleuze's approach through his novel concept of sense. This contrast is too deep to investigate in full here – and should be the subject of many academic projects in future – but it is helpful to point to some of its salient features. Prior to this, though, it is worth noting that analytic and Deleuzian defences of events share a common foe in the insistence that events are superfluous and/or supervenient on facts, that is that there is no difference that can be noted in an event that does not correspond to a fact-based difference. Why then speak of events at all and not stick with a meticulous empirical observation of the facts? Like Davidson, Deleuze's argument will be that it is not a question of reducing events to facts, but rather that we require events *and* facts, and events that are not facts, to explain the richness of language in relation to reality. Here is Davidson quoting the fact-based argument:

> It is often argued [. . .] that events are a species of fact. Austin, for example, says, 'Phenomena, events, situations, states of affairs are commonly supposed to be genuinely in the world [. . .] yet surely we can say of all of these that they *are facts.* The collapse of the Germans is an event and is a fact – was an event and was a fact.'
>
> (Davidson, 1980: 132)

And here is a clue as to the differences that will appear between Davidson and Deleuze in responding to the fact-based claims: 'There is a lot of language we can make systematic sense of if we suppose events exist, and we know of no promising alternative' (137). Deleuze's interest in events does not lie in this systematisation but rather in the conditions for language's resistance to systematisation. Where the gerund allows for a formal language that can account for events, Deleuze's use of the infinitive is to draw our attention to processes that sunder a given formalisation and hence explain how events have that same capacity. An event is then not a recursive thing that happens to be particularly resistant to fact-based identification, but rather a singular thing requiring a structure that does not depend on founding identities.

The first contrast between the analytic treatment of events and Deleuze's is that the form 'the spilling *of* directs the verb to what it qualifies in a much stronger way than the orphaned 'to spill'. This is important because Deleuze separates events and sense in order to preserve the independence of the latter. The sense in 'to spill' is not altered in each spilling, only its relation to other infinitives (the intensity of the relation of 'to spill' and 'to offend' can change, but the components cannot). Second, a spilling directs us towards an ongoing actual process that then invites the debate about whether there is indeed a process independent of its constituent facts. Deleuze's 'to spill' does not invite this comparison directly, since it goes beyond the actual process and into a virtual effect (in the relations between infinitives independent of actual things). However, this makes the engagement with a fact-based account even harder to sustain because Deleuze must then explain the relation of the actual side of the event to its virtual or 'infinitive' one. As I will show in the following chapter, he claims that they have a special transcendental relation: they are conditions for one another, but to the point of having special cause-effect relations. Third, the analytic difficulty around questions of where events happen – for example, in terms of the important challenge of locating exactly where a killing occurred, either with the murderous act or with the death and according to which definition of death – is 'solved' by Deleuze by saying it occurs in the actual side of the event, but also in its virtual side, and is therefore both well-located and infinitely extended through its effect on sense. However, Deleuze then has his own great difficulty in explaining how an event can be both well-located and infinitely extended in its virtual side. This is the recalcitrant Deleuzian problem of how to achieve any determinacy at all once we abandon spatio-temporal location and concept-based identity, a problem that is less strong in the analytic approach, though still at the heart of many debates. (*Where exactly is the spilling?*)

For example, in the raising of barricades, it is not only that the raising happens to a series of upturned carts and torn boards, it is that the relations of a series of infinitives (of effects that can happen again elsewhere – that are happening again elsewhere) are changed. In the raising, verbs that express resistance, hope, fear and many others change in the ways they relate to one another. They also therefore change in the way they can be expressed in other actual events. A useful way of thinking about this lies in the relation between a first actual event and a second one. According to Deleuze's reading of events and effects, the urgency for authorities to make sure that the first barricade is rapidly overcome, and that reports of it are suppressed and controlled, does not only lie in the actual crushing, but in the danger the first raising presents through its effect on sense and through the way that sense can be expressed anew in a second, third and any subsequent uprising. This is not to say that actual events are not important; on the contrary, the actual expression of sense is always necessary. It is to say that the relation between actual events can only be understood completely when we take account of their effects on sense. For Deleuze, there is an effect linking two barricades beyond their actual spatio-temporal location. They may become materially isolated, but from the point of view of sense, they communicate:

> This inexorable resolution so thoroughly impregnated the air of the 6th of June, 1832, that, almost at the very same hour, on the barricade Saint-Merry, the insurgents were raising that clamor which has become a matter of history and which has been consigned to the documents in the case: – 'What matters it whether they come to our assistance or not? Let us get ourselves killed here, to the very last man.'
>
> (Hugo, 1982: 959)

This ethereal communication described by Victor Hugo once again raises the problem of virtual effects and their causal relation to actual states of affairs. Deleuze is acutely aware of this problem and confronts it in the series 'on the communication of events'. There is something very beautiful in the idea of communication independent of actual causal relations, as Hugo shows with his barricades in *Les Misérables*, but there is also a philosophical revolution demanding a radical shift in our common-sense expectations, and more importantly in the expectations we have justifiably based on the natural sciences.

Rather than a well-located happening, sense is then more like a distant and disembodied destiny that different events intermittently connect to, feed off and alter for all other events ('Infinitives inherit from the communication of events with one another . . .', LoS, 185, 216). Deleuze's counter-actualisation of events is therefore not how you seek to repair what has actually been done. It is how these acts of repair redouble or replay what has happened, at the level of the intense relations of sense defined as the reserve of potential happenings. In the series on language this is rendered as a to and fro movement of linguistic actions and reactions setting up a circle in language (LoS, 184, 215). Counter-actualisation is therefore a reciprocally determining interaction between sense and the actual side of events. *How can we be worthy of the spirit of the barricades mounted by the Commune?* In the later Chapter 4 on morals, I will show how this allows for a replaying of what Deleuze calls the singular fault lines that run through a life. You may be a puppet controlled by anger and love, but these also make your life singular, mobile and difficult – in the sense of requiring constant creative responses. A useful test for understanding this stretch beyond facts and linguistic meaning can be found in miserable expressions such as 'I cannot believe that I did it again!' or 'Why must I always do it again?' The poignancy of these cries does not turn on the repetition of mere facts and actions, or in the straightforward meaning of an act. It stems rather from what the repetition reveals about a deeper sense, for example, of how a particular life unfolds, sometimes tragically, often joyfully, in relation to patterns of significance that actual acts express but do not capture fully. Or it stems from the way a particular repetition marks a threshold or passage from one significant state to another. The cry 'Why did I do it again for that one time too many?' is not only addressed to a matter of fact, or even to what that fact means, in the sense of a description of a state of affairs as distinct from the actual state. Its emotional intensity comes from what a given actual occurrence reveals about a changing set of 'value' or 'significance' relations and how it has effects in them. This kind of repetition and its relation to destiny, to the unconscious and to the return of forgotten, bygone and even illusory past events, partly explain Deleuze's substantial work on psychoanalysis in *Logic of Sense*.

Deleuze's novel way of thinking about sense and event allows for a better understanding of the term 'events-effects' and of the problems that drive his approach to language. Events-effects are the way the realm of sense is caused to change by actual occurrences; they are the 'surface' events that rearrange the intensities of the relations between infinitives like 'to love' and 'to rage'. It seems extremely odd to describe these as 'effects' related to causes, since we would ordinarily associate the cause-effect relation with associated changes in actual matters of fact (rain at place A at time 1 causes streams of mud as the topsoil floods away at place B at time 2). But, incongruously in terms of standard terminology, Deleuze would not call this latter relation causal because, until we introduce its significance, the association of rain and erosion is empty and arbitrary. It is empty because the statement about causality needs to be made determinate with respect to the senses it is supposed to relate. 'So what?' we might ask, when told of the causal relation, until we realise which ones of a great range of possible values are related by the causal claim. It is also arbitrary, since the decision to focus on a particular causal relation still needs to be founded. For example, erosion has many associations and brings together many series over time so why focus on rain in the causal chain, rather than quality of the soil? Why not dryness over time? Or over-farming? Or the destitution of the farmer that led to the mismanagement of the land? Or the way hope can emerge anew with a New Deal? 'This' rain and 'this' erosion do not cause each other where sense is concerned, they cause changes in relations of sense such as the waning of 'to hope' and 'to struggle' and their smothering by 'to bend' and 'to break' etched on the farmers' faces and starving bodies as 'this drop of rain and flow of mud' is the last one before the land is abandoned or a life lost: 'Here, in the faces of the husband and his wife, you begin to see an expression you will notice on every face; not worry, but absolute terror of the starvation that crowds in against the borders of the camp' (Steinbeck, 2002: 79).

When Deleuze describes the relation of these effects to the possibility of language as essential, he means that these events depend on language for their expression. This can seem rather trite if we understand it as 'We need language to express or describe events', but it means something much more profound, that is, that events are *in principle* expressible in language because of the nature of the relation of sense to actual occurrences. In other words, the causal relation of changes of matters of fact to changes in sense is essentially expressible in language, due to the way language is constructed. It is very important not to take this as meaning that any construction of language is necessary for events-effects and for sense, on the contrary, many will be shown to be unsatisfactory. It is also very important not to confuse the statement with the idea that expression in language is necessary for there to be events. To do this would be to miss the 'possible' in Deleuze's statement and to connect his claims to human-centred notions of significance and to arguments of the superiority of humans due to their capacity for or ownership of language. Nothing could be further from Deleuze's position. His philosophy is deeply inimical to anthropocentrism and 'man' could not be the centre or highest value of his philosophy because any human identity, or human value, would always presuppose depth (body) and surface (sense) – processes that belied any claimed centrality for a human essence. So language as a possibility for event-effects does not mean the possible human use of language, but the way language as process provides a set of conditions for the expression of sense.

Prior to passing to an explanation of the structure of language in relation to events, it is worth pointing out that many of the examples I have given in this book could lead to an anthropocentric or subject-centred reading of Deleuze (in the quote from John Steinbeck's journalism two paragraphs higher, for instance). This is because these examples are designed to trigger reflection from widely accessible experience in order to avoid exclusivity or narrow fields. A reader might pass from an example based on experience or forms of inner reflection to a mistaken belief that the experiencing subject is a foundation for Deleuze's thought. This would be a mistake. However, alternative approaches have their own risks in terms of interpretation. For instance, the scope and flexibility of his philosophy would be lost were readers to think that we can only understand Deleuze if we know differential calculus, or nouvelle vague cinema, or French philosophy of biology, or a rarefied field of art and music (avant-garde, marginal or canonical), or the whole of the history of philosophy, or only if we take our lives way beyond established social norms and practices. In my view (*oh, the irony*) the difficulties presented by starting from examples that encourage thinking about Deleuze in terms of experience are outweighed by the advantage of breadth and contact with the 'everyday' and with 'ordinary language'. Deleuze's assault on common and good sense should not be confused with an assault on the everyday; rather, his thought frees the everyday from the grip of layer upon layer of common and good sense. My refusal to lose 'experience' is part of a political position, in terms of a commitment to bring philosophy to bear on life as accessibly as possible and with as much flexibility and care as possible, to as many as possible. There is no doubt that this could fail badly and that it excludes equally, or perhaps more, valid approaches to the explanation of Deleuze. Nonetheless, I would not want to see his work become the claimed property of intellectual or social elites, or a self-selecting margin, or a revolutionary cadre. These should not themselves be excluded, but Deleuze's sensitive and open philosophy should accompany and shape many of 'us', through our thoughts, and our political actions, rather than remain in the possession of a few protectors.

UNFOLDING THE CIRCLE OF THE PROPOSITION: DENOTATION, MANIFESTATION, SIGNIFICATION AND SENSE

Two difficult but very important ideas situate Deleuze's philosophy of language. The first is that processes that we use to explain how language works with respect to truthful communication (denotation, manifestation and signification) form a 'circle'. Put simply, this means that neither the reference of language (denotation), nor its situation in relation to a speaker or point of writing (manifestation), nor its meaning as decipherable through the position of words in relation to one another (signification) are sufficient bases for understanding how language works. Instead, each one of these must be attached to the others for its own process to be complete. How a proposition refers to something in the world depends on how it is qualified by the moment when it is written or spoken by someone, and this in turn depends on how its meaning is set, for example according to dictionary definitions, but this is in turn incomplete without a reference. This is why Deleuze speaks of a circle in language: each ground given for deciding on, say, truth or meaning or validity requires further grounding outside itself, to the point where no hierarchy or fixed order of the components of language can be set. This claim is very radical and should not be read as the claim that each component of language is insufficient on its own only in some way, but as the much stronger but also more troubling claim that each component only works when it is with the others in a circle. So, for instance, it is not that we can refer to things in language and that this reference is crucial for deciding about the truth of a proposition but somehow incomplete when we need to decide on its meaning (in a statement about a matter of fact, such as 'The book is on the table', for instance). It is rather that *no aspect of denotation is complete without manifestation and without signification.* Paradoxical and productive circling is the essential process of language, not the correct positioning of different linguistic functions on the circle.

The second idea is harder than the first and develops the idea of the circle in a very original manner. It is that sense, defined in Deleuze's new way, breaks the circle and can be found in each of the processes set in the circling. What could this mean? It means that we cannot escape the manner we keep turning round and round from denotation, to manifestation, to signification unless we refer to an extra process in language. This additional key component is sense, as distinct from the other terms, but also as the way to stop each one failing, where failing means coming up against paradoxes that block its functioning without remedy. For example, when addressing a particularly obtuse interlocutor (over whom we have neither explicit power nor hidden influence) we may become caught in a frustrating circle passing through these kinds of questions: What are you talking about? Do you mean always or sometimes? What do you mean by this word? Each time we specify our denotation, motives and meanings this further specification is itself called into question. According to Deleuze, the only way to break out from the way each question throws us back to others is to pass to a different kind of question or problem: 'Why is this significant?' 'What is a stake here?' 'What does this situation change in terms of values, or emotional investments, or potential for changes?' The helpful experience of language to recall here is the way some dialogues fail to work until we suddenly grasp the motivations of the speaker, or what is at stake in the exchange, for example, when we are victims of a concealed sales pitch, or a hidden put down, or when we suddenly realise that we are the addressees of an emotional plea. *And the solution to all these woes is Dr Watkins's purple elixir . . . Why didn't you have the courage to tell me I was fired – I need more space and if you cannot understand why . . .* Each component of language is conditioned by another and this conditioning forms a vicious circle such that when we try to rest on a component to answer a question (such as 'What is truth here?' or 'What is the meaning here?') we are always pushed on to another question. This endless cycle is only broken by the role played by sense in each component. However, as Deleuze shows, this raises a difficult set of questions about sense and the event. In particular, it raises the question of what sense is, if not a reference, or a manifestation (a stating by someone), or a signification (meaning – as opposed to my use of significance or value).

The third series 'on the proposition' insists on the difficulty of the question, but it also provides a set of answers. These begin with an explanation for the insufficiency of each of the standard aspects of language, followed by an argument for the role of sense in each one, followed by a rather difficult but important definition of sense (there are many such definitions, in *Logic of Sense*, and that multiplicity is itself significant because sense is what allows language to evade limited final definitions). Deleuze's setting up of the circle that runs through denotation, manifestation and signification can be shown through an example. Starting from an argument between two people, the proposition 'I hate that thing that you do' might cause a difficult pause: the proposition is important, but it is also puzzling. It might seem that analysis of the referent (*that* thing) provides a way out of the potentially devastating dispute ('Well what is it that thing that I do?') Deleuze's point is that though this move can establish whether there is such a referent, this association of the proposition with a value of true or false (true if there is such a referent, false if not) is no good in solving the problem it presents in terms of the beliefs and desires invested in it. The proposition may truly refer to something, but until we study the beliefs and desires inferred from it, we will not get much further. These are the domain of the manifestation, that is the way the proposition is uttered by someone at a particular time inferring a set of beliefs and desires ('You don't care about me, because you are always looking elsewhere'). The uttering or writing of the proposition – its manifestation – allows for a set of checks that cannot be deduced from denotation alone (When? Where? Why? What are the stakes?)

Deleuze concludes, very rapidly, that manifestation is a prior principle for any possible denotation: 'Indication or denotation subsumes the individual states of affairs, the particular images and the singular designators; but manifestation, beginning with the "I," constitutes the domain of the personal, which functions as the principle of all possible denotation' (LoS, 13, 24). In other words, there can be no full reference without a manifestation because the set of beliefs and desires associated with the denotation require a manifestation (the way in which the dispute moves on to questions such as 'Well what did you think I was staring at?'). It could be objected, at this point, that Deleuze and this explanation are taking loaded accounts of propositions: loaded in the sense that they are emotional and subjective. If we take a different kind of proposition (such as 'The probability is 0.5') then manifestation does not seem to figure. The answer to this objection is that there is no proposition that is completely free of desires and beliefs that are themselves dependent on a manifestation. For example, in a technical scientific presentation, the earlier proposition about a probability could fit into a long set of conclusions and recommendations, all open to debate. Interlocutors, soon pass from something they can easily agree upon as true ('It is indeed at 0.5') to a set of much more contentious beliefs that do not leave the initial proposition free of manifestation type questions. ('Yes, it is at 0.5, but that does not allow you to infer that we must recommend this kind of treatment in all cases. 0.5 is meaningless without its context.') Deleuze's point is not that subjective emotions justify the primacy of manifestation, but that *inferences* from one proposition to another (to beliefs and desires) depend on their situation with respect to a manifestation. Moreover, such inferences are not only questionable when leading to subjective beliefs such as 'You lied!' but also to more factual ones 'Should we leave the probability at 0.5 despite this run of 15 tails or look at the coin again now?' In short, 'when', 'where' and 'who' determine truth.

The next step in the argument is the claim that signification, defined by Deleuze as the connection between a word and 'universal or general concepts', is a prior condition for manifestation. For any given proposition, signification is the chain of universal and general concepts implied by any one of its words or found as the conclusion of a chain of implications that includes that word. For example, in the proposition 'I only do it out of innocent habit', the word 'habit' could have a chain of signification that includes 'learning', 'biological conditioning', 'repetition' and the conclusion 'involuntary', as well as the antonyms 'freely chosen' and 'intended'. I have called this chain the meaning of the word and I have associated Deleuze's signification with meaning. There are some risks in taking this step because he is using the former term within the structuralist tradition where signification is logically deduced from sets of oppositions between words, that is from the place in a structure of other words and meanings, or more properly, structures of signifiers and signifieds (voluntary-involuntary-free-not-responsible and so on, and what they signify). Meaning, in the analytic post-Fregean tradition, is not the same thing as structuralist signification though it shares a search for objectivity and generality (universality is much more tricky and controversial). On the other hand, this use of meaning is certainly not what Deleuze is constructing with his concept of sense, nor what he signifies by manifestation. The demonstration of the priority of signification requires a split between speech and language (*parole* and *langue*). In speech, manifestation is prior to signification, because the person who speaks maintains a priority over the chains of signification (we can always ask the person to clarify an utterance and that clarification will alter what we took the significations to be). When we turn to language, though, signification must be prior because for propositions to allow for implications and conclusions, they cannot be allowed to vary at the whim of the person who makes them manifest. In language, things follow necessarily and this necessity must be prior to manifestation and to denotation. This is because misattribution of a denotation depends on the constancy of signification; we cannot make a mistake in referring to something unless we have a meaning attached to it.

However, having argued for this order of priority, with the exception of speech, Deleuze closes the circle with an argument for the priority of denotation. Once we take a proposition from a chain of signification as a true conclusion of the chain, we can refer to it as true of the state of affairs that it designates. For example, detectives can infer the perpetrators of a crime from a series of clues and deductions (a chain of inferences in signification) and then interview the presumed criminals (a denotation). However, they could only do this *without fear of failure* given two conditions: if the premises on which the proposition stood in signification were themselves true, so they in turn must be referred to a denotation; and if the detectives had a reliable account of what a valid implication was, which would require something external to the proposition that itself required a validation. In order to be certain that the interview will be with guilty parties, the detective has to be certain of the clues and of the methods of deduction, as Sherlock Holmes seems to be in this deduction, told within his account of the 'method of deduction':

> I knew you came from Afghanistan. From long habit the train of thoughts ran so swiftly through my mind that I arrived at the conclusion without being conscious of intermediate steps. There were such steps, however. The train of reasoning ran, 'Here is a gentleman of a medical type, but with the air of a military man. Clearly an army doctor, then. He has just come from the tropics, for his face is dark, and that is not the natural tint of his skin, for his wrists are fair. He has undergone hardship and sickness, as his haggard face says clearly. His left arm has been injured. He holds it in a stiff and unnatural manner. Where in the tropics could an English army doctor have seen much hardship and got his arm wounded? Clearly in Afghanistan.' The whole train of thought did not occupy a second. I then remarked that you came from Afghanistan, and you were astonished.
> (Conan Doyle, 2001: Part 1, Chapter 2, 'The science of deduction')

Against Doyle's absolute confidence in his method, Deleuze is making two important points with respect to weaknesses in signification. First, when true conclusions in a chain of implication in signification are referred to a referent in denotation, this re-establishes the priority of the referent (*Does he, in fact, come from Afghanistan?*) In other words, it does not matter how carefully you argue about the valid meanings implied by the use of a term in an argument, if you then go back to the referent and your conclusions do not tally with it, it is the signification that must bend to denotation, either in terms of the rules of inference or in terms of the premises. Second, establishing the truth of implication sets off an endless chain of justifications (A is true, because B justifies A, B is true because C justifies B, and so on). The way to block this chain is once again to refer to a denotation; in other words, the selection among chains of justifications of implication is made through a denotation. (*This is the decisive argument for the logic we shall work with.*) However, because of the dependence of denotation on manifestation, the circle continues to turn. In Conan Doyle's account of 'the science of deduction' the manifestation and signification work through Holmes in a troublesome series of ways, since the article on the science of deduction cited in favour of his argument has in fact been penned by Holmes and the reference to Afghanistan is loaded and open to wide interpretations and doubt, for example through Watson's injury there or through the partially true but deeply loaded and wildly influential story of Dr William Brydon, sole survivor of the British retreat from Kabul in the winter of 1842 (also referred to by Melville in *Moby Dick* and inscribed in visual memory by Elizabeth Butler in her painting *Remnants of an Army*). Drawing inspiration from Poe's Arsène Dupin rather than Holmes, and hence from Lacan's reading of Poe (to be discussed in Chapter 5) Deleuze concludes his discussions with the following assertion:

> From denotation to manifestation, then to signification, but also from signification to manifestation and to denotation, we are carried along a circle, which is the circle of the proposition. Whether we ought to be content with these three dimensions of the proposition, or whether we should add a *fourth – which would be sense –* is an economic or strategic question.

(LoS, 17, 27)

This conclusion calls for a list of critical questions about Deleuze's treatment of the proposition and his work on the circle. Answers to the questions provide important guidance on how to interpret and understand Deleuze's philosophy of language:

1. How seriously should we take Deleuze's very short work on denotation, manifestation and signification, given the vast amount of material available on these topics in specialist philosophical discussions?
2. What is the status of his conclusion on the circle of the proposition, given that such a conclusion contradicts the study that supports it? The chain of propositions given in the passage above itself depends on the circle and its validity must therefore be called into question.
3. How can a question about language be economic and strategic instead of a matter of knowledge? Should it not be a matter of whether we can know and understand sense, rather than opt for it, or weigh it up?
4. Is the 'circle' of the proposition a metaphor for a more precise linguistic or philosophical property? If so, what role does the metaphor play and what property does it point towards?

45

5. In evoking paradoxes in setting up the circle, isn't Deleuze moving too quickly, at the expense of careful exposition of the paradoxes and the search for possible solutions to them?

The main answer to these questions is that Deleuze's treatment of denotation, manifestation and signification is not his philosophy of language proper. It could not possibly stand up to scrutiny alone, when compared, for example, to the extensive work on denotation in the analytic tradition after Frege.

Instead, Deleuze's work is part of an argument for the extension of language into sense through an argument dependent on a series of paradoxes. His treatment therefore provides useful points of contact with other philosophies of language, but only as a way into his fully original position that depends on the relation of structure, sense and event. The statements about the circle therefore have three functions: first, they give an impression of how Deleuze's philosophy relates to *possible* flaws in denotation, manifestation and signification; second, they allow for a set of critical arguments for the extension into sense through each of the elements of the circle; third, they lead into a different account of language based on sense and structure. Much therefore remains to be done on the connections and differences between Deleuze's philosophy of language and other longer established theories. It is another of many areas ripe for extensive original research. This relative lack of development does not mean that the proposition is unimportant for Deleuze. The proposition in its relation to difference (and hence to sense) is treated at length in *Difference and Repetition,* notably in relation to the concept, and somewhat differently in later works on writing and language, with Guattari in *Kafka: Toward a Minor Literature* and in the important collection on literature *Essays Critical and Clinical.*

For example, echoing his earlier work from *Logic of Sense,* Deleuze studies variations on the proposition 'I would prefer not to' in the essay on Melville's 'Bartleby' in *Essays Critical and Clinical.* Deleuze shows how Bartleby's formula has an effect through sense without having clear denotations, manifestations or significations, or indeed exactly because these are lacking. According to this reading, Melville's story depends on the absence of easily located referents, motives and meanings for Bartleby's statements. What Bartleby would 'prefer not to' shifts and evades us; this is the source of the proposition's power. The meaning or signification of his preference, that is its implications in terms of his desires and beliefs, is equally slippery and evanescent. Bartleby fails as an instance of manifestation, as even the moment of utterance or inscription gradually disappears as the story unfolds, ending in his death as the final iteration of 'I would prefer not to':

> Strangely huddled at the base of the wall, his knees drawn up, and lying on his side, his head touching the cold stones, I saw the wasted Bartleby. But nothing stirred. I paused; then went close up to him; stooped over, and saw that his dim eyes were open; otherwise he seemed profoundly sleeping.

(Melville, 1995: 46)

Yet Bartleby's propositions have a great effect through something else that they transmit to hearers and readers alike. This, for Deleuze, is its effect through and on sense; it is why Bartleby is an event in the story and, more widely, why he serves as an example of resistance to the categorising demands of modernity and to the exchange requirements of capitalism. Bartleby refuses to stand as a locatable manifestation or referent, a cog in the modern machine; his proposition eludes a set meaning, something which could carry a value. So when Deleuze speaks of breaking the circle, he means breaking with the contradiction implied in the second critical question above, a point that he will also develop in a much longer study of paradox later in *Logic of Sense*. This break depends on sense and on the introduction of a necessarily economic and strategic aspect to language. As it flows through structure, sense operates in an economic manner in terms of circulation; we have to chart the flows of intensity in sense-relations. It carries strategic force because it is associated with a game-like interaction with events, that is events are approached through forms of replaying, or counter-actualisation, rather than knowledge.

SENSE AND THE CIRCLE

Deleuze gives the following arguments for the extension of denotation, manifestation and signification into sense towards the end of the series on the proposition; he gives very similar arguments in a discussion of sense in *Difference and Repetition* in a discussion of the sixth postulate for an image of thought. The main point is that sense cannot be identified with any of the three elements of the circle:

1. The sense of a proposition cannot be the denotation, because this appeal to a referent establishes the value of truth or falsity of a proposition, whereas propositions retain a sense independent of their truth or falsity, that is they can have an effect independent

of whether they are true or false (for example, in a poetic form or through the effect of a paradox or of a humorous nonsense proposition – 'We shall say "Ni" to you . . . if you do not appease us' (*Monty Python*, 1975). Moreover, the words of the proposition do not correspond perfectly to the referent; they convey something more and something less. This is why Deleuze repeats an odd comment about chariots passing through mouths, in *Logic of Sense*, in order to explain how word and thing retain a difference that cannot be resolved by mapping the words onto what they truthfully correspond to, since the chariot does not pass through your mouth.

2. The manifestation of a proposition cannot correspond to its sense because without sense or signification the manifestation becomes empty, that is the subject of the proposition, the 'I' uttering it, must convey a meaning and alter a series of values or lose the identity required to manifest anything. This rather odd argument can be explained through the difference between senseless sounds coming from a next-door cell in a prison, implying that there is no subject, no 'I', making the sounds, and the moment when the sounds start to signify something. Once we associate the sounds with meaning and significance, we can then construct a possible neighbour: 'It was a continual scratching, as if made by a huge claw, a powerful tooth, or some iron instrument attacking the stones' (Dumas, 1997: Chapter 15).

3. Sense cannot be the signification of the proposition because, if we define signification as the 'possibility for it to be true', that is, if we say that a proposition can only be true if it has 'meaning' and if we then define what form this meaning should take, then there must still be something in the proposition that allows it to be shown to be true or false in designation and to vary in its implied desires and beliefs in manifestation. We need a third term between the deduced truth associated with signification and the values of true and false established by correspondence in denotation. Put simply, if we fix the form propositions must take in order for them to signify something truthfully, we restrict their capacity to fail to be true when they designate something and to imply different beliefs and desires when manifested or uttered by someone. (*I know it should be the case, but look, the facts just do not fit . . . Yes, this is what it implies, but still my beliefs take it differently.*)

Yet all these points seem only to approach sense negatively, rather than as something with a clear definition allowing it to be recognised in a given proposition. Deleuze is well aware of this and discusses the problem at length. If sense is defined in such a way as to allow it to be grasped, as it were mechanically, or according to a formula, or through a technique such as its careful determination in a denotation, it would become fixed according to the elements of the circle it is supposed to break with (and must break with to displace its paradoxes). In order to avoid this, an *empirical* approach is required, that is sense must be allowed to emerge in various studies, none of which determine it as a final referent, set of intentions or meaning. However, though it has impeccable roots in Deleuze's early study of Hume, *Empiricism and Subjectivity* (1953), his empiricism is offbeat and must be distinguished from other forms of empiricism, such as repeatable and carefully constrained empirical experiments in the natural sciences or exhaustive empirical surveys and statistically extrapolated conclusions on empirical bases in the social sciences. He is not searching to reproduce a same result, or to produce a result that falsifies a claim or theory, under experimental conditions, or to find patterns of sameness or of statistical significance. Instead, Deleuze speaks of a 'higher empiricism', that is the creation of differential counters to events, variations and movements. These reveal novel differences and open up series to disjunctive syntheses that cannot be reduced to a single and self-same line; this creates connections by dividing rather than assembling around repeated identities. Deleuzian empiricism is therefore empirical in terms of an open-ended passivity to events, hence sharing the sceptical and provisional aspect of standard empiricism, but it is also experimental, not through setting up experiments, but by responding creatively to events. This shift from well-established views of empiricism as an ongoing, open and always revisable search for results verifying or falsifying claims, to one where creative experimentation accompanies emerging events is at the core of Deleuze's 'method'. It can come across as a rather mystical and wrongheaded project, until we realise two things: first, the precise arguments of *Logic of Sense* are an example of this experimentation, so he is not dealing in wishes or impossible dreams but in actual and rigorous arguments and studies; second, Deleuze's empiricism is not designed to exclude other forms, but to complete them and to interact with them critically and constructively. Each of his treatments of the proposition and its paradoxes are essays in allowing sense to emerge without tying it down directly; they are experiments on language, in the context of contemporary research, *aiming for the determination of sense free of its identification.* Deleuze's critical extended engagement with

Husserl on sense is another such experiment in *Logic of Sense* (it is studied at length in Chapter 3, below).

Deleuze's empiricism involves the creation of concepts, ideas, images, fields and disjunctive syntheses (terms that will allow Deleuze and Guattari to define philosophy as 'the creation of concepts' in *What Is Philosophy?*). Towards the end of the series on the proposition, he puts forward one of these creative accounts of sense with the following positive and negative moves that provide a context for his notion of experimentation on sense as event:

> *Sense is* inseparably *the expressible or the expressed of the proposition, and the attribute of the state of affairs.* It turns one side towards things and one side towards propositions. But it does not merge with the proposition which expresses it any more than with the state of affairs or the quality which the proposition denotes. It is exactly the boundary between propositions and things [. . .] It is in this sense that it is 'event': *on condition that the event is not confused with its spatio-temporal effectuation in a state of affairs.*
> (LoS, 22, 34)

Sense has been defined earlier as the alteration in the intensity of relations of series of infinitives (for example, 'He is green' alters the relation of 'to green', 'to blunder' and 'to excuse' when stated about a particular new recruit). But now we see that Deleuze also associates sense with a change in a state of affairs (greenness is a novel emerging attribute for a state that includes the recruit referred to in the proposition). It needs to be called emerging because it is not 'this' identified green property in 'this' well-spatio-temporally-located recruit, but rather what makes the recruit singular and non-identifiable in a set of oppositions and shared properties. Singularity here indicates a radical incomparability. The notion of emerging then tags a variation or pure difference, in Deleuze's usage.

The expressed and the attribute are different since the former involves constituents (infinitives) that are not changed by their expression, whereas the latter involves attributes that are only varied within states of affairs. 'To green' is invariable and only alters through changes in the intensity of its relations to other infinitives, whereas the attribute of greenness is singular to the state of affairs (it is the singular emerging greenness of this recruit). So when sense relates to a singular greenness in a new recruit, it also changes the *relations* among infinitives by making some stronger and some weaker; for instance, the relation of 'to green' to 'to blunder' or 'to weaken' builds up, if the recruit is particularly clumsy or weak: 'Private Pyle has dishonored himself and dishonored the platoon!

I have tried to help him, but I have failed! I have failed because you have not helped me! You people have not given Private Pyle the proper motivation!' (Kubrick and Herr, 1987). The strength of this division between the attribute and the expressed is that the infinitive can remain the same when the attribute and the expressed change dramatically. This is because the appearance of new attributes in the state of affairs changes the relations of the infinitives and not its terms. Kubrick and Herr's violent turn of events does not change the sense of 'to green' but expresses a hitherto obscure connection of the unknowing outsider with revolt ('With a twisted smile on his face Pyle points his rifle at Hartman'). It is crucial for sense to be on both sides of the attribute and state of affairs duality to avoid Deleuze's philosophy descending into a negative and contradictory form of philosophical dualism. He needs to avoid an opposition that would raise the question: how are the expressible and the singular state of affairs related at all if they are different? It is equally important, though, for sense to be confused with neither, because if sense were only the expressed his philosophy would be a new Platonic idealism (with the eternity of the infinitives), whereas if it were only the singular emergent state of affairs his thought would be a new materialism (one of emergent singular properties). In response, though, readers of *Logic of Sense* will quickly note the frequency of dual terms in the book (Aiôn and Chronos, expressed and state of affairs, series and structure). These dualities are found throughout Deleuze's work (for example, actual and virtual in *Difference and Repetition* or reterritorialsation and deterritorialisation in *A Thousand Plateaus*). The divisions provide theoretical power, novelty and applicability to his work, but unless the key middle terms of sense and intensity are taken into account, and unless they convince us, his philosophy will continue to be threatened by severe contradictions and misinterpretations.

SERIES AND PARADOX

Series 5 'on sense' begins with the same writing technique of misleading and failing connection as many others. This time the failing link is called by a dialogical rejoinder ('but') and an antecedent that appears to come in the middle of a chain of arguments ('but since'). The current translation misses this carefully crafted, significant and humorous quality of Deleuze's writing by eliminating the French beginning for the series '*Mais puisque* . . .' The series should really begin with 'But since' in order to prompt a vain search for the dialogue at the end of the preceding series, and then to prompt a – hopefully amused – reflection on the sense of its absence. This particular elision is quite subtle, because Deleuze has broken the connection for an implication in order to give a practical example of his point about the dependence of manifestation and signification on designation. The meaning of the 'but since' sentence eludes us due to the absence of a dialogical referent for the rejoinder – despite our perfectly good grasp of the signification of 'but since'. The subsequent collapse of our confidence in that signification takes the manifestation with it because we lose confidence in the authority of the writers and our confidence in their command over a series of implied desires and beliefs. *Not another French thinker incapable of clear syllogisms!* Of course, any such self-servingly rapid and viscerally charged conclusion would be straightforwardly wrong, since Deleuze is multiplying arguments rather than forgetting one (they are in all the other series). He is showing that manifestation is also multiple. We should look for layers of manifestation and their interaction, in particular in terms of effects between conscious and unconscious moments. Thus Deleuze's critique of intention need not be that it does not exist. It is rather than it is multiple: there is never a single originator of the intention. It is also perverse: the kinds of thing that can be identified as intending are much wider than human originators. They extend into the unconscious, which also has its intentions, however much we may hate it for it. *No! No! Don't go! What meant to say was* . . . But restricted intention is the easiest of Deleuze's targets; he is making the much broader point that denotation is a crucial process even without designators and a referent. In fact, his deepest claim is perhaps that denotation works best in terms of sense and productive experimentation when the referent is slipping away from us. He is therefore illustrating the frequently made point in *Logic of Sense* that sense is learned through the failure of the teacher to point to the 'right' reference, to provide an accurate and trustworthy manifestation, and to communicate the sole and exact signification.

After this witty start, which also plays on the lead set by all the failed dialogues of *Alice's Adventures in Wonderland*, the remainder of series 5 can seem dull and repetitive since it works through many of the paradoxes already covered elsewhere in *Logic of Sense*. However, as ever in the book and in his other works, the point is not in the repetitions, but in the way they vary. I want to draw out a single important point from this variation in covering the paradoxes set out in series 5. It is that paradoxes – and all series – are double, in the same way as sense was presented as double, one side as attribute and one side as expressed, in series 4. This should not surprise us since, if series were not double, then the suggestions made about sense in the previous section would fail. The really important point, though, is not the duality, but its detail: how things are double and the processes involved in explaining how sense works; how things interact across the duality; how some things remain on one side or the other; and the reasons given for each of these explanations. This returns us to Deleuze's great power as a philosophical engineer, something worth noting again because it conditions the originality of his work on paradoxes. Paradoxes are not only problems generated by formal systems or puzzles proper to particular models. They are constructed problems that have technical functions, creative solutions and a genetic power with respect to novel forms of thought. The style of *Logic of Sense*, its literary inventiveness and its historical position in post-1968 French thought, often associated with more 'poetic' ways of writing and thinking, could encourage us to dissociate Deleuze's work from the rich logical formalisms that emerged with Frege, Russell, Whitehead, Tarski, Gödel and many others – one of the most productive strains of twentieth-century philosophy. This division would be a great mistake. Deleuze's book is driven by similar concerns to many logicians and, although his responses can seem very distant, there are strong parallels to be brought out. (This is another exciting seam for researchers to work on, for example on set theoretical operations and Deleuze's concerns with symmetry and mirroring.)

Simple versions of the paradoxes covered in series 5 are listed below. The first thing to note is that Deleuze has given them two names, separated by the conjunction 'or'. This should not be read as an exclusive 'either, or', but rather as a disjunctive synthesis in the usage from *Logic of Sense*, 'both, and'. Even this shortening requires some qualification, though, because it is not 'both' as separate entities, but as series of transforming asymmetric relations, where asymmetric means that each relation is irreversible, it runs in one direction and a different relation answers it in the manner of a distorting mirror. Perhaps Deleuze's 'or' is best read as 'together, differently' with the technical more correct though ugly 'reciprocally determining, asymmetrically and in multiple ways' held in reserve for the most academic usage. A quick response to the criticism that all this careful definition of 'or' is at best redundant and at worst misleading can be found in the added subtleties allowed by 'together, differently' when compared with 'either, or' or 'and', for example when connecting terms of comparable types but carrying significant variations (heat or high temperature; cold or chill). *Her cold temper burned into his mind, and left it frozen.*

Paradox of regression or indefinite proliferation

This paradox corresponds to one that we have already discussed, also on regression. Each time we specify the signification of a proposition through the use of a further one, that second proposition can itself be given a further specification, to infinity. However, where sense is concerned, Deleuze introduces a subtle but crucial point: there is a regression of this kind in terms of the sense *presupposed* by a given proposition. Supposing that we do not – and cannot – say what we mean (the full sense we generate as a presupposition), the regression is then that each time we attempt to capture our presupposed sense we generate another one, to infinity. The introduction of a presupposed sense in the paradox of regression does not only generate the paradox of a chased meaning that never appears, but the much more disrupting paradox that each specification changes the sense of the whole infinite series, that is it changes its effect in terms of value and significance and not only in terms of meaning. An example of this kind of regression and of its relation to the unconscious can be found in the tangles we get into when we try to correct Freudian slips but generate an even worse one, or when we dig ourselves out of complicated lies by digging deeper, generating an ever more sticky and doom-laden pit; the first level of qualifications and excuses is accompanied by another level that transforms the first one making the chains of significance, of guilt and deception, greater each time. *I know I said we had firm evidence, but what I meant was . . .* However, this generation of new senses should not be seen as intrinsically negative, since the values come from the generated sense and are both negative and positive. This neutrality comes out in the second name for the paradox, deduced by Deleuze through a study of Lewis Carroll's use of chains of names and qualifications. The infinite chains are not series of qualified and qualifier propositions, but rather, for the later propositions to refer to the sense of earlier ones, they have to take names from them and give different ones for their sense. *You said 'bed', but you meant 'red'.* This implies that the infinite regression of qualified and qualifier propositions is also an indefinite proliferation of sense and names. What can seem like a negative paradox 'We never get to what we mean' is therefore also a productive one because sense proliferates indefinitely 'We always have more sense than we think'. Deleuze draws a

very important moral conclusion from this property: the proliferation of propositions ensures that no proposition can finally fix sense,
thereby offering a resistance to final moral judgements or the last
word on an event.

Paradox of sterile decoupling or dry reiteration

Though *Logic of Sense* proceeds through many paradoxes it would be
a mistake to say that there is a given number of independent ones.
Instead, the paradoxes are responses to one another and lead into
one another – something we have already seen in the construction of
the circle of denotation, manifestation and signification. So the previous paradox of infinite proliferation is answered by a further
paradox generated by an effort to solve it. If we attempt to extract the
sense of a proposition, by trying to express all its values or significance in a further 'dry' one, then we are left with a sterile sense that
cannot be used in the infinite chain it was extracted from. A good way
of understanding this lies in Deleuze's examples of this paradox in
the esoteric propositions 'God is' or 'The sky is blue' used to curtail
interminable debates about the nature of God, or the meaning of the
sky. Another way of understanding it is Deleuze's expression *dédou-*
blement that I prefer to translate as decoupling rather than division
(this latter term has a perfectly good French pair in *division* that
Deleuze does not use here). *Dédoublement* means to stop the double
lines of infinite and indefinite sense from the previous paradox by
replacing them with a single lone unit; sense is then decoupled or
uncoupled but at the cost of drifting away aimlessly like a wagon shed
from the back of a train. Such dry propositions may indeed claim to
rise out of and block long scholastic debates, but the paradox is that
they do so by expressing a sense that is sterile or powerless with
respect to the propositions it comes from – unless we break its sterility by inserting it back into the chain, and hence break its first function. Dry reiteration is another version of this decoupling, since to
repeat the proposition in order to give it its sense, 'It means just what
it says', leads to the same sterility or dryness. It can seem that this
paradox is the most 'negative' one that Deleuze presents, but that's
not the case, since both decoupling and dry reiteration allow for the
power of the 'infinite' paradoxes to be re-launched. That's why
Deleuze insists on the 'either, or' relation between the two – we can
either go with the infinite or with sterility – but the most important
factor is that in shifting from one to the other we re-energise movement or 'impenetrability' in exactly the kind of way interminable
scholastic debates can be helped by the impenetrability of an esoteric

term or the way a detached esotericism can be released through its insertion in chains of clarifying commentary: 'The two paradoxes, that of infinite regress and that of sterile decoupling, form the two terms of an alternative: one or the other. If the first forces us to combine the greatest power with the greatest impotence, the second imposes upon us an analogous task, which we must later on fulfil [. . .]' (LoS, 32, 44).

Paradox of neutrality, or of essences' third estate
Also following on from the previous paradox (as the next will on this one) this paradox turns on forms of independence between sense and the propositions it is expressed in. This is not a full independence, but rather that contradictions between propositions with respect to their different 'modes' are not reflected in their sense. The modes are denotation, manifestation, signification, possibility, necessity and reality. Propositions may refer to different things, be uttered at different moments and by different speakers, they may be negations of one another, some may be asserting reality, others possibility and others necessity, yet they all express the same sense. Crucially, this paradox does not work if we confuse sense with meaning – something that we must never do in reading *Logic of Sense*. It could be that there is no such thing as sense, but it is not the case that sense is meaning. This is because meaning changes with its propositions; for example, the meaning of 'to be green' alters with a proposition that states a new discovery, say of the frequency of light corresponding to green. This is not the case for sense which, for example, remains neutral for the sense 'to green' in relation to the propositions 'This tree is green', 'This grass is green', 'This is not green', 'Green is necessarily of this frequency', 'The possible green that may be a species of yellow', 'Green is a real property of this leaf'. At this point it is quite understandable and perhaps temporarily advisable to feel that we are entering a realm of complete nonsense: how can the sense not change in all of these? The answer is in the opposition to meaning. Deleuze is not stating that the denotations, manifestations, significations and modal states of the propositions do not change. Consistent with our intuition that meaning alters, he is allowing that the relations of intensity between different senses associated with the propositions can change; that is, their significance can change. Most importantly, he is also stating that this significance and its changes are not secondary to and do not supervene on any of the other moments or modalities of the proposition. However, the condition for this resistance to lawful correspondence

is the neutrality of sense ('to green' does not change though its intense relations to other infinitives do). A negation of a proposition, a change in denotation, signification or modality, does not have a necessary relation to a change in sense and hence in significance (though it does in signification). The significance of an event, which is both something expressed and a change in a state of affairs, is formally independent of the types of propositions that express it, where formal independence implies that there is no necessary law governing a connection, rather than a complete independence. There may indeed be a connection in terms of significance or relations of intensity, but this is not a necessary one. This distinction responds to the suspicion that Deleuze is not really dealing with a paradox here. It would certainly be paradoxical were the meaning of a sentence to be independent of its modes, but once the meaning and sense connection is broken it seems that Deleuze separates sense and modes by definition rather than through a deduction that could generate a logical paradox. Yet this suspicion is unfounded if we return to the 'value' and significance aspects of sense. The paradox is that propositions matter in a manner independent of modal operators. They have effects on values and on emotional investments independent of the rules that govern the modes of the proposition, for example negation or modality. This is not to say that 'X is a traitor', 'X is not a traitor', 'X may be a traitor' or 'X will be a traitor' have necessarily the same effect on significance, and certainly not that they have the same meaning. It is to say that they have the same sense (the infinitive 'to betray') and that the effect on the intense relations of 'to betray' to other infinitives cannot be deduced according to rules about modality or negation. *That failure is possible hurts me more than actual failure.*

Paradox of the absurd, or of impossible objects

The neutrality of sense joins Deleuze's work on language to analytic discussions of impossible objects (and to a potentially rich project of determining how Deleuze advances discussions of problems of existence and subsistence, possibility and impossibility, in the line of Meinong and against Quine – the former is a thinker he admires and follows in *Logic of Sense*, whereas it is arguable that the latter is at the furthest remove from Deleuze). Words for impossible objects may have no referent; we may argue that they therefore have no signification or alternatively that, since they include a contradiction, they have none such, but they do have a sense. So the 'round square', 'immaterial matter' or 'mountain without valley' all have a sense.

57

Once we become accustomed to Deleuze's definition of sense, this is fairly straightforward, since all of these names can appear in a proposition that has an effect that matters and changes values (for example, in the way the 'round square' could trigger enthusiasm for research in philosophy or mathematics, or the way 'immaterial matter' could have implications for a set of religious beliefs, or how 'mountain without valley' could describe the effect on a particular homeland: *after the clearances the Highlands became mountains without valleys*). Once again, the stakes lie in determining whether this is the locus for a paradox and why. The paradox is that though sense is related to the proposition, sense is immune to the law of non-contradiction (it is after all why the proposition matters rather than being an indifferent statement of a matter of fact): 'For the principle of non-contradiction applies to the possible and to the real, but not to the impossible: impossibles are extra-existents, reduced to this minimum, and as such insist in the proposition' (LoS, 35, 49 – I have preferred to translate *principe de contradiction* as 'principle of non-contradiction', to retain the right philosophical meaning, and not to introduce quotes around extra-existents, where there are none in the original. The use of minimum to describe extra-existents is to avoid defining them in opposition to existent, real or possible things, and minimum here is not a value term, as in 'lowest', but rather a description of a relation such as 'least actualised'). For Deleuze, what we ought to take to be absurd or impossible and hence dispensable or worthy of blame turns out to be the source of any significant 'ought' at all, because sense, despite being capable of generation in nonsensical propositions, is the source of significance and value for any proposition. Sense is part of any complete account of even that which we take to obey principles of non-contradiction.

STRUCTURE AND ESOTERIC WORDS

In the introduction to this book, I used a term 'structure' that has up until now seemed redundant in Deleuze's philosophy of language. This omission is due to the approach through positions that he wants to distinguish his philosophy from. As we move to a positive presentation, structure can be seen to play a necessary role in his philosophy and this can be shown through responses to two sets of critical questions which play off each other and highlight polarised types of opposition to Deleuze's approach. The sets of criticism focus on the 'neutrality' and 'evanescence' of sense. One set uses these essential characteristics to criticise any reference to sense at all, claiming that it is a nefarious and nebulous term, the other sees sense as the goal and direction of the philosophy, thereby rele-gating his work on series and on the specific detail and identities of actual language to secondary obstacles in the search for pure sense. There are important political stakes to these oppositions and each side can be taken in two directions; these can be associated broadly with a left wing and a right wing, or a progressive and a conservative mindset. Either, the focus on sense is an idealist and unnecessary dis-traction from a continuous and fragile reality that cautions us to remain within the slow, fragile, yet also powerful unfolding of life and values we must conserve. Or, the focus on sense is a distraction from a reality that includes points where progressive change is pos-sible if we will it. It is ironic to find Deleuze caught in a pincer between these opposed positions, but this can be understood through the way his use of sense can be painted as a superfluous and misleading dream. Sense is then either a delusion turning us away from a stark reality that demands an unstable mixture of conserva-tion and conflict, or a mirage that keeps us from a deeper reality that could underpin revolution.

The second set of oppositions is strongly related to the first, but this time criticise Deleuze for not having gone far enough in the direction of sense or of the Idea. However, they in turn split on the nature of sense. Is it an ineffable source of transforming power, something that can energise life and language showing us the way to an ever more free and 'different' existence on the edge of chaos and catastrophe? Or is sense more like a source and reminder of tran-scendence, of values that exceed knowledge and acts, thereby com-manding restraint, respect and a dutiful suspension of judgement? The technical split in terms of sense then turns on how it operates in attracting and directing the actual but illusory world it must be expressed in. Does sense operate as a liberating disruptor, showing the way to break through reference, meaning, logic, selves and sub-jects into a new existence as inspired creators? Or does sense func-tion as an inhibitor, not only of the goal of somehow breaking through, but also of any belief in actual grounds, whether they be in objects, meanings, processes, the self or the subject? It is less easy to draw these oppositions in terms of conservatism and progressivism, since this judgement depends on external circumstances; inhibition can be revolutionary in serving as an obstacle to conservative stasis or extremism, and a radical permanent revolution can be deeply conservative both in its zeal and its search for permanence in change. In essence, though, the turn to a demanding transcendence is reactionary in relation to Deleuze's position, while the call for ever-accelerating liberation is progressive but to the point of total destruction. More precisely, in terms of Deleuze's study of language, all of the above objections turn on the question of how sense and the event are related to series, given the assumption that both the event and sense retain an independence from the series they occur in.

The answer to this question and to its many political implications is given through another paradox, presented in the eighth series 'on structure'. Put simply, the paradox begins with two series where one is the signifier, which has a 'pointing towards' function, and the other is the signified, which has a 'pointed to' function (possibly, but not necessarily, as meaning or purpose). The former allows the latter to be expressed, somewhat like the way an outstretched thumb might signify that one is hitchhiking. According to Deleuze, there is always an excess of signifiers in the signifying series and a lack within a closed totality of relations in the signified series (a field of signifiers is always 'too rich' whereas a closed field of signifieds is always to be found wanting). So one series, the one that is expressed or explained in something else, inevitably puts across 'too many' signs and a great mobility within them, while the other series, the one that is expressed, always gives us a fixed set of relations and a whole that is 'finished' and yet lacking. Note that I am using 'sign' loosely here as signifier. In orthodox structuralism the sign is a signifier with a signified, but in Deleuze's work, the sign is neither the signifier not the structural sign. However, in all of these positions, there are no 'natural' signifiers or signifieds, they are defined by their function and not by what they are and a signifier can itself be signified (for example, when the words 'the hitchhiker's thumb' signify an actual hitchhiking thumb which itself signifies that someone wants a lift).

Why is this relation of excess to lack paradoxical? First, because the two series depend upon one another: given one we must have the other. We have already seen this kind of dependency in the treatment of dualities, above; the relation of signifier to signified is a case of wider metaphysical dualities in Deleuze's philosophy. So no signifier without signified and vice versa; and no language without either. Second, what each series necessarily provides is at odds with what the other one does. One gives too much openness and changing unstable variety, the other gives too little flexibility and too many fixed relations: hence the paradox of excessive and lacking series yoked to each other but unable to balance each other out. Of course, this would not be a problem were it not the case that language has to have both series, so it must deal with a contradiction that cannot be resolved (the next section on paradox gives Deleuze's arguments for this claim). The dual nature of paradoxes for Deleuze also comes out well here, since the paradox can be seen negatively as a lesson about the failure of signs in two ways: on the signifying side they are too mobile and open, whereas on the signified side they are too complete and fixed. The paradox can also, though, be seen as productive, since the fixity on one side is responded to by the productivity on the other, and the chaotic openness on that side is kept in check by the restrictive closure on the other. At this point we can once again glimpse Deleuze's engineering in a response to the outlined objections, since his paradox means that the separation of revolutionary productive creativity from conservative fixed preservation cannot be made – they have to live with one another imperfectly and cannot dream of pure separation.

In greater detail, this paradox can be seen as part of Deleuze's work on structuralism and on the anthropologist Claude Lévi-Strauss. Deleuze is not a poststructuralist if this is taken to mean a thinker who repudiates structuralism. Instead, Deleuze's work on structure tries to open up and stretch the way structure works in order to allow for the work of events on series. This approach to structuralism can be found in his important essay 'How do we recognise structuralism?' from the collection *Desert Islands and Other Texts* that shares many arguments and ideas with *Logic of Sense*. The argument also connects to the influential appendix to the book, on the novelist Michel Tournier's version of Robinson Crusoe (*Vendredi ou les limbes du pacifique*, 1972). Deleuze's point applies to the relation between the known and the unknown in the sign and to the effect of each upon the other. The signifier, people standing by the side of the road as we drive past, for instance, presents us with an open puzzle or question comprising many potential signifiers: how their body is shaped, their facial and physical behaviour, their clothes, their relation to a background, the time of day, and so on. The signified, on the other hand, can only work if it is a network of simultaneously given but mutually excluding forms of knowledge. The thumb means the search for a hitch or a Roman sign for execution, the behaviour can mean violence or friendship, the clothes can mean wealth or poverty, that bush swaying in the background can mean a group of hidden fellow-travellers or a gentle wind, the time of day could mean someone returning from work or an early reveller. All of these forms of knowledge are interlinked and connected according to a grid of mutually confirming and excluding chains of implication. Deleuze is interested in the way this allows the two series

61

to interact without merging into each other, since the excess of the signifier becomes a forced movement in the signified (in the way your thought processes reassess your knowledge when challenged by the many signs in the hitchers) but also in the way the search for knowledge runs something through the many signifiers, turning them into ordered series (in the way your knowledge puts a pattern in the trail of your eyes across the figures and their background). *Shall I stop? Will they stop?*

Deleuze draws out two crucial technical terms from this interaction of series: the 'empty place' in signifying series, and the 'non-situated' or 'placeless' 'occupant' in the signified. These allow for interesting studies of works of art with a Deleuzian take on structuralist approaches, which is also a good way of understanding the terms. For example, in his *Annie Hall* (and in many of his films), Woody Allen (1977) builds up a humourous paranoid tension, explicable through Deleuze's concepts of excess and lack. In the film, Annie's brother Duane has made the following confession to Alvie, the character played by Allen: 'I tell you this because, as an artist, I think you'll understand. Sometimes, when I'm driving . . . on the road at night . . . I see two headlights coming towards me. Fast. I have this sudden impulse to turn the wheel quickly, head on into the oncoming car.' A short while after this unasked for and disturbing information, the film cuts to the following scene: 'Duane, behind the wheel stares straight ahead. It is raining very hard, the windshield wipers are moving very quickly. The headlights of another car brighten the interior of Duane's car as the camera shows first Duane, then Annie, then Alvie staring straight ahead.' The tension and humour come from the way we accompany Alvie in his fearful and fated calculation of what is to happen. On the one hand, like a moving beam shed by the car lights, we search for indications of the impending twitch of the wheel. We therefore pass an empty place along the excess of candidates (the hands, the neck, Allen's own face, Annie's unknowing one, the engine note, the sound of tyres). Each one is invested as an empty place as we alight on it during the search across them and as the question passing between them unites them into a series: *Is this the sign of fate?* The empty place is then carried by Alvie's gaze and mind, and ours, as they run across the excess of clues. The minds are not the essential thing here, however, since Deleuze's point is that the empty place is the condition for the excess of signifiers: because what they signify is not fixed, but empty, each sign and all series are necessarily open. Woody Allen's paranoia plays on and reveals this kind of desperate search amid too many threatening signifiers of doom (hence also his hypochondria, guilty fantasies and capacity for mishearing innocent terms as insults or menaces).

On the other hand, at the level of meaning or the signified in the film, we have the crash that may or may not happen, we do not know, and because we do not know we cannot place it in our current knowledge of the characters, the plot, the message of the film, its jokes, and so on. The crash is not given and it has no place, it is supernumerary until it happens, yet its lack plays through all the meanings. The two terms work off one another in the scene, since the moving search displaces the crash and its meaning while the possible crash motivates the search, in the same way as a placeless meaning motivates the paranoia ('they want to persecute me'), or the hypochondria ('I am terribly ill'), or the guilty restlessness ('I have committed a crime and they know it'):

> It is necessary to understand that the two series are marked, one by excess, the other by lack, and that the two determinations are interchanged without ever reaching equilibrium. What is in excess in the signifying series is literally an empty square and an always displaced place without an occupant. What is lacking in the signified series is a supernumerary and non-situated given – an unknown, an occupant without a place, or something always displaced.
>
> (LoS, 59, 65)

Deleuze's notion of structure is itself therefore marked by a lack of equilibrium and by processes of reciprocal determination where each reciprocating side determines the other, but only as something in movement, resistant to identity and disruptive of any settled structure, for example of knowledge. So when we squirm and twist in embarrassment and amusement at Allen's predicaments, it is not because they are fixed, but on the contrary, because they are open. It is the impending event and its effect, through series, on established meanings and changeable signs that explains the humour (and the role of sense as this event): 'And – and uh, there's gonna be all that tension. You know we never kissed before and I'll never know when to make the right move or anything. So we'll kiss now we'll get it over with and then we'll go eat. Okay?' (Allen, 1997).

This necessary reciprocal determination between an essentially excessive series and an essentially lacking one allows Deleuze to make the following political statement:

> It is this disequilibrium that makes revolutions possible. It is not at all the case that revolutions are determined by technical progress. Rather,

they are made possible by this gap between the two series, which solic-
its realignment of the economic and political totality in relation to the
parts of the technical progress.

(LoS, 49, 64)

So against conservatism and reactionary politics, but also against a
government by supposedly progressive technocrats, Deleuze insists
that it is in the nature of series to produce an excess that demands
revolution, that is a creative experimentation with novel signs and
events beyond any totality of forms of knowledge, including a meta-
understanding of how technology is associated with progress. It is
impossible to be conservative, because the things that we ought to
be conservative about are excessive and lacking. However, against
utopian revolutionary politics, Deleuze's structure requires this
excess even within any utopian image and therefore defines that
image as a form of lack itself demanding a creative and transforming approach. Instead, Deleuze speaks of a 'permanent revolution'
but this does not mean a permanent total revolution since revolutionary events and their replaying are generated by excess (new
signs demanding revolution) and by lack (insufficiency in current
social structures), that is by a relation to ongoing and transforming
series rather than absolute novelty. Totalitarian revolution is impossible because events happen between series, rather than at their end
or pure beginning: 'The technocrat is the natural friend of the dic-
tator – computers and dictatorship; but the revolutionary lives in the
gap which separates technical progress from social totality, and
inscribes there his dream of permanent revolution' (LoS, 49, 64).
The Deleuzian revolutionary politics is therefore between any final
ideal of a society based on a universal model and an opposing view
where society explodes into individual and contingent interests.
This can seem very suspicious, since it appears to evade a commitment to either side, while also drawing on the values of both. It is
worth asking whether this is a general property of his appeal to paradoxes: Do they make claims to an impossible middle ground and
to its contradictory extremes? More technically, can Deleuze put
forward workable models based on his deductions of paradoxes?
Can practical modes of life, for example political ones, be based
around those models?

In the seventh series 'of esoteric words', Deleuze provides
responses to these questions through a development of properties
of the duality of series with respect to a number of procedures based
on his reading of Lewis Carroll. It is natural to interpret these
approaches in a literary manner first. *Logic of Sense* provides us with

a new structuralist literary theory, though again such a convenient label is risky and 'a new pragmatics on the structural becoming of texts and events' is more accurate, if unwieldy. This second name captures the way Deleuze's structure is mobile, focused on events, and avoids any limitation of the literary around a closed text or body of texts. However, there are dangers in associating this work with literature and aesthetics, since, as we have seen with the series on structure, Deleuze sets his book within political, philosophical and moral horizons and challenges. The following 'procedures for serial development' from the seventh series are therefore not only ways approaching a particular type of literature, but much broader practical methods derived from his work on structure. Series can develop in the following ways:

1. Two series of events with very small differences between them can relate to one another and be set in motion through a shared strange object.
2. Two very different series of events can be regulated together through a shared proposition, onomatopoeia or sound.
3. Two very disparate series of propositions can be regulated by an esoteric word (an internal and secret word such as 'Snark' in Carroll).
4. Strongly ramified series can be regulated by portmanteau words (words with multiple meanings constituted by the fusion of other words, such as squiggle fusing squirm and wriggle).

It is straightforward but a little restricting to see how these procedures work in Carroll's books as literary devices. Broadly, they hold together differing tales, storylines, forms of expression, tropes and realms through words, sounds and objects that bridge between them yet do not conflate their differences into a single narrative or stylistic unity. These intermediaries share a similar puzzling set of properties such as strangeness, lack of meaning and ambiguity allowing them to switch between strands while resisting their reduction because of those properties; for example, ambiguity allows two accounts to be connected through the fact that the word belongs to both yet it also keeps them apart since it has different meanings in them. However, the function of these mediating terms is much greater than as a literary device in *Logic of Sense*, since they explain how the empty place and placeless occupant work practically in series within structures generally. Furthermore, they explain how events, series and propositions are, at the same time, synthesised and contracted, yet kept apart and subdivided. They are then one of the detailed accounts of Deleuze's important concept of disjunctive synthesis. Even this does not capture the full strategic importance of his moves. This lies in two processes set up by the procedures releasing the power of disjunctive synthesis: revolutionary critique and creation (an inseparable duo repeated in the title of another literary critical collection with much greater horizons than the purely literary: *Essays Critical and Clinical* – the clinical is necessarily creative for Deleuze).

The answer to the critical question posed earlier is therefore that specific and practical procedures allow us to criticise, create and transform political situations, in such a way as neither a totalising nor an isolated individualist theory can emerge. So it is a mistake to think that Deleuze's 'in between' position is impossible or unworkable. It is also an error to believe that a position avoiding extremes is incapable of revolutionary actions, or that it complies with an established order. On the contrary, he provides well determined practical procedures that set out precise critiques of the extremes, invite creative expressions of new practices and revolutionise stagnant or corrupted situations. The apparent impossibility of his determination of sense through paradox becomes a practical and effective assembly resisting reduction into a unified whole. Here is the wider interpretation of the procedures listed in the work on esoteric words:

1. Apparently stable structures relating two social and political series of events can be set in motion through the release of a shared strange object. For example, a model for working practices may relate, order and allow the control of two apparently similar tasks. The comparison strengthens the claim that the ordering is natural or necessary. It can be resisted when the related series are shown to be different in relation to a strange object that the ordering is incapable of claiming as its own (when specific spaces and times, or values and qualities, are used creatively and rendered inassimilable in order to resist the hold of a repressive model, for instance in the seditious use of meeting places, or in an unpredicted resistance to the imposition of a particular time-constraint).

2. If two series of events are proclaimed to be from completely different political groups, social classes, cultural practices or economic functions, thereby justifying a form of social order based on that difference, then propositions, outcries and physical revolts or attractions shared between the series can be deployed to question their division. A creative attention or voicing of

well-chosen propositions allows for a critique of the order and changes within the series and between them, without having to claim they are 'the same' (when tastes, affects, emotions and statements cross sexual, economic and cultural divides, independent of a theory that unites them, for example in disruptive statements such as 'Animals think' or 'Murder is always murder' or 'We love each other just as you do').

3. Two apparently distinct social models and their systems of knowledge and justification can be brought into line through a shared esoteric word or term, that is one that is significant in both without being fully conceptualised. A disruptive shared word attracts other propositions and gives them a common direction yet sits uncomfortably with them, creates ephemeral yet deeply powerful heterogeneous movements. For example, when different lines can unite briefly around resistance to a common foe and dreams of a future without its return – '*solidarity*: unions and church against tyranny' or 'students and workers against *fascism*'.

4. An order based on multiple radical separations on individual lines, groups, units or subjects can be disrupted through the emergence of a dream, goal or wish that crosses the separations and unites them temporarily around a new word or direction, interpreted differently because it is nascent and still mysterious, but maintaining the differences together in resistance and forward movement nonetheless (for example, when a multifaceted slogan such as 'Enough!' or 'Justice!' or 'Peace!' or 'They shall not pass!' expresses a common thread running through a society or across many societies allowing disparate interests and groups to move away from an old order).

These practical procedures provide a strong response to criticisms about lack of cutting edge and abstraction in Deleuze's work, but their roots in his work on paradoxes and language allow other related criticisms to persist. Notably, each of the points listed above contains ambiguous, vague, 'secret' and 'strange' terms that fulfil the function of relating series without fusing them together with the function of allowing series to resist an analysis according to more fundamental grounds, such as a form of knowledge, an ideology or a theoretical framework uniting all of them. The terms are supported by his study of paradoxes and structure, since the former allow for elements of language that slip from one function to another (from denotation to signification, in terms of truth, for instance), while the latter defines the most general forms of 'disjunctive' terms in the 'empty place' and its power to convey excess, and the 'placeless occupant' and its release of a lack into a structure. What if the vagueness and ambiguity are signs of a fundamental flaw in Deleuze's approach (as could be argued from debates on vagueness in analytic philosophy, for example, as put forward by Timothy Williamson)? In the same way as the concept 'vague' can be criticised as merely a lack of knowledge that can be removed by careful measurement and definition, or in the way ambiguity can be resolved through more precise definition of terms, could it not be that Deleuze's paradoxes and his paradoxical terms can be eliminated through more careful analysis and definition? If so, would it not be better to seek to construct language in order to avoid generating paradox, rather than celebrating it and focusing on its capacity to generate and make space for novel creative responses? From a more practical point of view, could we not take each of the linguistic formulae from the procedures and subject them to a critical analysis that would eliminate them or replace them with better terms? This would not necessarily be reactionary politically, since the elimination of vague or ambiguous terms might allow for more effective reforming activity underpinned by a stronger and more convincing relation to truth, for example as supplied by the empirical sciences? Why appeal to paradox and nonsense when we have scientific truth and its capacity to unmask obscurantism?

PARADOX AND NONSENSE

Deleuze answers critical questions about the necessity and form of paradoxes and of nonsense in the eleventh and twelfth series 'of nonsense' and 'on paradox'. Put simply, his arguments are that nonsense is not the absence of sense but rather the presence of an important kind of sense that can only operate through nonsense. Paradoxes are not puzzling and detrimental contradictions generated within logical systems, but forms that reveal how contradiction is generated, thereby revealing the limits of common sense and good sense, and making space for a different sense sited in language and in things that embraces impossibility against common and good sense. Nonsense has the dual function of breaking with the demands of denotation, manifestation and signification, and opening up an additional realm of sense. So though a word or chain of words may appear to have no reference, no reasonable meaning and may call into question the reliability of anyone that utters them, they still work and operate in language in two positive ways: they undermine false denials of the circle of language, that is they belie claims to secure and well-founded denotation, manifestation and signification; and they allow for the production of sense between different series. A good way of understanding these functions is through the capacity of creative poetic language to debunk priggishness, grammatical or otherwise:

> (i do not know what it is about you that closes
> and opens; only something in me understands
> the voice of your eyes is deeper than all roses)
> nobody, not even the rain, has such small hands
> > (e e cummings, 'somewhere I have never traveled', 1994)

Nonsense works. It can wound and delight, sooth and excite. When it does so, not only are sensations and affects transmitted, but claims to corral them through proper use founder. Cummings rejoins Deleuze and provides a manifesto for sense in his 'since feeling is first'. The poem releases sense by breaking its bond to syntax, meaning and clear reference, strengthening a sensual side and releasing words from the demands of syntax and proper reference:

> since feeling is first
> who pays any attention
> to the syntax of things
> will never wholly kiss you;
> > (e e cummings, 'since feeling is first', 1994)

Deleuze determines two figures for nonsense by studying the way nonsensical words work in Lewis Carroll. Such words connect series within language and series within objects and therefore act as unstable but functioning empty places *and* placeless occupants: 'To account for this correlation and this dissymmetry we have made use of a number of dualities: it is at once excess and lack, empty space and supernumerary object, a place without an occupant and an occupant without a place' (LoS, 66, 83). This leads to a definition of nonsense words far removed from standard understanding. In the logic of sense nonsense words 'say their own sense'. In turn this is defined according to two properties of nonsense words with respect to how the sense of a word can be given. First, for standard words, sense is given through a further word that defines it or it is given through a denotation, yet neither of these work for a word such as 'Snark' in Carroll and, instead, the word denotes or refers to itself. (*Show me the Snark – I cannot, so we must look at its sense – What is its sense? – Well, I cannot give you another word, it's 'Snark'.*) Second, again normally, a word cannot lead to an opposition that implies it; if we

69

define A as 'B and not-B' we know that we have an impossible term or a false definition. However, portmanteau words, such as smog (smoke and fog) can lead to such contradictions (since there is fog that is not smoke). These words only give their sense when we take it that one side gives the sense of the other and the reverse (the sense of smog is 'smoke and fog' or 'fog and smoke'). When we claim that nonsense words 'say their own sense' we imply that their sense cannot be determined elsewhere and that this sense is itself contradictory; the sense is acquired through self-stating and through the stating of a contradiction.

It could be objected at this point that Deleuze is using sense in a confusing way in these arguments, since on the one hand it is operating as meaning, on the other as sense redefined as changes in the intensity of relations between processes, themselves expressed as infinitives. There are two related answers to this criticism. First, given the non-linear and partially independent nature of series, each one starts afresh without presupposing the others. So the series on nonsense is opening the way for the new definition of sense by slipping from sense as meaning to sense as intensive process. Second, sense is an example of a nonsense word for Deleuze, because it must have the double structure of, for instance, portmanteau words, and it must express the dualities contained in the concept of sense (excess in the expressed, lack in the expression). It is therefore necessarily both sense as that which is expressed and meaning as the expression, where these also subdivide into infinitive and intensity, word and object. This duality rather than opposition is one of the key points of the series on nonsense. Nonsense says its own sense, not as that which has no sense, as in the idea of no-sense, rather saying one's own sense is expressing the duality in its resistance to demands for oppositions and for words that stand on one or other side of an exclusive divide (either sense or no-sense). Here is the long passage that explains this move away from the principle of non-contradiction stating that a proposition cannot be true and false:

> This is indeed the most general problem of the logic of sense: what would be the problem of rising from the domain of truth to the domain of sense, if it were only to find between sense and nonsense a relation analogous to that of the true and the false? We have already seen that it is futile to go from the conditioned to the condition in order to think of the conditioned in the image of the conditioned as the simple form of possibility. The condition cannot have with its negative the same kind of relation that the conditioned has with its

negative. The logic of sense is necessarily determined to posit between sense and nonsense an original type of intrinsic relation, a mode of co-presence.

(LoS, 68, 85)

The stakes of Deleuze's logic of sense are shown well here. He is claming that the realm of sense is the condition for the realm of signification (the ream of identified meanings determined according to the principle of non-contradiction) and for the realm of denotation (identified actual objects). However, this use of condition takes it as a real condition, that is, not as what is possible in the actual words and worlds it will be expressed in, but as related to them through mutual determinations. The realms interact as determining conditions for one another; put simply, sense conditions the intense significance of actual things and words, whereas the expression of sense in them gives it a determinacy allowing it to avoid a descent into chaos. These determinations would collapse the two realms into one real one, were there not an asymmetry between the two realms, that is were there not a difference between the relations that hold in both – otherwise the relations would become the laws that conflated the two, for example through a shared principle of non-contradiction or even a law of excluded middle stating that a proposition is either true or false. Deleuze's critique of Kant's transcendental philosophy is in the background here (as prefigured in his *Kant's Critical Philosophy*, 1963, developed in *Difference and Repetition* and still a concern in his last essay 'Immanence: a life . . .'). He is developing a new transcendental philosophy that seeks to avoid the mapping of the condition on what it conditions, thereby allowing both an openness through the asymmetry of their relations and a form of reciprocal determination. The worst fate would then be to destroy that asymmetry through a shared formal logic based on non-contradiction.

Yet, what value is there in embracing the co-presence of the true and the false or a proposition and its negation? Are not all the paradoxes produced when we do this representative of positions and systems to be avoided and blamed? The straightforward answer is once again that Deleuze's position is consistent with the operation of the principle of non-contradiction *as a response to paradoxes*. He discusses this in context of objects that lead to paradoxes, such as Russell's paradox. The wider point is, though, that the laws and rules are developed because other propositions that do not obey them allow paradoxes to be generated and, therefore, sense and nonsense are prior to and constitutive of the logical laws. Deleuze calls this the determination of signification in terms of principles of non-contradiction, or law of excluded middle, or Russell's theory of types. Whatever value we assign to such laws though cannot apply regressively to the paradoxes that give rise to them without forming a vicious circle, not in a strict logical sense for that would set off circles within circles, but in terms of our explanation of the genesis of laws and language in relation to sense: 'The interest of the determinations of signification lies in the fact that they engender the principles of non-contradiction and the excluded middle, instead of these principle being given ready made; the paradoxes themselves enact the genesis of contradiction and exclusion in the propositions stripped of signification' (LoS, 69, 87). We therefore miss something crucial about thought and its laws if we apply the law retrospectively and thereby fuse condition and conditioned.

What we miss is nonsense as a 'donation of sense', that is, of the appearance of significance and singular intense investment in an event. Once sense has been distinguished from reliable signification and denotation, once it appears with nonsense as it generates a paradox, uniformity and repeatability of the same meanings and references are lost. This means that nonsense must appear as an event, or better, with an event: hence Deleuze's use of 'donation' understood as a singular gift of sense rather than an identified and registered exchange of meaning. Each time the 'nonsense' of cummings's poems are stated their sense changes with the saying, with its when, who and how. Sense is therefore produced rather than exchanged or reused and Deleuze's wider lesson is that this is potentially as true for all words as it is for nonsense ones. Sense is therefore also an effect of the stating or saying, it is produced, but it is also latent prior to that production – hence the insistence of replaying, re-enactment and counter-actualisation in the production of sense. Cummings's poems are remade each time because their sense and hence all else is allowed to float and drift in them:

not so
hard dear

you're killing me

(e e cummings, 'raise the shade', 1994)

It is this drift that Deleuze values in structuralism each time it finds a floating signifier or each time it claims that all signifiers are floating, that is, that anything that signifies does so contingently and can equally well signify something else (for example, when we use a code that moves each letter in the alphabet along one and 'ibse' signifies what 'hard' used to). This drift is not the meaninglessness of total lack of sense, as we have seen in his novel definition of nonsense. On the contrary, it allows philosophy to 'displace frontiers' and open up new connections, directing thought to new creations rather than tying within ever more fixed structures. This explains the absence of positive references to an existentialism of the absurd and the critical remarks on Camus in *Logic of Sense*. The absurd situates existence through a lack of sense and its main events are stunting removals and destructions ('One always finds one's burden again', Camus, 2005: 24) whereas Deleuze determines events as excessive and as a donation with no prior negativity. The danger in the absurd is the emptiness it leaves us with and then how we fill it anew; the risk in Deleuze's higher empiricism is that it might donate too much for us to bear or select within.

In developing Deleuze's response to questions about the value of nonsense and paradox, the twelfth series 'on paradox' repeats many of the points from the series that precedes it, but it adds a discussion of their strategic consequences and context. These are characterised by a contrast drawn between different modes of thought with respect to the allocation of what they think about or the events they think with. So the difference between a world conditioned by sense and by disjunctive syntheses, and a world conditioned by the principle of non-contradiction, as well as other resolutions of paradoxes, is mirrored in two further differences: first, a distinction drawn between conscious cogitation and thinking with the unconscious; second, a distinction drawn between a thought that assigns categories or enclosures (common sense) and then assigns beings to those categories (good sense), and thinking in relation to events before and free of such assignations. These oppositions are consistent themes in Deleuze's work; they are developed at greater length in Chapter 3 of *Difference and Repetition* for the critique of common sense and good sense, and in *A Thousand Plateaus* for the critique of spatial assignment as opposed to flows free of boundaries, in the distinction drawn between smooth and striated space. I will study the consequences of this in relation to thought, the unconscious and the event in Chapter 5 below. Here, I focus on the critique of common sense and good sense, because this Deleuzian response is an answer to some of the critical points made above about the cost and risks of abandoning standard logic and of embracing nonsense words, vague objects, excess in the signifier and lack in the signified. In short, Deleuze's view is that the underlying presuppositions of these critical approaches betray and reinforce the negative and illegitimate hold of common sense and good sense on thought.

His first move is again to describe a set of paradoxes that explain the genesis but also the insufficiency of common sense and good sense:

1. The abnormal set (for example, the set of all sets that are not members of themselves, leading to Russell's paradox: if the set of all sets that do not contain themselves does not contain itself, then it contains itself, but if it does contain itself, then it does not).
2. The rebellious element (an element that belongs to a set that must exist since the element does, but that then belongs to two mutually exclusive subsets that it determines – the round square could be an example of this, but note that Deleuze's views on existence are moot here and further study of impossible terms, in particular mathematical ones, is important for later work on *Logic of Sense*).
3. Infinite subdivision (the present is always either passing away into an infinitely subdivided past, or moving into a similarly divided future, but it is never simply present).
4. Nomadic distribution (a distribution that determines an open space rather than filling a closed one – but how is a distribution that does not define categories or distinct spaces a distribution at all?).

All these paradoxes are barriers to a well-ordered distribution that assigns things to sets or categories and thereby gives them an identity defined positively and negatively (belongs to A, does not belong to B). They therefore hinder common sense by putting the reflection that determines categories into question (we can construct paradoxical sets). They also obstruct good sense by determining things that cannot be placed in any category (there are elements that belong everywhere and nowhere).

The main thrust of Deleuze's argument is not about the formal problems raised by these paradoxes, but lies instead in a critique of a dominant image of thought, general opinion or *doxa*, a common social and intellectual order. In broad terms this *doxa* reinforces the following presuppositions:

1. In terms of direction, thought should seek to move away from difference and towards order (in the sense of finding all the categories to which things belong) and thereby eliminate pure differences, that is differences that are not based on oppositions or negations.
2. In terms of function, thought should assign things in a fixed and well-determined manner: a 'sedentary distribution' such as the repartition of land for farming or the division of economic functions into sectors.
3. Thought should move from the singular, that which is incomparable, to the regular, that which can be brought under laws.
4. It should change the remarkable into the ordinary.
5. Thought ought to direct time from past to future as the direction determined by the four previous points (that is, the future is more ordered than the past, which is what gives time its direction).
6. The key activity in this direction takes place only in the present.
7. Thought then is about prediction and possibility: how we predict and delimit the movement into greater order by weighing up what is possible and likely.

We shall see how Deleuze shows that all of these presuppositions miss the creative role of the unconscious in relation to events in the later chapter on thought, but, to conclude this discussion of his philosophy of language, it is important to disentangle it from three misunderstandings my dialectical reading may have imposed upon it. First, it is not that there is a language or thought eternally free of *doxa* and residing in a pure realm of paradox. On the contrary, sense and nonsense require *doxa* and fall back into it: 'the gift of sense occurs only when the conditions of signification are also being determined' (LoS, 81, 100). Second, the event of language is as much sensual and bodily as it is about thought, or more precisely, language, thought, the unconscious and body are inseparable in a fragile event that creates sense as it disappears into signification and meaning: 'This tableau of a total deployment at the surface is necessarily affected, at each of these points by an extreme and persistent fragility' (81, 100). Language and paradoxes are creatures of passion: 'It is here, however, that the gift of sense occurs, in this region that precedes all good sense and common sense. For here, with the passion of the paradox, language attains its highest power' (79, 97). Finally, it does not follow from this reciprocal determination of meaning and fragile sense that they are equal partners in a symmetrical relation, since novelty and creation, intensity and value, can only come from sense and nonsense:

nothing which we are to perceive in this world equals
the power of your intense fragility: whose texture
compels me with the colour of its countries,
rendering death and forever with each breathing
(e e cummings, *W [ViVa]*, **XXIX**, 1994)

3

Philosophy as event

Logic of Sense marks a turning point in Deleuze's way of doing philosophy. Up to this book, his style was one of critical and incisive reading of other thinkers (Hume, Bergson, Kant, Nietzsche and Spinoza) or of the creation of a highly complex weave of philosophical arguments and concepts (*Difference and Repetition*). With *Logic of Sense* experimentation with a style of writing and a more free approach to the tradition break out and allow novel ideas and a different ethos to guide philosophical thought. In order to understand the depth of this shift it is helpful to situate Deleuze's philosophical training at the Sorbonne. He was perhaps the most talented heir to a profoundly academic form of textual analysis, deeply indebted to a rigorous search for structural consistency, historical situation and conceptual power in philosophical works in relation to contemporary concerns such as discoveries in science, new political ideologies, innovation in the arts and historical events. For example, at the Sorbonne, Ferdinand Alquié and Martial Gueroult, though often disagreeing with one another, were masters in the historical reading of modern rationalism, notably Descartes and Spinoza. Deleuze continued this reading through his own extraordinarily detailed and rich study of Spinoza, *Spinoza: Expressionism in Philosophy*, which appeared a year before *Logic of Sense*. Jean Wahl, on the other hand, introduced empiricism and pragmatism as well as the works of Whitehead into French thought and Deleuze's work, thereby offering a contrast to Jean Hyppolite's reading of Hegel. Deleuze was also inspired in his early years by Sartre and then later by Nietzsche and by French thought developing Nietzsche's ideas and spirit (partly explaining the long appendix on Klossowski in *Logic of Sense*). This intellectual background led to Deleuze's early studies – models of clarity and scope – and to a long series of reviews and review essays, many of which address the philosophical works of his teachers with modesty, admiration, but also some devastating critical points. Almost all of these reviews and articles are used in little altered form or as the source of notes and remarks in later books; this does not mean that there is an exact continuity between the works, but rather that his early academic studies provide philosophical material for the creation of new concepts and structures. What then led to the move away from this historical approach, with its commitment to reflection in relation to contemporary issues through close critical reading, to the more creative and experimental writing of *Logic of Sense*? More significantly, given this change, what is at stake for what we understand philosophy to be? Finally, how does this alter the way Deleuze is positioned as a philosopher?

The eighteenth series of *Logic of Sense* 'of the three images of philosophers' is a good start for answering these questions. It is an interesting series from a bibliographical and concordance point of view, since the idea of 'images of thought' in relation to philosophy is also developed in the third chapter of *Difference and Repetition*, whereas the remarks on Nietzsche draw on Deleuze's *Nietzsche and Philosophy*, while the spatial and event-driven approach leads into work on thought and event, notably the concept of haecceity in *A Thousand Plateaus*, and the remarks on philosophy and illness connect to ideas in *Essays Critical and Clinical*. Above all, though, every one of these points is taken up and added to in Deleuze and Guattari's *What Is Philosophy?* where philosophy is defined as the creation of concepts on different planes occupied by conceptual personae (such as Diogenes Laertius's reinvention of Empedocles as a persona on a plane determined by Etna, by the event of his death in the volcano and by the sign provided by his remaining bronze sandal – an example found in *Logic of Sense* and then twenty-two years later in *What Is Philosophy?*). These connections and the endurance of questions about the nature and legacies of philosophy demonstrate Deleuze's ever-present reflection on philosophical practice in light of philosophical tradition. *Logic of Sense* is the first book where radical experimentation on the practice takes place at the same time as this reflection, perhaps because Deleuze was aware that his own thought marked a new and potentially influential departure. (Of course, his other works are also inventive, but style of thought and novel form are united more strongly in the sense and series book.)

There are two main facets to this turn and reflection: first, Deleuze begins to study images of philosophy in terms of movement; second, these movements are explained and drawn in bodies and propositions as they express events happening to them which they then resonate with. Rather than a logical timeline, or conceptual classification, or historical situation, or ideological narrative, Deleuze gives us a *diagram* of event-driven and event-creating movements. Only after these have been drawn does he risk classifications and judgements, and even then these are always set against underlying tensions and connections, as well as stakes relative to the occurrence of further events. This production of images of philosophy is itself a form of his 'superior empiricism': a creative but also self-destructive fusion of experiment and experience, refusing the ultimate legitimacy of any procedural abstraction, while working with its persistent return through images of thought. A Deleuzian diagram is an apparatus expressing a series of dynamic transformations; it is a concept he develops beautifully in his book on Francis Bacon, *The Logic of Sensation* (1981), in relation to Bacon's preparation of the ground for his paintings, and in his book on Foucault, *Foucault* (1986), in terms of movements within layers of what is seen and what is said. These movements are not displacements of things as the effect of forces, but changes in things as they move and encounter others. *A diagram is then itself in movement and designed to convey displacement and change, rather than provide a static representation of a given state or even a representation of a passage from one static position to another.*

The diagram is not a map, but a series of directions and processes rendered in such a way as to combine many sensual and linguistic interactions in a domain. For example, a map could be drawn of the path of an ambulance escaping enemy territory across a desert, but this would be mainly a representation of a set of spatio-temporal locations and not a full diagram of the flight. This latter would only be achieved when the flows of intensities (variations in love, hate, suspicion, ideas and life-forces) in the ambulance were expressed in relation to the path, to the desert, to heat and to encounters with enemies and so on: *as it gets hotter you will quarrel . . .* An evocative title capturing the direction and hopes of the journey, such as 'Ice cold in Alex', is a better sign for a diagram of the changing flows of fears, weaknesses, thirsts and energies than a simple representation of a set of spatial facts. Note, though, that this opposition of representative map and diagram is itself a matter of degrees of relations rather than an analytic difference. Maps are diagrams, but to a low degree in relation to a particular series of events, that is the intensities and movements are captured and set in motion poorly. For example, compass points carry a minimal set of physical associations dependent on hemispheres and on which degrees of variation are monitored, so according to Deleuze's approach no map is strictly 'intensity neutral'. Indeed, were there such pure representations then his philosophy would become limited to a particular domain, rather than a claim about all of them.

HEIGHT, DEPTH AND SURFACE

In order to convey three different images of the processes and sensations of philosophy, Deleuze's diagram works on three axes: upwards (height), downwards (depth) and on the surface, or simply 'surface'. The first two are not on a single vertical axis for exactly the same reason that a diagram is not an intensity neutral map. How the movement upwards works is not the logical negation or the spatial opposite of the downward movement. On the contrary, the two movements or directions involve different determinations of one another such that downwards on the upwards axis does not mean the same as downwards on its own axis and vice versa. This philosophical separation of vertical movement into different axes of elevation and descent can be understood through the concept of sense. In a world framed by values associated with elevation, a fall has negative connotations, but if a world is framed through values of descent or material depth, then elevation can be seen as a negative detached loftiness. *Revere the sublime thinker! With his head in the clouds . . .* Similarly, the surface or surfacing must not be understood as simple movement on the horizontal plane but as an event determining depth and elevation yet different from both. Surface is neither a space between two others, nor a separate independent realm. It is instead a condition for processes in the other realms that retains an independence from them in one aspect yet is determined by them in another.

The surface is a real effect between actual causes (depth) and ideal propositions (elevation). It could be imagined as an opaque and unstable surface between a liquid and a gas. The roughness of the sea's surface alters sense from the point of view of an 'upper' airborne perspective and from a lower sea-dwelling one; it is independent of both, yet also the medium for their mutual transformations – hence the creative richness of worlds that encounter one another through such a medium, from Jules Verne to Disney's *Finding Nemo*: 'I was beginning to accustom myself to the sight of this interesting fishing, when suddenly, as the Indian was on the ground, I saw him make a gesture of terror, rise, and make a spring to return to the surface of the sea. I understood his dread. A gigantic shadow appeared just above the unfortunate diver' (Verne, 1994: Chapter 3). There is a different 'image' of the gas–liquid relation from both sides and the condition for these images and for their difference is the surface between the two. To the objection that shared laws relate gas and liquid, we could answer that contemporary science questions this through emergent properties resistant to reductionism, understood as the search for the most simple general laws unifying a set of apparently disparate laws and processes: 'Thus, none of the properties of water vapor are emergent, regardless of what people thought in the past, but some, if not all, of the properties of liquid water and ice may turn out to be irreducibly emergent' (Hull and Van Regenmortel, 2002: 4). Such an answer would be hostage to discoveries in science, either in firming up a reductionist approach, that is by confirming more fundamental laws holding for both media, or in changing our concept of emergence, for example by denying any role for the surface. It is arguable that this latter possibility is in fact the case when emergence is defined strictly in terms of incompatible local laws and that we therefore require a non-scientific support for the concept of surface. I will provide a full version of the need for this type of support in a later section setting out a refutation of materialist readings of Deleuze in relation to *Logic of Sense*.

For a different literary example of Deleuze's conception of the role of the surface, here is a passage from Virginia Wolf capturing the emotional power of a surface between water and air close to his ideas:

> And then, letting her eyes slide imperceptibly above the pool and rest on that wavering line of sea and sky, on the tree trunks which the smoke of steamers made waver upon the horizon, she became with all that dower sweeping savagely in and inevitable withdrawing, hypnotized, and the two senses of that vastness and this tininess (the pool had diminished again) flowering within it made her feel that she was bound hand and foot and unable to move by the intensity of feelings which reduced her own body, her own life, and the lives of all the people in the world, for ever, to nothingness.
>
> (Woolf, 1997: 72)

The surface of the pool and its relation to the sea and horizon are reserves for ideas of vastness and tininess, free of a simple logical opposition of vast and tiny, and caught instead in a productive pendulum-like tension: the sense at work is vast and it is tiny, and it is not one without the other. As such, it communicates the attraction and threat of the sea, compelling and hypnotic yet also annihilating through these affects. The surface connects pool and sea, reflective surface and horizon, allowing the passage from the safe and the familiar to the distant and obliterating. The two-way passage is important, but less so than its power to generate new images and to retain this power. The sea and air are kept from an essential or natural function by their relation through a third term, the surface, and its relation to thought. This 'becoming' within the thought, as mesmerised not into a state of immobility but rather into movement towards the border of a compelling danger, is Deleuze's sense as expressed in the intensities of an individual's feelings. Sense is incomplete without this expression, but it is not captured in the feelings, as a final meaning, nor does it cause them on a single plane regulated by natural laws. Sense and surface resonate with their expression in a relation of mutual determination, where significance appears differently in both through a shared two-sided event: '. . . listening to waves crowded over the pool . . .'

It is not enough, therefore, or even quite wrong to consider the axes defining images of philosophy independent of the events that determine them for different individuals (not human individuals but rather singular perspectives on worlds determined by events). Depth, height and surface are different for different events and for how they are expressed through individuals. These events communicate but cannot be reduced to one another or to laws that hold for the axes. If we wanted a slogan for these views, then it would be 'A different individual for each event, in a different world, but always communicating with all others'. The axes are ways of accounting for this communication, they also allow for temporary classifications of how they interact and the effects and legacies each one has, but on no account should they be taken as final values associated with well-determined classes. Any reader drawing a conclusion such as Plato-height-bad, Nietzsche-depth-better and Stoicism-surface-best would be making a mistake, by missing the dynamic interconnection of all and their dependence on the events determining the reader and its world. Deleuze's criticism of common and good sense with their attendant divisions and classificatory judgements would simply apply to his own thought, were we to allow a new demonology or division of species to rise from it. Instead, the following important passage explains the crucial role played by the event:

It is like sense which, on one of its sides, is attributed to states of life and, on the other, inheres in propositions of thought. There are dimensions there, times and places, glacial or torrid zones, never moderated, the entire exotic geography which characterizes a mode of thought, but also a style of life.

(LoS, 129, 153)

This means that though sense has two sides, one in language and one in bodies, it only has them when they come together through an event, which in turn does not take the form of an essence or nature, or factual state or well-determined process. Instead, *the event is the way in which a disjunctive synthesis of series of differences determines an individual, which itself connects to all of life and communicates with all other individuals.* Where philosophy is often described as the search for indubitable truths, for the essence of things, Deleuze replaces this with essays on expressing the haecceities determining individuals. These are alterations rather than fixities, characteristics rather than properties, inclinations rather than predicates, but they are also boundlessly and immanently interconnected and therefore any supposedly external direction or value must be considered in relation to the event and to the individual, rather than providing an external scale from whence to judge them.

When Deleuze associates height and the drive to elevation with Platonic philosophy, with idealism as a form of sickness characterised by manic depressiveness, and with the image of philosophy as 'in the clouds', this should not be understood as implying that these terms are always associated in this way, but rather that they are latent connections which may be expressed in further events. As speculative associations rather than deduced categories, the images of philosophy are cautionary rather than necessarily determining. As creative innovations rather than the products of induction, they are invitations to react and recreate rather than bend and reflect. The associations do allow us to learn about the connection of images of thought, actual sickness and real types of ideas, but as forms or potential patterns rather than necessary classes or groups. Equally, when Nietzsche's thought is characterised as a move into depth from height through surface, that is into the body as source of health and sickness against elevated abstractions, Deleuze is not giving the antithesis of Platonic thought, but an image in tension with it. Plato and Nietzsche bequeath a mobile and treacherous landscape which other thoughts have to inhabit but also transform. The Stoics change the sense of thought in 'a reorientation of all thought and of what it means to think: *there is no longer depth or height*' (LoS, 130,

83

155). We could interpret this as a move beyond philosophy as the search for pure and healthy but ultimately doomed ideals, and as escape from the deep wounds and violent rends of the body, but Deleuze follows his definition of Stoicism with a long and important discussion of the concept of 'mixtures' in relation to the surface. His point is that *a philosophy of the surface and of the event is always caught in a struggle with violent and destructive mixtures of bodies; it is always trying to give sense to a life of violent shocks, invasions and punctures* (for example, in the way a body ingests others, is inhabited by parasites, has to procreate through contact with the outside and give birth to strangers – all mixtures fraught with danger and destruction, poisons, viruses, desires, loves, passions and sacrifices). It is also that the surface must struggle with the temptation of height, that is with a desire for immobility and abstraction conveyed through ideas. This elevation is always at risk from its relation to depth: it dreams of being able to classify mixtures into eternal goods and evils, when they belong together, and only allow for good and evil in relation to each individual and event: 'Contrary to what Plato believed, there is no measure on high for these mixtures, no combinations of Ideas which could allow for definitions of good and bad mixtures' (LoS, 130, 156).

What are we to make, though, of the hyperbolic and lyrical style of this eighteenth series? Of all of them it is perhaps the most light on argument, evidence and close study. It is prone to brutal gener-alisations and multiplies images to the detriment of precision and consistency. Is this really the heir to the rigour and historical fidelity of Deleuze's teachers? Or has philosophy taken a speculative liter-ary turn too far that only deserves a rapid counterblast in the name of real scientific empiricism and of true, classically logical, rigour? Even if we accept the interpretation that the images are speculative provocations, are they not bad speculations, too crude with respect to the past to generate genuinely new ideas, too blunt to offer rea-soned arguments in the present, and only open to the future for dangerous fools who prefer a romantic simplicity to truth? The first answer is that the work on the images of philosophy must not be read in abstraction; it is not a hermetic article, but a member of a series (as all articles are). It belongs with the others and it only works in full when balanced by their arguments and detail. The images are designed to dramatise a position, or rather a new direc-tion, as if Deleuze had been asked 'Where do you situate your phi-losophy in the tradition?' or 'Are you anti-Platonic and therefore Nietzschean?'

His answer is very subtle; it is that *positions and directions in philosophy only work to the extent that they guide thought in relation to events for individually modulated but communicating problems.* As such, it is inaccurate to claim oneself to be Platonic, Nietzschean, Hegelian or Deleuzian – or even free of any such historical classification. This is because any creation in relation to an event brings these directions into play in different ways and to different degrees. The directions allow us to feel what is at stake in different choices and reactions. The work on the surface and on Stoicism gives a dramatic rendition of these necessary connections and risks, but it does not justify them or show the detail of their processes: 'Surface, curtain, carpet, coat, this is where the Cynic and Stoic reside and what they wrap themselves in. The double sense of the surface and the continuity of right and reverse sides come to replace height and depth' (LoS, 133, 158). Philosophy gives rise to and works within images, and the image of the surface cancels dreams of a discontinuity or natural order for images, whether directed by a search for elevated ideals or for base facts. So after the series on this surface in relation to mixtures we still have the questions 'Why?' and 'How?' Why are events the starting point for thought and philosophical constructions? How do events determine individuals or individual responses to questions concerning good and bad mixtures? These questions are answered in greatest detail in the series on singularities, the problematic and the two series on static genesis. However, before passing on to them it is important to make the following remarks on individuals in *Logic of Sense* on the basis of a reading of the last paragraph of the series on humour.

INDIVIDUALS

As shown in the discussion of the nineteenth series on humour in my introduction, the series presents a transition from irony to humour as forms capable of thinking with events. This involves an important argument clarifying the role of the individual in Deleuze's work. Irony appears to resist foundations and therefore it seems to remain open to events by avoiding the trap of forcing them into a pre-given frame. Its sceptical power depends on taking up a proposed foundational truth prior to leading it to a nonsensical conclusion. However, this strategy is flawed. When faced by the question 'Who speaks?' irony returns to a form of ground in the individual. Philosophical irony, that is the sceptical dismantling of claims to certainty from Socrates through Kant and on to the post-Kantian romantics, depends on the ironist as an indivisible and unique source: the individual who speaks or plays. According to Deleuze's reading, this source takes different forms: with Socrates, it is the individual thinker, named and characterised; with Montaigne and then developed in Kant, it is the person, any and all subjects, the 'I' as a class; with the romantics, it is a poetic creativity, capable of taking up all expressive possibilities, of playing any role (Deleuze takes this version from Kierkegaard – quoting him at length). The flaw here is that, unlike humour, 'irony encloses singularity within the limits of the individual or person' (LoS, 139, 165). In other words, with the individual there is still a form of identity restricting thought and inhibiting its openness to events; this can be a character or human (Socrates), a form (the 'I') or a power (the romantic poet). In each, it leads to two destructive consequences. The weaker is that openness is merely an appearance, the individual remains stuck with its commanding identity. The stronger – generated and dramatised by the negation of the weaker – is that each figure of the individual is threatened by a terrible 'undifferentiated ground', a bottomless and terrifying chaos with no order or sense. This happens when the valued individual dies murdered or committing suicide, when reason abandons the subject or person, or when poets lose their power and descend into madness. These versions of the individual are therefore tragic, yoked to a sceptical task returning them to an illusory freedom, but ultimately destined to a senseless end. But then, given this tragic destiny, why does Deleuze still use the concept of the individual? Even if he could abandon it, as he does in some of the series, how can he explain the role of individuals in the images of philosophy? What gives rise to them? More seriously, how can *he* reply to the questions 'Who speaks?' and 'Who is the Deleuzian superior empiricist?'

The answer lies in a disavowal of all the ironic figures of the individual in favour of an *individuation*. This is defined as a closed structure of singularities, in relation to an open series of all singularities, where this relation is determined by a problematic structure and by an actual expression according to a dual and two-fold static genesis, and a counter dynamic genesis, that give genetic priority to singularities over individuals. This is a strange and difficult formulation that requires definitions of singularity, problem, static and dynamic genesis, duality and structure from other series. It will be taken apart and explained at length in the following sections (the concept of dynamic genesis is explained in Chapter 5). There are good reasons for this esotericism and baroque form: Deleuze is describing complex and ubiquitous enfolded processes that cannot be framed in a language that allows a return to prior identities. The danger of this return is a key factor in his account of images of thought, since the mere repetition of traditional terms increases the risk of pre-supposing the images we wish to escape by strengthening their hold through habits of thought. (A useful exercise for understanding this grip of grammar on thought processes is to take your 'natural' incli-nation for your voice in writing, for example your use of 'I', 'we' or a neutral form 'It is said', and to swap it for one far removed from it, to see if what you say still feels the same. *And if words do not suit you, try it with clothes or gestures.*) The return and reinforcement of images of thought in words, syntax and style explains Deleuze and Guattari's later insistence that philosophy must be the creation of concepts. It also explains the complexity and fondness for neologisms in Deleuze's thought and its closeness to another great twentieth-century inventor of concepts, Whitehead, whose philosophy stresses adventure and novelty as well as conceptual innovation for very similar reasons:

> This backward looking traditionalism came in at the Renaissance. It wasn't Greek. My own department, philosophy, has been especially a suf-ferer from it. That is why I have attempted to invent new terminologies for new concepts. There is a jargon of thinking that gets in the way of thought itself.
>
> (Price, 2001: 55)

This multiplication of concepts invites critical points transferred from the analytic debate about philosophies of the event, where the concept of event is attacked for failing tests of metaphysical parsi-mony and ontological economy. We should have no more meta-physical concepts than we need to explain phenomena and, since facts will do, the concept of event is redundant and should be dis-carded. For example, Quine argues that events should be identified with physical objects in space-time:

> Physical objects, despite the vagueness of terms that denote them, are individuated to perfection by spatio-temporal coextensiveness. No wonder: our conceptual apparatus of space, time and physical objects is all of a piece. Space-time is a matrix that stands ready to cast objects forth as needed in the course of introducing logical order into one or other branch of science or discourse.
>
> (Quine, 1996: 113)

Similarly, we should not have concepts that commit us to more onto-logical entities than we require and, since events seems to subdivide into infinitely many classes (all gerunds or all infinitives) and into infinitely many different occurrences (each occurrence of an event as different) we should avoid allowing events as beings. Why commit ourselves to extra beings such as 'spillings'? Why commit ourselves to events that proliferate because they are claimed to be different each time (the spilling at t1 is never the same as the spilling at t2)? Here is an answer by Jaegwon Kim to the problems of recurrence and economy raised, among others, by Chisolm against Davidson: 'The proliferation of events with which my account of events is often charged is not in itself serious; for "the number of events" is very much like "the number of things" or "the number of facts"; "event" is not an ordinary run of the mill count noun' (Kim, 1996: 129). This response connects to some of Deleuze's intuitions, since Kim's argument points to relations of inclusion between events, which counter accusations of proliferation, since it will only be proliferation in one sense responded to by a capacity to simplify through relations of inclusion. In the same way, Deleuze also has great proliferation but always in terms of wider and wider circles of the folding of events into one another.

I hope to show that Deleuze's philosophy is not metaphysically wasteful and passes the test of metaphysical parsimony: all its terms play an indispensable role. It is also noteworthy that his philosophy involves implicit criticisms of both the demand for parsimony (or Ockham's razor) and of the belief that facts will do. I have already discussed the latter in the previous chapter and will do so again later. For the former, Deleuze provides the argument that parsimony is not necessarily a value, or desirable, since metaphysical richness and creativity participate in the construction of the world of phenomena and cannot then be discarded from it without hiding its real nature. So the question is not how few concepts do we need to reflect a fixed world, but which ones should we continue to invent, discard, renew and transform in relation to worlds already in motion and inevitably destined to remain in motion. The principle of parsimony should be replied to by principles of gift and genesis. Have we donated well? How shall we participate in the evolution of our worlds? According to these principles, parsimony may be negative through its conservatism, which fails to see the becoming of the world, and through its repressiveness, which fails to acknowledge the necessity and value of the new. The form of the demand for parsimony reflects these flaws, since it focuses on phenomena rather than on the creative experience, and depends on an idea of redundancy in relation to phenomena rather than on a relation of enrichment between established and novel concepts, and between creation and new phenomena. Philosophy creates and preserves worlds, whether it wants to or not. Parsimony is not necessarily a good principle for this creation. Indeed, according to Deleuze's understanding of the priority of disjunctive series over synthetic ones, parsimony will tend to encourage forms of thought incapable of examining their own conservatism and repression. In terms of ontological economy, Deleuze's philosophy is concerned with relations of determinacy rather than numbering of types of entities. So the concern that we are committed to too many entities is not relevant since he denies that they can be counted in that way at all. *The problem will not be about number but about the capacity to determine ontological entities against a connected and undifferentiated background. Determination will allow for counting and numbering, but only of illusorily distinct entities.*

Notwithstanding this debate about the redundancy and profligacy of concepts, Deleuze's definitions are amenable to more simple and accessible descriptions. The individual in Deleuze is a *process* of individuation rather than an individual with a given identity. This process and its aspect of becoming, difference or pure variation are prior to any secondary identity that it gives rise to. This 'expression' in actual identities is in a relation of reciprocal determination with the pure differences. The process explains how individuals emerge, rather than setting them up as grounds for any possible explanation or its sceptical questioning. This emergence comes out of a realm of all singular variations (like all the potential infinitives such as 'to grow', 'to sadden', 'to shrink' and 'to anger' presented in the previous chapter). It gives them an individual determination by selecting the distinct closed structure of some of them against the obscure background of all. This means that individuation is doubly a two-way process; this double reciprocal determination is the basic form for processes in *Logic of Sense*, because there are always two series operating on each other in two ways as excess and lack. First, individuation determines actual individuals as selections in relation to the virtual and thereby determines the virtual realm of infinitives or variations, stopping it from becoming an undifferentiated chaos. I use 'virtual', defined as the real but non-actual condition, because of its dominant role in Deleuze interpretation after *Difference and Repetition*. However, sense replaces this term in *Logic of Sense* and is in many ways a more subtle and precise term which, through its two-sidedness, counters the dualism or overvaluation of the virtual (and devaluation of the actual) that can be read, in error, into the virtual-actual distinction. Second, individuation sets the actual things in motion, by determining them in relation to virtual variations, thereby also setting the variations in motion at the level of alterations between distinct and obscure structures. As we have seen with the relation of signifying to signified series in language, series always work in asymmetrical pairs in *Logic of Sense*; each member of the pair then itself subdivides according to the asymmetrical relation, and each of these also subdivides, ad infinitum, since no series is the final grounding one: *it is dual asymmetric series all the way down.*

To return to the example from Woolf, the process of individuation lies in the selection of the pool, sea and horizon, and of the idea of annihilation against an infinite set of other objects capable of determining her characters. Other selections, for instance, of sand and sea creatures, would lead to a different individuation. Indeed, different selections take place around the pool, with characters choosing each other and more 'human' desires rather than the vastness, thereby creating misunderstandings and break-ups, or what Deleuze calls the problem of the communication of events. Selection sets characters in motion, makes things significant and gives them value, by expressing the potential in sea and pool, or in body and flesh. However, as we have seen, the objects selected are themselves set in motion in the experience. It is not the perception that sets them in motion, rather affect is motion because of what it conducts and, when it is separated from this, it loses its mobility and force, to become mere perceptions or sense-data, illusory psychological identities or facts thrown over a differential reality. As Woolf shows, sensations, affects and thoughts are prompted by the pool and sea. However, it is not only identifiable properties in them that accomplish this, but 'abstracts' set in unstable relations and carried, not by properties, but rather by a potential to connect and to convey (shimmering, varying in colour, expanding and contracting). These 'ideas' are the virtual variations expressed in the actual potentials ('to tend to vastness', 'to vanish', for example). They are not concepts or the contents of the mind, but rather conditions for what will occur in these actual things. By relating to these conditions, Woolf's selection therefore also selects in the virtual realm of all pure variations. However, this virtual selection, unlike the actual one, works only by making some forms of significance more distinct, some less so. The answer to the question 'Who speaks?' in this description of individuation is then not Woolf, nor the actual pool, nor an actual experience, but rather the virtual conditions for the movement, for the dramatic change and events she describes. These conditions are Deleuze's 'sense'; they are prior to anything actual, even if they must be in relation to it. Sense speaks and not individuals. To the objection that selection by Woolf is the necessary ground for these processes, Deleuze answers by tracing the work of the conditions for this selection back to its conditions in sense and, as we shall see, 'singularities'. This is not to devalue authors, or to replace them by a set of material conditions, but to situate all of these in wider geneses.

SINGULARITIES AND SENSE

Like sense, singularities are two-sided: both actual and virtual, or the actual expression and the sense that is expressed. A relatively simple definition of them is that they are turning points determining an actual thing as a process but themselves resistant to identity – such as the tension between sensations of vastness and tininess determining Woolf's character Nancy. That determination is only their actual side and they are also the intensity of a relation between infinitives in sense (to become vast, to become tiny). Deleuze's definition of singularity is taken from mathematics, notably from the French mathematician and philosopher of mathematics Albert Lautman. (This is not the only concept carried over from Lautman, since Deleuze's use of problem and genesis can also be traced back to his work on mathematical structure and genesis in Lautman's *Essai sur les notions de structure et d'existence en mathématiques* (2006).) This mathematical source will be studied at greater length below through a reading of the ninth series of *Logic of Sense*. Singularities determine a thing as a series of 'becomings', that is zones and neighbourhoods where there is change and inflection, such as all the places where a living being is becoming something other than it currently is in an open, tense and unsure manner. Consider the changing geography of your face in the mirror in the morning: the singularities are the new lines and shades constituting turning points in the many identities contributing to your personal identity, such as image to others, sense of self, self-image, self-identity, health and subjectivity. The first grey hair or the line where slight elevation of the brow becomes baldness intimating hair-loss is a singularity. In reality, every point of your body is such a singularity or turning point; each is potentially the locus of an inflection or change. So though we often become fixated on standard thresholds, such as flecks of grey or new lines, this is often at the expense of missing more intense ones that remain imperceptible yet determine us more strongly as individuations nonetheless. Note that these are not positive or negative in themselves and only what follows them can determine this – and

91

only provisionally and under a perspective. In short, series of turning points or singularities determine an individuation, which itself settles into series of individuals.

The two-sidedness of singularities also gives things their value or significance, but in a way that keeps both of these beyond compare. Thus the singularity in baldness is not only the actual line but the turning point at the level of ideas or propositions ('to bald' or 'to grey'). They therefore answer the questions 'How is this different?' and 'How does this matter?' but without saying what it is or why it matters in terms of a given identity. On the one hand, a singularity is an intensity determining something as singular because it is itself singular and incomparable, for example what makes you 'you' and no one else, or what makes a thing singular as opposed to a particular member of a given general class, determined as particular by a given identity (has property 'a') or negation (does not have property 'b'). On the other hand, it is also that which determines the singular significance of this actual singularity, that is the cut or selection in all potential senses which allows something to become distinct against the background of all potential values or variations as captured in infinitives. A way of understanding this is in the great variety of different turning points for human individuals: for some these may collect around appearance, for others around intellectual agility or social connections and so on. The way a turning point is meaningful therefore also involves different concentrations on the ideas accompanying them ('to age' is related to 'to lose looks', 'to gain wisdom', 'to sicken' in different ways for different singularities and therefore to different individuations and individuals). Like the shift from the virtual to sense, singularity adds to the concept of intensity from *Difference and Repetition*; this twist allows Deleuze to connect singular determinations to intensities, that is to variations resistant to final limits and measures.

Fixed limits and measures would allow comparisons cancelling the incomparability of the singular thing. This is also true, though, if the location of singularities is fixed for any given individuation. One of the crucial aspects of Deleuze's philosophy is therefore that *all points in any given process or function are potentially singularities.* When using the mathematical definition we could assume that there are few turning points (such as (0,0) for the function $y = x^2$ where the function shifts from a descent to a rise). This is a mistake because for Deleuze a singularity is about relations between series of series themselves all dual (actual and virtual) and therefore turning points are determined by encounters between series such that, for example, (1,1) could also be a turning point of $y = x^2$ in relation to a series synthesised around the idea 'equals its square'. Or, perhaps more prosaically, the turning point on the baldness line might be determined in relation to a series synthesised according to the idea 'Looking like X'. *It was the morning when my father stared back from the mirror.* This leads to another definition of singularities such that they are all the turning points coming together as an event to determine an individuation. The ubiquitous potential of singularity explains how events very distant from a perceived or conceptualised identity can occur in a deep and meaningful manner to it. The new series brought by the event pick up on the latent potential of points that did not appear to be singularities before the event. For instance, in terms of design, we might believe that we can at least tend to fix the singular points for any given task, designing a ship, say. However, because ships are connected to all other actual and virtual series, the known singularities (when it keels over, when it loses buoyancy) are always supplemented by many other ones that not only add more and more turning points to factor in, but also raise or diminish the role of established ones (for example, where ship design includes the idea of raising the hull out of the water above a certain speed).

The concept of singularity responds to many of the critical questions posed in the previous section. These criticisms can be viewed in two ways: as technical issues raised by the structure of Deleuze's philosophy, but also as inherent problems of his approach in contrast to ones that eschew talk of 'pure difference', 'the virtual' or 'sense' as conditions for actuality:

1. How do singularities allow the process of individuation to avoid posing a new ground or foundation, with its own identity and set of metaphysical presuppositions? Is Deleuze not committed to an incoherent project which seeks to argue for pure variations or pure difference, from which other actual things emerge with a temporary and fleeting identity, but with no substance for that virtual matrix? *Singularities are a non-identical determinant of individuation, because they determine the process, but are themselves always variations or turning points across changing series rather than things with a fixed identity and location.*

2. Can singularities be part of two-way processes of reciprocal determination, yet also support claims for the asymmetrical properties of these processes? Has Deleuze an incoherent account of reciprocal determination which should allow us to trace interaction between different realms or fields, yet breaks that track with the

concept of 'asymmetry'? *The triple nature of singularities (expressed in actual things and in propositions but synthesised on the surface, that is with series of other singularities) allows for this asymmetry in the neutrality or impassibility of that which is expressed with respect to its expression.*

3. If singularities are part of a process of reciprocal determination, why are they given priority in the answer to the question 'Who speaks?' Aren't identities as much necessary aspects of this answer as singularities? If they are, should we not say that identity in the actual individual, or in facts accessible by this individual, comes before the so-called virtual conditions, since if there is any positive ground in Deleuze's account it comes from the actual and not from the virtual (which may indeed be superfluous)? *Singularities have a priority with respect to change and to significance. Novelty does not come from an actual identity, but from its turning points or singularities. (This in turn shows the importance of the singularity as universal potential, rather than as a fixed part of the identity of something.)*

4. What is the meaning of condition in Deleuze's work? If a condition is a cause, then it is a mistake to call it a condition, unless it is a necessary cause, which would contradict the different conditions implied by Deleuze's selection. What does it mean for things to be in relations of reciprocal determination as conditions? How can a condition be conditioned by what it conditions, since this would defy relations in time – as if a cause were caused by its effect – and it would deny the notion of a condition as something formal and unchanging, thereby making conditions particular causes once again? *The meaning of condition in Deleuze's philosophy is not 'cause' but source of determination across different realms (virtual/ actual, proposition/actuality, sense/expression).*

The fifteenth series 'of singularities' begins with a direct consideration of these objections through a difficulty posed by the principle of impassibility in Deleuze's structure. How can something be impassive and yet also operate in the genesis of something else? We have already seen this principle at work and a justification of it in his philosophy of language. Sense is supposed to be neutral, that is not to vary with denotation, manifestation and signification, yet each one of these is incomplete without the work of sense as a process. If something works with something else as reciprocal determinations, do they not change one another, and if so how can one be called impassive? The solution in the philosophy of language is due to a distinction drawn between sense, in the infinitives such as 'to grow', and their expression in, for instance, a denotation 'To grow is expressed *in this way in this*'. This expression did not alter the sense of 'to grow' but only its relation to an open series of other infinitives, where the relations changed in terms of degree (such as stronger or weaker). Sense is then a neutral reserve that changes in its relational degrees and these degrees correspond to the terms 'distinct' and 'obscure' in the account of individuation I gave above: the strongest degrees are distinct and the weaker obscure, but none disappear completely and the condition for this persistence is the neutrality of sense or its impassibility. Neutrality or impassibility justifies the asymmetry in Deleuze's account of individuation: though sense is expressed and changes in its relations, its components remain neutral and unchanged.

This argument from the philosophy of language is made more precise in the series on singularities through another description of neutrality in the modes of the proposition: quantity, quality, modality, relation and type. I will explain these rapidly in the example of the infinitive 'to waver' taken from Woolf. The sense of 'to waver' is expressed on the horizon, in plumes of smoke, or in a small rock pool. In each it is different, but to be different it must be the same in some way, yet it cannot be the same as something that does not vary, because then how could it be different in each case? The solution is that, as sense, 'to waver' does not vary but only its expression in denotation, manifestation and signification and its concurrent relations to other infinitives, in the way Woolf introduces a surprising relation to 'to withdraw' for instance. Sense does not change in terms of 'quantity'; by this Deleuze means that it is not a universal (where there is no capacity to change in different expressions), nor particular (which would attach it to a particular actual case, such as the pool), nor personal (which would tie it to a particular manifestation). In terms of 'quality', sense is the same whether affirmed or negated (to waver, not to waver), which is also true for 'modality', that is the kind of sentence leaves sense unchanged ('Does it waver?' and 'It wavers!', for example). It is also invariant in terms of 'relation' (what it is related to in terms of referent, utterance or meaning). Nor does 'type' alter sense, that is it remains the same whether is imagined, perceived, willed or understood ('I want it to waver' or 'I imagined that it wavered'). It should be noted that none of these points are proven here and again Deleuze's speed and insight need to be tested through further research in the philosophy of language.

One rich area of comparison available here would be with work on universals in relatively recent analytic metaphysics, since problems concerning universals have interesting connections and contrasts to the problem of sense in Deleuze, for example in David Armstrong's treatment of universals and D. C. Williams's work on tropes:

> Socrates is a concrete particular. The component of him which is his wisdom is an abstract particular or 'trope.' The one general wisdom of which all such wisdoms are members or examples is an abstract universal. The total Socratesity of which all creatures exactly like him are parts or members is a 'concrete universal,' not in the idealistic but in a strictly accurate sense.
>
> (Williams, 1953: 7)

This debate then connects back to historical work on universals and haecceity in Scotus, whose work is discussed in Deleuze's research on impassivity. Another area of interest would be in terms of problems of parts and wholes dating back to Plato: if the whole is the sum of its parts, then it cannot be the same if one of its parts changes, but then we would want to say that some things are still themselves even when some of their parts change (when we break a nail, for example). So the whole must be more than the sum of its parts. How can this be? In all these metaphysical discussions, the three great innovations introduced by Deleuze are the distinction between infinitives (universals) and their common relations, the neutrality of infinitives but variation of relations, and the asymmetric dual processes relating infinitives to actualisations (concrete individuals).

A surprising example is used to demonstrate the impassivity of sense. Deleuze argues that battles remain independent of the experience of different combatants and of the wide range of actual occurrences at different stages of a conflict. This is not controversial if it is taken as the common view that many different perspectives exist on any given battle, but this is not Deleuze's lesson. He is not giving us a theory of interpretation where different standpoints cannot be reduced to one another and where a complete interpretation faces the challenge of bringing together an open-ended set of incommensurable perspectives without reducing them to one another. Instead, Deleuze asks himself two related questions: What is the condition for this persistent range of perspectives? What does this condition imply for the perspectives, for the battle and for all other conditioned actual things? We do not have a number of perspectives on an actual battle, but rather a virtual battle as sense and event rendered through those perspectives and the illusion of the one true actual conflict in the battlefield. The key to this point is Deleuze's further concern with the eternity of the battle. This is not an odd concern if considered through the suffering and death implicated in the battle. The perspectives he focuses on are not those of disinterested participants, but of dying soldiers. The battle is not a battlefield but an element drawing together those deaths, this violence, that suffering. It is therefore 'the Event in essence' because it captures the need for sense beyond the insufficient meaning and facts of the battlefield. This does not demonstrate the necessity of sense, but presents the passage to eternity required for sense to be worthy of its effectuation. The scandal of presenting a death in battle as meaningless for soldiers or for civilians is a sign of the battle as 'eternal truth' at work in thought. Even the most 'senseless' violence, for example as described in Anthony Beevor's *Stalingrad* (1999), is the motivation for a search for sense. The crux though is the form this sense must take to both interact with the actual facts and yet maintain a kind of impassivity.

TRANSCENDENTAL DEDUCTIONS

Unlike humanistic or world-historical redemptions of senselessness in battle, Deleuze does not turn to actual counters to the horrors of war, for example to acts of kindness transcending the violence, to lessons for the future or to a dialectical logic of history explaining its necessity and positive outcomes. Instead, he adopts and alters a method in philosophy, transcendental deductions, in order to demonstrate that there is always more to reality than actual experienced things and their causal relations. This turn to the transcendental is designed to avoid the need to appeal to something transcendent or outside this world while also side-stepping reductive explanations in terms of natural laws and/or facts. Deleuze is therefore constructing a complicated and many-sided type of immanence, where all things are within a same world, but differentiated in terms of how they are in it. Nothing, though, is strictly independent and of a separate realm, for example in the way some interpretations of the role of God work to absolve Him of the crimes of Auschwitz, the slave trade or 'natural' disasters such as the Lisbon earthquake or the 2004 tsunami, by claiming that He created the world but is not now part of it. Whether Deleuze manages to avoid transcendence or an overly reductive immanence is one of the main general critical questions around his philosophy. The other is whether one should wish to avoid either of these responses, that is whether some kind of transcendence, through God or human values, or some mix of naturalism and essentialism, for example through universal and eternal natural laws, is a more appropriate and valid basis for thinking about the human condition.

There is also a counter-position to Deleuze that attempts to construct a mid-way arrangement somewhat akin to his position but retaining the 'evidence' and compatibility of human action and human freedom with a naturalist approach. His model is completely at odds with this kind of compatibilism with its appeals to the latest science for its naturalism, its evolutionary account of free will and ideas, and its common-sense approach to the value of free will and the retention of human values:

> . . . by sketching out the non-miraculous paths that can take us all the way from senseless atoms to freely chosen actions, we open up handholds for the imagination. The compatibilism of free will and science (deterministic or indeterministic – it makes no difference) is not as inconceivable as it once seemed.
>
> (Dennett, 2004: 306)

From Deleuze's point of view the argument that freedom evolves and is the result of evolution – and a singularly valuable result due to its connection to reasoned action – is still a limited position, despite its sophistication. This is because it underplays the role of change and novelty within evolution and, more importantly, it ignores the conditions for such openness to the future (in the past and in the present). It is also because it overplays the role of freedom in relation to action and to reason, not in a causal sense (which is why the framing of the debate in terms of freedom and determinism is already an error) but in terms of the relation of thought to events. For Deleuze, the problem is not how we can be free and part of a determined or probabilistic nature, it is rather that when we think we carry with us much more than inherited characteristics and ideas. So the challenge is how to think with a series of conditions (past, present and future) rather than how to combine free will and a current understanding of nature. This excess over free will includes ideas, past events, emotions, desires, impulses *and their conditions.* Key questions then become: How can there be novel events? What is their sense? How can we think in a way that is worthy of them? This is not to deny freedom or the advances of science, but to be wary of the metaphysical and evaluative presuppositions they carry with them when attempting to work with a great momentum inherited from the past in relation to openness to the future. The important point carried over from Deleuze's work on presupposition in language and on images of thought in philosophy is that any vocabulary and syntax carry such presuppositions and images irrespective of their origins. Sourcing concepts in scientific discoveries and insisting on their empirical and transient nature is not enough to cleanse them of metaphysical baggage. In fact, to make such a claim is to reinforce the very metaphysical ballast we hoped to shed.

In the development of Deleuze's position the transformation of the transcendental method, notably after Kant and Husserl, is as important as its adoption. Loosely, Kant's transcendental philosophy seeks the a priori conditions for any possible appearance, where a priori means independent of experience. The guiding question is then: what forms are necessary for any appearance rather than this or that particular appearance? The answer, also put simply, is a synthesis of space and time, which is the condition for the unity of an intuition in space and time without which we would be left with a fragmented chaos or 'manifold'. How can we have intuitions in which appearances appear? The answer is: if the intuitions are united in space and time rather than chaotic. This synthesis allows for the deduction of a set of categories or conditions that any possible experience must bend to, 'pure concepts of the understanding which apply a priori to objects of intuition in general' (Kant, 1999: 113). An example of this kind of condition would be that quantity must either be unity (one), plurality (many) or totality (all). It is impossible for us to experience anything else except as an illusion of reason. Note that this does not mean that anything else is impossible 'in itself', but only in appearance. If Deleuze is a philosophical engineer seeking to construct a system adequate to the way series are synthesised by events, Kant is constructing a system capable of handling any possible appearance in intuition. So he asks 'What is the pure form of these appearances?' since to merely construct in terms of known forms would be inadequate in terms of new and different appearances. The pure form then allows him to deduce sets of conditions: the a priori synthesis of space and time. This in turn allows him to deduce a set of categories that hold for any appearance given this synthesis. Note how this loose analogy shows an inherent weakness of transcendental philosophy: it seems to prejudge what can appear when setting the categories. What if experiments demonstrate that the categories are wrong or need to change? What if the pure form is merely an abstraction from current experience? Then the whole method is shown to be suspect, since the categories cannot have been a priori and necessary but a posteriori or after experience and contingent on what occurs. This is a fundamental weakness of Kant's approach that shows up particularly strongly in the coherence of the categories with Euclidean geometry, but incoherence with later discoveries, for example in terms of Riemann's differential geometry. It is a weakness that both Husserl and Deleuze are aware of and seek to remedy.

Husserl's use of the transcendental is related to Kant's but the possible experience and pure forms of intuition are replaced by a search for the essence of consciousness through a reduction or 'bracketing' of all aspects of consciousness that are open to doubt, or are inessential. Husserl's 'eidetic' thinking, as in a series of brackets working towards an essence, is then the deduction of the essence of consciousness. For example, you may be conscious *of* a dog, but the dog and its existence are inessential to the consciousness – it could well be a cat or there might be no dog at all, merely a projection or illusion of one. But the directedness of consciousness in any consciousness-of, its to-ness or intentionality, is its essence; any consciousness-of is a directedness which we discover when bracketing the inessential things we are conscious of: 'The realm of transcendental consciousness as the realm of what is, in a determined sense, "absolute" being, has been provided us by the phenomenological reduction' (Husserl, 1983: 171). Husserl's question is then: 'What is essential to consciousness when we operate a reduction of all that is dubitable in it?' The interesting difference between the two takes on transcendental philosophy is that Husserl's method starts with phenomena, then brackets them, arriving at the essence, whereas Kant starts with the pure form in intuition and searches for its necessary conditions. It seems then that Husserl is closer to an empirical method and arrives at different essences (pointing towards a transcendental science), whereas Kant is distanced from actual experience and arrives at categories (conditions for any possible science). This does not mean that Husserl is a classical empiricist – quite the contrary, since he is opposed to the radical scepticism implied, for example, by Hume, which would imply that the essence is itself open to doubt. He is also critical of models of the subject implied by classical empiricism, which ironically presume too much about the nature of experience and the experiencing subject. Empiricism is destined to contradict itself, unless it is grounded on a form of transcendental reflection:

For experience we therefore substitute something more universal: 'intuition;' and by so doing we reject the identification of science taken universally with experiential science. Furthermore, it is easily recognized that by defending this identification, and by contesting the validity of purely eidetic thinking, one arrives at a scepticism which, as genuine scepticism, cancels itself out by a countersense.

(Husserl, 1983: 37)

This countersense is that we cannot make the claim that all knowledge must come from experience without presupposing a principle which itself does not come from experience. In this search for a philosophical position free of dogmatism or the uncritical adoption of ideas, but also free of thoroughgoing scepticism and the bending of all philosophy before the natural sciences, Husserl and Deleuze rejoin Kant:

Critique of reason indicates here the true middle way between the dogmatism against which Hume fought and the scepticism which he wished to introduce in opposition to it – a middle way which, unlike other middle ways, one is not advised to determine for oneself as it were mechanically (a little of one and a little of the other), and through which no-one is any wiser, but a middle way that can be determined exactly according to principles.

(Kant, 1953: 128)

Deleuze's transcendental philosophy has elements from Kant, Husserl and Hume. It takes the deduction of conditions from the first, the work on an actual starting point from the second, and the flexibility and requirements of repetition from the third. Against Kant and Husserl, it neither starts with intuition nor with consciousness, but with events themselves – and not events *for* a consciousness or *in* an intuition. Again against both, it is neither interested in any possible experience, nor in any absolute essence. Deleuze's fundamental insight is that to start with consciousness or intuition is contingent and detrimental to thought; instead, we are given multiple variations that cannot be reduced to one another and he therefore seeks the conditions for this irreducibility and multiplicity. In addition, unlike Kant and Husserl who are both seeking forms of certainty against scepticism, Deleuze is not primarily concerned with truth but with explanation. He is not asking 'What can I know for certain?' but 'How does this arise and under what conditions?' So where the two earlier thinkers seek to anchor intuition and consciousness on something solid and invariant that replicates them, Deleuze reverses the problem and asks why there isn't this

101

solidity: Why is there variation and novelty rather than identity? This type of enquiry is itself a version of Leibniz's principle of sufficient reason which states that there must be a sufficient reason for anything that happens. Leibniz then asks 'Why is there something rather than nothing?' and eventually arrives at God's choice of the best of all possible worlds. Deleuze replaces the 'something' with change and enquires after the sufficient reason for alteration prior to identity, eventually arriving at the realm of sense and of singularities. His transcendental philosophy therefore takes off from a requirement to convince us of the becoming in any event and of its priority over identity. Difference must therefore be defined independently of identity as 'difference in itself' (the title of one of the main chapters of *Difference and Repetition*) rather than as difference between identities or the negation of an identity. In turn this implies that reduction or bracketing is an inappropriate method for Deleuze's work, since the direction of the reduction is towards that which is indubitable and essential, whereas Deleuze wants to determine the conditions for that which is inessential (and only taken as negatively so, when viewed from the point of view of a set identity). His work moves towards the genesis of difference and variation in ever wider structures and, instead of bracketing, it needs to extend, connect and yet differentiate. This explains why his method is best understood as proceeding through disjunctive syntheses rather than reductions.

A useful way of looking at this is to see the demands for invariant truths and for identity as desires and consequences rather than necessary conditions for thought or hidden properties of reality (as a priori conditions or essences). It must be stressed that this move is not to deny that there are truths or identities, it is to deny that these are primary or foundational, necessary or essential. Deleuze's transcendental philosophy deduces the primary role of difference prior to identity and of multiplicity prior to unity and this is why he seeks to demonstrate the independence of sense as impassibility (to ensure its priority over actual identities) and the genetic role of sense (to explain how change and variation determine actual identities). The key move is to split sense and singularities into invariant pure differences and varying relations of distinctness and obscurity so that they can be determined through a relation to actualities and yet remain impassive. This allows Deleuze to situate his philosophy between the transcendental determined by resemblance between identities and their supposed opposite in an ungrounded abyss: 'We seek to determine an impersonal and pre-individual transcendental field, which does not resemble the corresponding empirical fields, and which nevertheless is not confused with an undifferentiated depth' (LoS, 109, 124). However, the use of 'seek' in this passage is telling, since where Kant and Husserl provide some of the most deep, extended and difficult arguments to support their deductions, Deleuze *appears* not to. This does not mean that he does not provide arguments, but rather that the nature of the deduction is itself necessarily different. This difference and the question of the validity of Deleuze's work will be studied in greater depth in the section on Husserl, below.

Transcendental deductions have to start somewhere: in the given that they then deduce the conditions for, for example intuition or a pure form. They are also usually intended to go somewhere, or at least to enquire whether it is possible to get somewhere, such as absolute certainty or a ground for scientific investigation free of sceptical doubt and dogmatic presuppositions. This allows us to understand the differences in terms of development of deduction between Deleuze and Kant and Husserl, because the latter have a well-situated given to start from (intuition or consciousness) and a long historical series of truths to be sceptical about, whereas, like Hume in his empirical historical studies in *Enquiries Concerning the Principles of Morals*, Deleuze has an exploded and wide ranging 'given' to survey: 'As this is a question of fact, not of abstract science, we can only expect success, by following the experimental method, and deducing general maxims from a comparison of particular instances' (Hume, 1975: 174). Where Deleuze adds to Hume, or develops a 'superior empiricism' (Deleuze's humour and Nietzschean playfulness again, *or impudence when viewed from Edinburgh*), is in returning to the transcendental method in order not to draw out generalisations but to seek the conditions for variety, that is: the conditions for the necessary suspension of the generalisation from accession to a necessary law; the conditions for the recurring inner plurality of each experience and each event; and the conditions for the connections of all events and all experiences as various, resistant to identity and always in movement. Of course, the main critical question remains whether empiricism can be added to in this way, or whether Deleuze betrays it in returning to conditions when we should only work with facts. His reply depends partly on the point made earlier that such facts carry conditions with them however carefully we seek to preserve them from metaphysics.

Deleuze includes Kant and Husserl's positions in the list of things to bring sceptical thought to bear on. This explains his critical discussions of Husserl, of consciousness and of the subject in *Logic of Sense*, but it also explains how his deduction is spread throughout the book rather than concentrated in a linear account. This is in contrast to the two deductions, A and B, of Kant's *Critique of Pure Reason* (1999), or Husserl's tracing and recreation of the transcendental moment in Descartes in the *Cartesian Meditations* (1999) where the Ego has been reduced to an 'I think' or cogito free of all its 'natural' interests, contexts and attentions. These deductions allow a condition to be deduced as certain and universal, because free of all these contingent and variant aspects (which the Cartesian method of doubt has already bracketed off – rendered by Husserl through the concept of 'epoché'):

> In *transcendental-phenomenological* reflection we deliver ourselves from this footing [of the world already given], by universal epoché with respect to the being or non-being of the world. The experience as thus modified, the *transcendental experience*, consists then, we can say, in our *looking at* and describing the particular transcendentally reduced *cogito*, but without participating, as reflective subjects, in the natural existence-positing that the originally straightforward perception (or other *cogito*) contains or that the Ego, as immersing himself straightforwardly in the world, actually executed.
>
> (Husserl, 1999: 34)

However, Deleuze operates a reverse reduction to Husserl's. He extends it to the cogito itself and changes its destination in terms of the search for certainty. So instead of starting with a ground that is beyond doubt in a reduced experience, Deleuze shows a ubiquitous multiplicity of singularities or varying turning points prior to any emerging identity: 'When a world teaming with anonymous and nomadic, impersonal and pre-individual singularities opens up, then at last we tread the field of the transcendental' (LoS, 103, 125). Note that Husserl also makes great use of the concept of singularity and many other concepts also used by Deleuze, so in the discussion to follow it will be important to investigate differences between the two positions in these concepts.

Deleuze's transcendental philosophy therefore takes place across all the series of his book, where each series shows how variation and difference precede and give rise to individuals that are then engulfed again in difference and variation. This transcendental thought is itself necessarily a multiple deduction with many claims to identity to undermine and trace back to a genesis in becomings or singularities. So when we ask 'Why does Deleuze add the account of singularities to this account of sense?' the answer is that the concept of singularity gives a different and more complete version of the connection of neutral sense or impassible 'virtual pure difference' to actual expression, because instead of linguistic processes such as denotation, we can refer to actual things, that which is denoted. The concept of impassibility, as incapacity to feel pain or suffering injury, is important in bridging between the metaphysical aspects of Deleuze's arguments and their moral ones, since it is the impassibility of sense which will allow for a suspension of actual suffering ('Impassibilité stoïque', in Littré, 1872). Singularity is a dual term, present in the neutral realm and in the actual one, but 'selected' in the latter, that is limited in terms of what it is related to, whereas only gradated in the former, that is giving rise to relations of distinctness and obscurity. This turn to that which can be denoted (put simply, to things in the world) extends Deleuze's compass to include biological processes and beings, which also explains why it is a response to problems concerning individuals. It also explains why it would be a mistake to simply oppose Deleuze to evolutionary accounts of, say, freedom, reason and ideas. His thought is about such evolutions, but it adds a series of philosophical concepts to them, because he views the scientific account as requiring a philosophical transcendental critique and extra-scientific forms of creativity, including the arts and literature. These additions are not in the service of science by providing examples and attractive formulations, they are challengers, critics and co-creators. This extension is very important, if somewhat underplayed in *Logic of Sense* when compared to *Difference and Repetition* and *Anti-Oedipus/A Thousand Plateaus* where biology and, in particular, the works of Simondon and Uexküll play extremely important roles. This in turn emphasises a literal reading appropriate to the concept of genesis outlined earlier and to be studied shortly.

If approached from naturalist accounts or the brute empiricism criticised by Husserl, Deleuze seems to be putting a philosophical structure 'before' an empirical study of genesis in biology. Yet this is not necessarily a scandal, in the sense of a divisive and egregious mistake. It is rather a challenge from a new kind of transcendental philosophy applied with great candour to a science we have come to see as empirical alone. Deleuze is adding fields and principles to scientific enquiry, not in order to limit it in any sense, but in order to provide critical and creative principles which guide us to points where science is unnecessarily closed or not open enough. This is never to say what can and cannot be discovered, or which theories

105

are possible or not. Such terms are completely at odds with Deleuze's superior empiricism. Instead, he explains how any theory and conceptual framework can come to be illegitimately closed through its metaphysical presuppositions, through the images it gives rise to and thrives upon and through the way its theories become fixed in thought and acts. He also explains how any science is necessarily open through its singularities and through the series it synthesises. These explanations are rich and precise, with a vast and productive array of concepts, arguments and novel images. But on their own they can never say exactly how any actual situation will unfold. This is not predetermined, nor determinable by his philosophy. Thus, in the series on singularities, when he speaks of the openness of skin, it is as a condition and not as particular fact:

> 'Skin is the deepest' must even be understood biologically. Skin has at its disposal a properly superficial vital potential energy. And just as events do not occupy the surface but haunt it, superficial energy is not localized at the surface, but linked to its formation and reformation.
>
> (LoS, 103, 126)

There is a great deal at stake in how we interpret this passage. It could be read as saying that biology teaches us that skin and the surface have a potential energy that cannot be located but that appears in the formation and reformation of skin or surfaces. To which Husserl and many other thinkers would quite rightly insist adding the preface 'on the basis of contemporary science it is probable that . . .' But in my view, because Deleuze is also a transcendental philosopher, the right reading of the passage is:

> The deduction of surface and sense applies to and is expressed in skin when it shows its vital potential energy, its capacity to adapt, change and renew itself. As an expression of surface and sense, actual skin is connected to its transcendental condition in sense. This explains its capacity for formation and reformation (but not the actual processes in a given case).

Skin is necessarily open to change, but we can never say exactly how without science. This is not 'philosophy first' or 'philosophy second', but 'philosophy and science'.

SINGULARITIES AND SERIES

Deleuze lists five characteristics that can be found across all his series when we search for a world determined by singularities rather than by individuals and by founding identities. The characteristics have a dual function that shows the deduction not only of difference but also of determination, as a counter to the accusation that we can only have thought where we find identity (even in naturalistic empiricism) and that without this we only have a dark chaos:

1. Singularities and events do not form stable or unstable series, but rather heterogeneous series that are meta-stable. There is a potential of differences that can be distributed into further series: it is stable as potential but unstable in itself, or as a series. This can be also understood through the concept of a stable reserve of unstable differences waiting to be expressed anew.
2. Series of singularities are brought together through a mobile element that runs through them and allows them to resonate. Deleuze describes this element as the empty place in his work on language and structuralism: series are synthesised by a shared element that resists identification and thereby also brings a disjunction into the series, as they change to adapt to the excess implied by the element they cannot handle.
3. Singularities are a matter for the surface, that is for the surface between the depth of bodies and the height of ideas, where 'between' means operating in both. This surface also has particular manifestations, for example the limits or borders of things. So singularities or turning points take place at the limit, but where limit is not that which determines the identity of something, but rather the insecure boundaries of identity – where identity breaks down and becomes other.
4. This surface is the place for sense, which not only means that value and significance take place between body and idea, but also that sense is neutral with respect to its effectuation in particular bodies and ideas. It gives sense to them, but they do not restrict or cause it to be one way or another.
5. Singularities are distributed in a problematic field, or they determine problems that actual things and ideas respond to and transform, but do not solve; the problems of sense are therefore paradoxical rather than of a question–solution form. The problems of sense are about how an individuation unblocks and alters a paradox rather than eliminating it.

These points can seem arcane and unclear, so it is helpful to see them in a practical example first, then turn to two areas where they are explained in greater depth: the series on singularities and the series on problems in *Logic of Sense*.

107

A good set of examples suited to explaining Deleuze's argument can be found in the adaptability of objects between different uses and roles. His point is that a bent stick, or a musical instrument, has a series of intense points which allow it to be included in many practices and games. Children can take the stick as a weapon, a marker, a projectile and so on. Its shape, smoothness or roughness, length and weight are all opportunities or hooks for many adaptations. These can be seen as the singularities held in reserve in the series described as a stick – in Deleuze's hands the stick is not a well-identified object, but rather all these series held as a potential for all the expressions. It brings them together, but without providing an overarching rule or logic. The stick is the mobile element relating all the games, but it also has such mobile elements running along it (such as 'to bend', 'to flex' and 'to fly'). These elements or singularities are on the surface, but only if it is in turn defined as that which brings together the full reserve of potential aspects open to different uses and the ideas around them. The surface is then not the surface of an actual object but the condition for openness and change in the object both in terms of actual uses and ideas.

Thus, for example, in the case of a ball projected a certain distance within a certain set of rules, the surface and singularities are the open potential of moves and shapes of the ball and the bodies that throw it, when these are viewed as between all the actual throws and uses and the ideas and rules that accompany them. When a reserved potential is revealed, for example when the ball can be made to bend in flight, then the sense of the rules changes (they can become obsolete or need refinements, for instance) and the sense of the bodies changes (we may need to change their shape, different players may come to the fore and others may be left behind). The stick or instrument is then itself determined as a Deleuzian surface through the paradoxical problems set by the singularities on them, by the different series opened up and brought together by weight, flight, shape, sounds, portability and fragility and so on. From this point of view, changes in the laws of sport are responses to processes set in motion by singularities such as the potential changes in sense where a ball can be roughed-up on one side or made to bounce 'dangerously'. The surface, as rough spot or steep bounce, brings together depth (the physical injuries, a feeling of outrage) with height (ideas of fairness, talent or dastardly behaviour) and calls for a creative response.

These simplifying examples need to be treated with caution, especially those taken from sporting realms with their tendency to elide emotional and technical complexity through their supposed obviousness or accessibility. It is not the case that there are special surfaces where sense and singularities come into play, but rather that how we respond to an event determines those surfaces. So singularities are a potential 'everywhere', not only in the shape of the ball or in the changing capacities of bodies. Moreover, depth is not only in objects – in fact it is not in objects at all, but in points where living things change and adapt in relation to their extended environments. The same is true for height. It is not in ideas in the mind, but in the way virtual ideas are expressed in actual things as expressible in propositions. The depth, height and surface relations are then about actual becoming and its stresses and strains, about ideas and their propositional expression, and about the surface determining depth and height in terms of sense. Thus, in the following telegram sent to Britain from Australia during the infamous bodyline cricket tour in 1932–3, where English bowlers bowled fast and directly at the body causing injury through 'unplayable' deliveries, it is not the case that singularities are necessarily in the players' bodies and the field settings. Depth is also in the feelings of the writers and of the general public in both nations; the ideas are in the field as much as in the rules; and singularities are working everywhere when there is intense change beyond established structures of identities:

> Bodyline assuming such proportions as to menace the best interests of the game, making protection of the body by the batsmen the main consideration. This is causing intensely bitter feeling between the players as well as injury. In our opinion it is unsportsmanlike. Unless stopped at once it is likely to upset the friendly relations between England and Australia.
>
> (http://www.334notout.com/bodyline/main.htm)

So bodyline, as Deleuzian event, is not restricted but necessarily reverberates through time and space with no intrinsic limit. It is this kind of principle about limits and restrictions that requires a transcendental deduction in Deleuze's philosophy beyond any given science of the game or social science of its context.

Two objections allow us to refine this example further; they both work on two levels: practical and ideal. These levels are in tension with one another, which is a point that Deleuze exploits answering them. First, can't we give an exhaustive scientific account of all the actual points on an actual stick or in an actual game? If we can, or if we can at least tend towards this, isn't Deleuze wrong to move into this metaphysical and transcendental treatment, since it brings in an

109

unnecessary and obscure account of things we should know through experiment rather than speculation? It is in response to these objections that we can see the importance of Deleuze's transcendental moves and definitions of surface and sense. The singularities aren't the actual knots and bends in the stick, but the relation between these and the ideas surrounding them. It is true that a stick may always break when taken beyond a certain pressure point, but it is truer that, even after it has broken in two, a child will create a new game relating to the earlier one: *it was the escape pod docked into the mother ship, silly.* The surface is then neither ideal nor actual, but the condition for the open renewal of the relations between the two. But, second, what if we consider these two realms to be the same and the child's mind just another more complicated stick? What if we then learn from (recent) history and say that all worthwhile advances of understanding and explanation have come from the natural sciences? Therefore, given the absence of other approaches that have not been discredited, we should always trust in scientific methodology and discoveries, rather than philosophical deductions. The answer to this second leg of the argument is 'Yes'. Yes, we should turn to the natural sciences and away from dogmatism and opinion; indeed, that has more often than not been the point of transcendental philosophy and is certainly one of Deleuze's points. Though it is a 'Yes, but', because the practical point of transcendental philosophy is to unearth and rectify remnants of metaphysical presuppositions and beginnings of fixed images and restrictive laws and concepts in science and its methods. This transcendental philosophy takes its place in the dynamism of thought and in favour of this open creativity, not without boundaries, since it is always within a given series, but seeking to be free of dogmatic presuppositions (including the bolstering of common sense and opinion by the sciences).

PROBLEMS

The ninth series of *Logic of Sense* 'of the problematic' expands on the concept of singularity while also explaining the relation between problems and questions. The features that I want to focus on first are caught in two very short but enigmatic sentences from the series: 'Events are ideal' and 'The mode of the event is the problematic'. These statements are important because they articulate the connection between individuation and events, something that the series on singularities and the work on conditions tend to elide. Deleuze's transcendental deductions do not arrive at universal conditions but at modes which determine individuated ones. What does this mean? It implies that his work on conditions arrives at the *form* rather than *content* of relations between surface, depth and height, or between sense, bodies and ideas. The form is universal, but it determines a content that is individual, or more accurately, individuation. It is as if we were given a condition such as 'All must pass through this grid' but also the qualification 'How each one passes is necessarily individual'. The form does not determine the substance, or the process of individuation does not determine each individuation as comparable in content with all the others. It could be objected here that Deleuze's philosophy is about eliminating distinctions such as form and content, because series cut across the elements of any given categories. This objection misses the role of structure in his philosophy. The structure of reciprocal determinations and of series is the 'form', whereas the singular determinations are the 'content'. The form does not override the *singularity* of the content, but equally that singularity cannot negate the *structure* in the form. Together they lead to what Deleuze calls 'the universal individual': *individuation is all there is and it is universal in a well-structured manner. Series and events are all there is, but they occur and develop according to transcendental principles governing structure.*

The two sentences from the series on problems are connected and, together, they mean that events are necessarily ideal. As such they occur as problems, themselves defined as series of tense relations between Ideas (in *Logic of Sense*, Deleuze usually uses 'Idea' when he is referring to the virtual Idea and 'idea' when he is using the term closer to the common usage of idea). Problems are not resolvable questions but problematic knots to be retied differently, because the Ideas that constitute them are neither reducible according to sets of laws or common principles, nor eliminable, rendered to nothing or to total insignificance. Indeed, if there is a principle regulating ideas it is that each singular element of the problem resists incorporation in a fixed category or set. For example, an event such as communication in a city may give rise to an economic, social and technical problem, such as how best to allow maximum communication without exclusions, at the lowest possible emotional drain on living beings. Deleuze's point is that this event is determined by the problem as something ideal, that is as something that expresses a series of different 'pulls' or Ideas such as 'to reduce', 'to flow', 'to grow', to 'include' and 'to communicate'. I have rendered the elements of the problem as the infinitives in sense, from

111

Deleuze's philosophy of language. The infinitives are determined when they are expressed in actual cases and in propositions: the problems are replayed when they too are expressed in actual responses and propositions. There is therefore a parallel between problem, Idea and sense in Deleuze; each gives a different angle on the structure determining individuation and the genesis of worlds and individuals. An example of the kind of principle regulating the form of the problem is that for any given problem the list of elements is necessarily endless and there is no principle for limiting this extension. 'To flower' and 'to love' are parts of the problem of communication, though perhaps very obscure ones for modern individuations. However, the content of the problem is determined in actual responses where different Ideas are made more distinct and others move back into an obscure but necessary ground in terms of their relations. The Ideas do not fade or become more distinct, their intense relations do.

Deleuze's point that problems are not questions is then that when a problem is replayed in an individuation (in the genesis of this actual series of physical changes and this series of propositions) the problem is not resolved such that the tensions between Ideas disappear forever. Questions give the impression that they are either answerable ('Yes', 'No', 'This way', 'This is how') or poorly formulated, or unanswerable and hence uninteresting. If they are answered then the question disappears. If they are poorly formulated then they should be corrected then answered. If they are uninteresting then they should be passed over. Questions are therefore either important but ephemeral, or uninteresting. Deleuze's view is that for problems, on the contrary, the background Ideas remain in reserve or as a potential to reappear in a different manner and for different novel individuations. This does not mean that questions do not matter in his philosophy. They do. But they retain their full force when they serve to draw out a problem. The kinds of question he therefore wants to rehabilitate are paradoxical and difficult ones, since their attractiveness yet lack of answers is a sign of the underlying problem. Simple resolvable questions define false problems, whereas webs of questions that pull against each other reveal a true problem, one that cannot be made to disappear in an answer. This distinction between true and false problems according to the resilience and reach of the problem is the basis for Deleuze's move into forms of truth adequate to sense, rather than definitions of true and false based on denotation or signification. However, we need to be careful here. The judgement of truth and falsity for a problem is

112

still dependent on its expression and there is no way of providing an essential classification of true and false problems. Similarly, whether a question is valuable or not is dependent on given individuations of problems, rather than a property of questions as such. 'Is the cat on the mat?' may or may not be interesting and how we surround it determines different answers: the more staid and the less productive a question becomes in terms of intensity and connections is one way of determining this. Perhaps the main feature to retain from this shift of truth to problems is that truth becomes a factor of *how and why* things are done rather than of *what* they are.

In the problem of communication and the city, an actual city may make the problem appear more strongly in terms of the idea of 'to accelerate' but this may reach a limit when the problem reappears, for instance when 'to accelerate' is changed in terms of the intensity of its relation to 'to breathe' and 'to flourish'. We can now see in more concrete terms how problems are events, insofar as the 'reappearance' of the problem with different intensities of relations accompanies a concrete event (*The city cannot breathe anymore* or *Communication is failing in the city despite its acceleration*). Deleuze's concepts of problem and event therefore insist on their returning nature, thereby capturing the wisdom associated with worries about hubris. Stupidity in any kind of design will then be to pose a question one knows to be answerable, to answer it and then to declare a true problem solved. This kind of approach is deeply inimical to his work on events, Ideas and problems. Deleuze is moving away from any type of thought that affirms that a problem has been resolved, and towards seeking ways of replaying problems better, criticising their fixing in an image of thought and creating new concepts at the cutting edge of the return of the problem.

The following passage shows why Deleuze is anti-utopian and opposed to ideas of linear progress:

> The problem may well be covered by solutions, yet it subsists nonetheless in the Idea connecting it to its conditions and that organises the genesis of those very solutions. Without that Idea the solutions would have no sense. The problematic is both an objective category of knowledge and a perfectly objective kind of being.
>
> (LoS, 54, 70)

We cannot finally solve a problem because the significance, value and aptness of the solution depend on the ideal tensions expressed in the actual problem. The ideal side is a real part of the problem that subsists even when solutions lose their temporary sense. This reality is underscored by Deleuze's insistence on the objectivity of the problem; it may be virtual or ideal, but as such it is an objective category of knowledge and an objective kind of being. It is therefore not speculation but objectively verifiable that problems recur and call for new solutions. Here, objectivity must not be understood in a simple empirical sense, where objectivity is a factor of correct correspondence of proposition and an identified empirical object or set of facts. It is rather a factor of conditions *and* actual things: it is objectively verifiable that ideal problems are conditions for actual situations. This explains the bemusement we sometimes feel at seeing old solutions to problems. (*Why did they turn to brutalist modernism?*) It is that we have become disconnected from the sense captured by those solutions. The fatal error, then, would be to think that these solutions share nothing with our problems. On the contrary, it is their problem recurring differently for us. (*What is the legacy of brutalism in our shared ideal problem?*) So Deleuze's objection to empirical objectivity is that it is partial, in both senses of the word; it conceals its ideal presuppositions and only tackles part of the event. Every object is generated by a problem it cannot divest itself of. (*It is never just a building.*)

Another formal – and objective – principle of problems is therefore that they must be 'returnable'. This can be understood by following Deleuze's reading of Nietzsche's doctrine of eternal return, from *Difference and Repetition* and his *Nietzsche and Philosophy*, where only difference returns eternally while the same never returns. As something ideal with elements expressed as infinitives, the problem returns because it has eternal and impassible elements, but any actual identified 'solution' never returns because the problem it responded to will have moved on and because without its ideal side it is only a partial, if necessary, aspect of reality. The reason why reality necessarily moves on can be traced back to the instability and impassibility in Deleuze's deduction of sense and of singularities as an unstable potential. The Idea does not have a fixed identity and is instead always in movement because it is constituted by singularities and their relations. As movement, though, the Idea or problem is impassible and cannot vanish – it only changes in its relation of distinctness and obscurity. *There is no concept of nothingness in Deleuze's metaphysics, nowhere for things to vanish to, so things only ever go elsewhere, differently.* So each expression of a problem in actual solutions is a cut within something that proceeds beyond that rupture, recording its passage as a trace in the Idea, but one that fades away. This does not mean that we can know when and how a problem returns, it means that thought should look for the most ideal and tense problematic relations underlying actual practical problems and the propositions that surround them. Two legacies of Deleuze's early work can be drawn out well here: the practical power of his work in *Anti-Oedipus* and *A Thousand Plateaus*, and Deleuze's rich reading of Foucault's work on statements, the seen and the said in his *Foucault*. The powerful extension and yet precision of the concepts created in the work with Guattari benefit from the lessons learned in defining problems as objectively real yet neutral with respect to each actual replaying of them. Foucault's work on knowledge in relation to what can be seen and what can be said as articulated through rare statements has powerful resonance with Deleuze's distinction drawn between actualities, propositions and sense, in particular through the concept of the diagram which can be understood as the diagram of a problem.

THE CONNECTION OF EVENTS

The claims about the eternity and necessity of the problem and the passing nature of any solution are somewhat rarefied but very important. A good way of understanding them is through the idea that all thought is strategic for Deleuze, that is any thinking has a series of presuppositions with respect to desires, sensations, individual interests, group interests and so on. Thought is therefore always an interaction with the problems raised by these desires and their limitless communication with other desires and events. For example, the design of a meeting space will reflect a series of overt and hidden impulses, dreams, phantasms, ideals and sensations, as captured, for instance, through the building and boardroom table in the Coen brothers film *The Hudsucker Proxy* (1994): 'Tracking down the length of the boardroom table. Executives line either side. We are approaching the man at the far end of the table, to whom the report is being directed.' *How can I get them to focus only on me?* Problems can be rendered through a series of ideal pulls and turns, that is they are born of unstable series of infinitives ('to grow') and turning points ('to grow/to burst'). These are eternal but ever-changing conditions for any design for communal spaces, revealed through questions such as 'What are the abstract motivations of this design?' So, by strategy, Deleuze does not mean a particular strategy in relation to actual fixed goals, such as 'this many people happily conversing in this space'. It means a necessarily partial interaction with abstract and ideal pulls. The space we construct at a given time can rapidly become redundant through other actual changes, but the key from

Deleuze's point of view is that these changes are also in relation to necessarily interconnected ideal connections; these ideal problems connect, recur and doom any actual solution to eventual redundancy. When we return to texts, bodies, spaces, techniques and designs from the past, the reason we can still learn from them lies in the reawakening of their struggle with problems we still connect to. It is because thought is strategic and because strategy deals with eternal but varying problems that the past can be and must be revived: only difference returns and not the same.

To understand this interconnected nature of problems and Ideas fully we must add the statement that a problem is a set of singularities to the statements on the ideality and problematic nature of events. I refrained from starting with this claim because it seems to embody all that is difficult about Deleuze's philosophy: everything melts into everything else and there appears to be no conceptual discipline or rigour. Singularities are defined in terms of sense and surface, now they define Ideas, problems and events. What is going on? The answer lies in the two-sidedness of singularities and of surface. When approached from individuation in terms of actualities, singularities explain the genesis of change and movement in the individual in terms of sense, for example in terms of the singularities determining an individual as a changing singular thing in relation to changing values and significance. However, in the series on problems, Deleuze is approaching from the other direction with the question: 'How are Ideas, events and sense determined?' The answer is also with singularities – the same ones – but this time focusing on their side in sense. Here, the translation of singularity into turning *point* is less appropriate and it is best to understand the term as *turnings* or *pulls* as captured in the infinitive of a verb. These have the same crucial property of singularities as resisting identity, which only occurs relatively with an individuation when the relations between singularities become distinct and obscure in an event or problem.

The following passage describes the two sides of the event as a set of singularities, raising two very important fields for Deleuze's discussion of events in *Logic of Sense*, mathematics and history:

> What is an ideal event? It is a singularity. Or rather, it is a set of singularities, of singular points characterizing a mathematical curve, a state of physical things, a psychological and moral person. Singularities are turning points, of inflexion, etc.; bottlenecks, knots, foyers and centres; points of fusion, condensation and boiling; points of tears and joy, of health and sickness, of hope and anxiety, so-called sensitive points.
>
> (LoS, 52, 67)

Note Deleuze's humour and knowing style here. The series on problems is written to reflect the passage from a question-solution structure to a problem-event one. He has started the series in the middle again, with a question seemingly coming from nowhere 'What is an ideal event?' and with a firm answer 'It is a singularity.' However, the answer is rapidly made more complex and less certain, transforming the question into a problem, or rather unfolding the problem that the question presupposed. This problem concerns the relation between the two sides of the singularity: on the one hand it is an actual turning point, a physical emergence or an emotional spilling over, but on the other hand it is also turnings in sense, changes in hope or the appearance of a novel significance. How must the singularity be understood to perform this relation?

Deleuze's response is to turn to the mathematical definition of singularity as a singular point on a curve or a function. These allow him to describe the behaviour and nature of singularities without tying them to one or other realm but adequate to both. This is why the beginning of the series is careful to distinguish singularities from actual or ideal identities; without this distinction they could not underwrite resistance to identity in the virtual or actual. His claim is then that singularities determine an ideal and an actual event – and their relation – in the following ways:

1. Every series of a structure corresponds to a series of singularities.
2. A series of singularities extends from any singularity to any other.
3. So any series is a series of converging series.
4. All series communicate in a single and same Event.

These determinations mean that any structure is always a structure of related turning points, but the singularities that determine it are also turning points towards all other series. All series therefore converge on one another, but they do so through their divergent points or singularities. In other words, *everything is connected, but always through connected series of differences or divergences* (and not identities, oppositions or negations).

The idea of history as constituted by series of critical points is taken from the French writer Charles Péguy's posthumous novel *Clio*. Deleuze only quotes a short passage from the closing sections of the work and, though he acknowledges Péguy's greatness in tracing the role of the event, he never offers us a full reading (the same passage is also quoted in *Difference and Repetition*). However, the main lesson taken from Péguy is that history is not only series of turning points, but many such series, all interlocked and playing off each other when a singularity 'redistributes itself in another set (two repetitions, a bad one and good one, one that enchains and another that saves)' (LoS, 53, 68). The reference to the two repetitions is an answer to the question of how singularities come to be part of a set at all: it is because they are expressed in an actual series, one that identifies and therefore enchains, and in an ideal or virtual one, one that repeats difference and hence opens up and saves. This actualisation and ideal differentiation themselves work through the two processes described in Deleuze's account of series associated with the study of structuralism in his philosophy of language. An empty place (itself a singularity) runs along the ideal series of singularities creating a synthesis, but a disjunctive one, because the creation is one of excess, whereas a placeless occupant runs along the actual series, also creating a disjunctive synthesis, but one of lack forcing the actual series back towards the ideal one that 'feeds it'. We can take an example from Péguy's beautiful but terrifying book to show this at work. The closing passages are synthesised around the questions – in the actual – 'When will I die?', 'When must things die?', 'What will it all have meant?' These questions bring the many disparate parts of the book together through the shared lack of a precisely dated and significant death, the placeless occupant indicated by the question, 'Where is death to be?' These questions are answered in many different contexts throughout the book, but they reach a deeply disquieting climax in its last passages where Péguy foretells the age at which he will die (leading his troops in the retreat on Paris the day before the battle of the Marne that turned the German advance, in September 1914). The baleful search for a final identity in death is renewed through another series in *Clio*, this time synthesised through the idea of glory which brings an excess to a wide series of ideas – religious, historical, personal, aesthetic – drawing them together but never reducing them to the same. In *Clio*, the value and excess of glory provide sense for the lack running through actual life in relation to death, but the grounded, limited and many-formed actual decay provides determination to the abstraction and excessive scope of glory. Péguy captures this most movingly in refusing to idolise the life of a goddess in conversation with a mere mortal. She envies and needs the precision and heights of mortal passion, as much as he searches for intransient meaning in her immortality. To modern ears the appeal to glory may seem naive and deserving of the twentieth-century disasters that followed *Clio*, but Péguy is much closer to Deleuze's concept of an Idea than any reductive and thin analytic definition. 'To glory' as an Idea in

118

Clio means worthiness as *deserved* fame and honour; it is to have been worthy of times and events, to have created new forms in art, but not to have outshone divine glory. It therefore already responds to hubris and to the duty to bend ideas of glory to events and to quakes in time.

Part of the greatness of Péguy's book is that, like *Logic of Sense*, its form reflects its message. *Clio* deploys many series of turning points through history in extremely diverse fields, ranging from mathematics, through literary theory, interpretation of the classics, theatre criticism and politics and on to theology. None of these quite coincide, except in the 'individuation' of Péguy himself, in debate with Clio, the muse of history, in every part of the book. We can understand Deleuze's qualms about irony and its focus on the individual better, when we see the damage that the search for the well-defined individual has done to Péguy's legacy and indeed to the significance of his death. Different interpreters have turned him into a saint, a left-wing politician, a right-wing nationalist, a literary theorist manqué, a not-quite philosopher, novelist, critic, editor and poet. Deleuze's point is that he is all of these, because each one connects to the turning points in the series of others; for example, in the persona of Joan of Arc, or Péguy's role following Hugo as a defender of Dreyfus, or his editorship of *Les cahiers de la quinzaine*, a precociously modern journal whose contributors became key actors on the left and on the right, or in his tragic, glorious, vain, contingent and foretold death. However, this eclecticism and breadth resistant to a single unified ground poses a problem for Deleuze. It could seem that the mathematical definition of a singularity is the ground for his philosophical work on the same concept. In turn, this would make mathematics the ground for *Logic of Sense* as a whole, inviting a wide range of criticisms, not only of the thinness of Deleuze's references around the mathematical concept, but more deeply in terms of criticisms of the privileged position that it, and any branch of mathematics, can claim for itself in relation to other branches.

A pure mathematical foundation is explicitly renounced in the book. Not only does it clash with its transcendental method, it also focuses too strongly on philosophy as justification rather than as explanation. The mathematical concept of singularity explains the transcendental role of the philosophical concept; it does not justify it. The mathematical series is in a productive disjunctive synthesis with others through the concept of the problem, but the problem itself cannot be a purely mathematical concept:

We can then conceive of the connection of mathematics and man in a new way: it is not a matter of quantifying or measuring human properties, but on the one hand to problematise human events, and on the other to develop the conditions of the problem as so many human events.

(LoS, 54, 70)

Singularities and mathematical analysis can fulfil this measuring role, for example when an equation is used to represent human behaviour or the properties of a technical apparatus. The reason they are not limited to this is because the number and place of singularities is not restricted and can be multiplied through additions of new series. The problematic, in all its variety, explains this absence of restriction and openness to novel additions without limit on kind. The problem for Deleuze cannot be fundamentally mathematical, because the problem cannot be fundamentally anything.

THE IDEAL GAME

When Deleuze turns to an explanation of the fourth determination of the ideal event that all series communicate in a single and same Event, in the tenth series 'on the ideal game', he does not rely on mathematics, but on a consideration of games as developed in literature, notably in Carroll, Borges and Mallarmé. The argument turns on a distinction drawn between different kinds of game. 'Known' games, the games we usually play, have the following principles:

1. There is a prior set of categorical rules.
2. The rules determine hypotheses dividing chance into gains and losses.
3. The hypotheses organise the game into distinct plays operating a distribution, falling under different cases.
4. The consequences of the plays are victory or loss.

For example, in a simple game of noughts and crosses, the categorical rules that must be followed include the rule: 'Players can play either noughts or crosses.' The hypotheses are, for instance, 'If you put a cross here, then you will lose, because this will lead to a line of noughts there.' The distinct plays are each inscription of a nought or a cross, which determines different patterns or distributions for the game, some winning, some losing.

Deleuze's ideal game has the following principles running counter to those of known games:

1. There are no prior rules, since each play invents and bends to its own rule.
2. The set of plays affirms the whole of chance, branched out at each play, rather than dividing it into numerically distinct plays.
3. Each play is a series as a distribution of singularities, but the set of plays is itself a play of all the singularities.
4. Such a game is the reality of thought rather than any actual reality.

These principles can also be understood through the example of noughts and crosses, but where the game is always included in a wider creative game of thought. So the first principle is that we can think of new inclusions of noughts and crosses where the rules are changed through the addition of wider contexts, for example when you take pleasure beating children at games rather than helping them to learn: to win is to lose, or when the game is only part of a wider timed exercise: to spend too long winning is to lose. The second principle is that there is no limit to these inclusions, so in principle the whole of chance is affirmed in the game, for instance in the way a game may turn out to have been the secret for a life, or the nub on which world events turn, or in the way a loss at one game may teach us how to win another more important one.

As opposed to 'known' games, in the ideal game chance does not fit recognised boundaries and each play branches out the whole of chance, because it changes the set rules for everything it is connected to. In the latter case, chance is not captured through probability but through the principles Deleuze has set out. This is not a standard mathematical chance, because such a distribution would stand as an invariant set of rules as in the first type of games. Instead, his ideal principles define the relation of thought and events to a transforming openness pervading all that precedes and that follows it. The choice of literature to explain this is therefore based on the power of words to rebound back through their narratives or contexts, changing fates and outcomes, creating new branches, elevating minor events and crushing large ones, damning winners and anointing losers into ephemeral victors. Probability is not enough to explain the power of the literary *coup de théâtre*. This is because the dramatic turn revises and changes the path leading to it, while itself remaining open to further change, for example in the way Juliet's plan to evade marriage and rejoin Romeo is set in a cascade of events, each turning the former from the route to happiness to tragedy, until all are dead. So a move invents its own rules and branches out chance in this invention by creating a series of turning points or singularities (the character of a child, the fate of a parent, the roll of dice, the taking of a poison). There can be no limit to this series of singularities, for this would limit thought in its capacity to remake them, so each move is the play of all singularities; Juliet's attempt to use a sham singularity turns into a real one nonetheless. It is not the whole world that is played each time, but all of its turning points, because the significance of each one plays through all others. No 'known' game can contain all these points, but thought itself can replay them, due to its open creativity. In the ideal game of thought, rules are limited and transient, there is never a final winner and loser, and all games and events are interconnected, because new ways of expressing Ideas will be created and these Ideas will necessarily be connected in the changing distinctness and obscurity of their relations. Deleuze is therefore offering an opposition to the subjection of philosophy to game theory, because he believes that any such theory misunderstands the nature of the openness of events. In reality there are no known games, since they are only illusory impositions of a boundary around a pursuit. These impositions can certainly be useful and there is no objection in principle to using game theory in philosophy. The opposition is to the limitation of the openness of thought by an illegitimate model for events. Once again, Deleuze's radical empiricism comes to the fore here: there is no induction for rules whether derived empirically, imposed or deduced rationally, because every play responding to an event puts those rules into question even if it obeys them.

The series on the ideal game is an extremely difficult and complex one. This is because it is responding to the following objections: How can a turning point in a game change the whole of chance forward and back in time? How can a turning point be a branching of the whole of chance without committing us to as many 'wholes of chance' as turning points? How then do these many wholes or worlds communicate? Are there not final points, such as death, that do not connect? Are not the dead, Romeo and Juliet, losers forever? Deleuze's definition of time as a process of reciprocal determination between two incompatible times, Aiôn and Chronos, is developed in the series in order to explain that events are both eternal and passing. Actual death engulfs all actual identities, but this death is not final, in the sense of leaving no further trace, nor effect:

> The other present, the living present, passes and brings the event into effect. But the event nonetheless retains an eternal truth from this

passing, upon the line of the Aiôn which divides it eternally into a prox-
imate past and an immediate future, and which never ceases subdividing it and pushing away past as well as future, without ever rendering
them less urgent. The event is that no one ever dies, but has always
just died or is always going to die, in the empty present of the Aiôn, in
eternity.

(LoS, 63, 80)

Deleuze's answer is therefore that although Ideas (or infinitives)
must be expressed in actual passing things in order to become
events, this actual passing only acquires significance and value
because it expresses Ideas. However, because they can always be
expressed anew – for example, due to the neutrality of sense discussed earlier – Ideas are eternal (in Aiôn). So the event has an
actual passing side (Chronos) and an eternal but differential side
(Aiôn). Though Romeo and Juliet actually die, the significance of
their death is due to their expression of a 'to love' in relation to a 'to
hate' that are eternal in their potential for repetition in different
ways and at different chronological times – all of these connect
through the infinitives 'to love' and 'to hate' in all their virtual relations, constantly changing in distinctness and obscurity. This does
not mean that Juliet or Romeo are eternal as immortals – quite the
contrary, all actual beings are necessarily mortal and only participate
in an eternity that cannot rest on permanent identities but only on
the conditions for actual change: Ideas or infinitives. By 'differential' I therefore mean that what is eternal cannot have a fixed identity, which would destine it to passing like the fixing of an idea onto
an actual thing, a symbol, say. This is why Aiôn is strangely subdivided and subdividing in the same way as the plays of chance. Each
eternal event is always being replayed and altered *in the same time.*
Deleuze's idea of eternity is one of eternal differentiations determined by actual expressions.

Critical questions about the branching of time and the movement of events back and forward in time therefore turn on the necessary relation of reciprocal determination of Aiôn and Chronos
and on the impossibility of conflating the two into a single time. The
importance of paradox and recalcitrant problems to Deleuze's work
is shown well here, since his theory depends on an oscillation
between the times that contradict one another: on the one hand,
reality is eternal differentiation or changing but contemporaneous
relations of Ideas or infinitives (the virtual); on the other hand,
reality is an always passing living present that carries the past with it
into an open future (the actual). On the one hand, all relations are

123

connected, but to different degrees depending on how they are expressed in the actual: the branching of time and its movement back and forward in the same time. On the other hand, nothing is solely self-identical because any actual thing is a process contracting the past and projecting into the future, where this process is determined through the expression of the virtual. This is an extraordinary and – perhaps to some – non-intuitive model of time. One way of imagining it is as a series of fragile parallel planes immersed in a viscous liquid. When a plane (an actual world, with actual individuals and persons) vibrates, it moves all the others, not by touching them, but through the virtual liquid medium. Reality is the medium and all the planes, but it is also a perspective from any given plane. From that perspective it is easy to think that the chosen plane is all there is and that all others are but possible worlds. Deleuze wants to remind us that we live with many potentials (the ongoing movement of liquid) and with many worlds (all the perspectives that energise ours without actual causal relation to it). To understand this co-presence of worlds and individual in relation to Ideas we have to turn to Deleuze's concept of static genesis.

STATIC GENESIS

The two series on static genesis explain how Deleuze's definition of sense, Ideas and infinitives can lead to an account of the genesis of identified actual things. The ontological static genesis can be understood as the genesis of actual beings that are literally but only partially static or unchanging, most notably individuals, persons and worlds. The logical static genesis accounts for the genesis of the logical component of the proposition, in particular identity in signification (meaning), for example in the concept as a limited set of predicates or the definition of a being as a set of properties. The definition of static physics in French (*physique statique*) provides a useful clue, as does the meaning of *statique* in general. It is the physics of things in equilibrium, as opposed to in dynamic states and *statique* refers to states in equilibrium or to immobility. These series chart the relation of identities to dynamic processes and the source of dynamism in actual static things from virtual intense ones. Deleuze is therefore explaining the role of difference in the occurrence of states in equilibrium. This account is necessary for at least three reasons. First, if he cannot connect difference to identified actual things, and if we accept that there are such things (which Deleuze does), then without this connection some aspects of actuality will be completely independent of an ideal or virtual determination. This would destroy the connectivity of the processes described elsewhere in *Logic of Sense*. Second, not only would there be a failure of connectivity, but identified beings and logical elements would provide a counter ground for philosophy, contradicting Deleuze's claims for the priority of differential processes, for example in the asymmetric reciprocal determination of the virtual and the actual, that is of Ideas and their actual expression through identified things and meanings. Third, Deleuze needs to avoid the claim that he is committed to the necessity of static things independent of their role in the determination of Ideas and their genesis from them. Though I have claimed that Deleuze accepts that there are identities, this is a dangerous statement unless qualified by the remark that this existence turns on issues of status. Through the static genesis, he will show that *when viewed completely* actual identities are illusory or in movement. However, when viewed as one side of inseparable processes, we can speak of identities and of their genesis.

Static genesis is therefore a two-way process. In Chapter 5, I will show how the same is true of dynamic genesis and it is therefore very important not to think that static and dynamic geneses are defined in terms of opposed directions; they are different but on the basis of how they work, and not in which direction. Though each series on the genesis begins with an account of the genesis of the determination of static individuals, persons, significations and worlds as singular, they lead to a reverse account of how these identities are sundered by this genesis, or solely identified as things that must change. This allows for a clearer definition of genesis in Deleuze's usage. It is the emergence of the singularity and hence dynamism of identified things, rather than their creation or birth as such. Deleuze is not committing the dogmatic fallacy of stating that he can rationally explain the identity of a given individual (an animal, say) by tracing its metaphysical origins in infinitives and Ideas. This explanation of actual genesis is for experimental scientists working on many genetic and social chains. Instead, he is explaining how, in principle, the individual significance and value of identified things is determined by Ideal conditions. For example, the actual genetic background of a child is for biologists to discover by tracking its genes, but the reason it is this meaningful child for itself, for you, for this world, for this evolutionary step, involves conditions added to (and interacting with) those biological conditions. The questions directing each enquiry are again different: 'What are you?' for the biologist and 'Why and whither you?' for the philosopher. Of course, this is too simple; both need each other's questions and responses for a complete view, even from their own perspective. We must be scientists, artists and philosophers to think with all the sides of our genetic emergence and ongoing creation. There's something of the renaissance in this comprehensiveness and the free-ranging quality of Deleuze's thought. The world will not be left to specialists, regulated by markets and protected by a deliberate impoverishment of social and political thought.

The mode of static genesis is limitation. It limits the series of Ideal singularities. To show this, Deleuze departs from the series of all ideal turning points or the ideal Event of all events, described earlier. Limitation of the series is the condition for singularity in the world, individual or person: a world is singular as the convergence of an infinite series of singularities against the background of all converging and diverging ones; an individual is a finite selection from the infinite series of singularities of a world; a person is the classification of an individual under a class or property, hence a limitation on the singularity itself (from turning point to form of recognition). An analogy of these limitations could be taken from an artist's pallet. Ideally, the colours can mix and cover infinite series of shades and shapes. When the artist sets these into convergent series of textures (*this* warmth and roughness) and shapes (*those* lines and planes) we have the conditions for a world. An individual then emerges once a limited number of colours, shapes and textures are selected on the canvas. A person emerges when a critic says: 'This is the combination of *identified* green and red dapples defining X.' We move through ever more restricted cycles of singularities until their openness and potential for turns is bound in the identity of a concept. The point of the series on static genesis is twofold: the steps of limitation pass the transforming potential of the singularity to each successive identity, making them only singular identities as things in movement and opened out by the singularities they limit; the limitations are themselves necessary conditions for all the ideal singularities, not as conditions for the singularity of identity, but rather as conditions for the determinacy of infinite diverging series as series of distinct and obscure relations. The ideal pallet is a chaos until the artist brings convergence to it, but the identified person is cold and lifeless unless its singularities are released – until the colours and shapes shimmer and resonate. Ontological genesis explains the singular value of things as open to change and the determination of an apparently chaotic ideal condition.

Much of the series on ontological static genesis is thereafter a response to a particularly difficult objection dealt with through a discussion of Leibniz and Husserl. I shall cover the Leibniz section here, leaving Husserl to a wider discussion in the next section. The problem for Deleuze is that in providing an account of static genesis he also sets up a possible reversal of his philosophy through the necessity of types and forms of identity. For example, are some worlds necessary within his account? Or are some individuals, or even persons? Is there a necessary form for a world and for an individual? If so, does this form take precedence over differential processes, making the limits required for genesis prior to the dynamic processes that they restrict? This is why Deleuze is careful to deny that the limitation of singularities applies to them as Ideal or virtual, insisting instead that the limiting processes are only effective in actual identities. This has double value for him, because it preserves the neutrality of Idea or infinitive, while instituting the lack in an identity that demands an energetic input from the Idea:

> To be actualised or to actualise oneself means to extend over a series of ordinary points; to be selected according to a rule of convergence; to be incarnated in a body; to become the state of a body; and to be renewed locally for the sake of limited new actualisations and extensions. Not one of these characteristics belongs to the singularities as such; they rather belong to the individuated world and to the worldly individuals that envelop them.
>
> (LoS, 110, 134)

The concepts of envelopment, where an individual is said to envelope rather than contain or 'be' a set of singularities, and the concept of expression, where a series of infinitives are expressed by an actual proposition rather than appearing as predicates in it, are central to this balance between having a dynamic role but not being identified or altered by it. To envelop is to determine something in its relations without setting it within fixed boundaries – something like the difference between the poem and the dictionary's use of a word. To express is both to allow something to acquire an actual series of connections, yet also remain neutral with respect to them – something like the an artist's use of a colour where, say, yellow is given a vivid and novel role, yet also remains as something that other artists can use differently, yet also in contact with former actual uses (and later ones).

The concern with predicates is at the heart of Deleuze's work on Leibniz in *Logic of Sense*. This is because there is an alternative and perhaps more intuitive way of determining individuals that Deleuze wants to resist at every turn. This alternative is one possible inter-pretation of Leibniz's work on predicates and a reading that Deleuze is trying to counter. Put simply, an individual can be defined in Deleuze as an actual distinct expression of a closed series of infi-nitives: the individual expresses 'to A, to B, to C, to D, to green, to grow, and so on' *against an obscure background of all others.* Alternatively, though, an individual or subject could be defined by a set of properties or predicates: the individual 'is A, B, C, D, green, growing and so on'. There is a lot at stake in the difference because in the latter case green can be finally determined as a general prop-erty or predicate, not when it is ascribed to the individual, but when it is itself defined according to a further set of predicates: to be green is to be A, B, C. As the green in this individual it is not fixed, but it is in a mode of defining that leads to the static determination of indi-viduals and of predicates or properties. This does not mean that the green cannot be in other individuals; it means that when it is in others, it is so as the same – once it has been defined. This is not the case for the expression of 'to green', since it is only fixed in its actual expression, and free to vary in other expressions because its deter-mination as an infinitive is through its changing relations to other infinitives rather than as an independent entity. Another way to look at this is through the concept of the event. For Deleuze, an individ-ual is determined by a series of events and he wants to resist a counter-definition of the individual as something with a fixed iden-tity determined by a set of properties or predicates to which events then happen as well-defined identical things or gerunds.

This work on predicates and on propositions rejoins studies from Deleuze's work on language, because his efforts to show the priority and neutrality of sense run parallel to maintaining the priority of infinitives, or what is expressed, over individuals and persons. For him, sense must be independent of propositions that attempt to determine the properties of infinitives. Each of these studies is double, since they are trying to resist identification while explaining and providing models for a study of actual individuals as necessarily dynamic and in movement due to their genesis in sense. Once we abandon the claim that sense or infinitives must themselves be iden-tifiable and of the same kind as actual things, we escape the paradox of something that is at work in something else, yet is unaffected by it:

> The very idea of static genesis dissipates the contradiction. When we say that bodies and mixtures produce sense, it is not by virtue of an indi-viduation which would presuppose it. Individuation in bodies, the

measure in their mixtures, the play of persons and of concepts in their variations, this whole ordinance presupposes sense and the neutral, pre-individual and impersonal field where it is deployed.

(LoS, 124, 149)

So where there are identified persons, there must also be non-identifiable sense as a condition for the individuation of persons, individuals and worlds. This sense explains their individuality as things that change and as things determined not only by a set of predicates but by a series of events. In the next chapter, on morals and events, we shall see this leading to a form of moral thinking about individuals where living with transforming impersonal events takes precedence over identifying oneself and maintaining that identity. In Chapter 5 on thought, we shall see how these impersonal and pre-individual fields of sense explain the importance of the unconscious in any thinking process. Conscious persons exist against a background of unconscious and impersonal events standing as the conditions for any identity.

DELEUZE AND HUSSERL

References to Husserl occur at key times throughout *Logic of Sense*. Deleuze cites his texts widely, quoting from *Ideas Pertaining to a Pure Phenomenology and to a Phenomenological Philosophy* (in the French translation by Ricœur), *Logical Investigations* and *Cartesian Meditations*. These references are not merely illustrations or cross references, or examples of types of philosophical reflection, or 'images of thought', or cases of errors or critical contrasts. Instead, Deleuze is making important distinctions between his transcendental philosophy and Husserl's, in order to show how his 'superior empiricism' departs from phenomenology, not only in terms of its technical interpretation of transcendental thinking, but more significantly, in terms of the strategic consequences and ontological commitments these differences lead to. My intention here is therefore not to give a complete assessment of Deleuze's relation to Husserl – a task far beyond the scope of this book. Instead, I will track the readings of Husserl, showing the detail of Deleuze's arguments as they apply to different conceptual innovations made in different series of *Logic of Sense*. This study will start with the fourteenth series 'of double causality', partly because it has been omitted up to now and partly because it includes an interesting version one of the most difficult problems for Deleuze's transcendental work.

129

I have alluded to objections regarding causality before. These turn on the difficulty of affirming two sides to reality, involved in reciprocal determinations (doubly), yet free of relations or laws that hold across the two sides – hence their asymmetry and the neutrality of one with respect to the other. The possible crossover law that Deleuze is most worried about in the series is causality, or a causal law holding across virtual and actual processes. He approaches it through short discussions of physics – or 'nature' – in the Stoics. The depth of the difficulty comes out most strongly in one of the rare heavy and clumsy concepts of Deleuze's work: the 'quasi-cause' (taken from the Stoics, but adopted by Deleuze, for example, in *Difference and Repetition* as well as *Logic of Sense*). This concept is accompanied by rather stretched analogies with physical processes such as surface effects. This is to the point where it seems that the work on sense and surface as conditions for actual things is at risk from an unnecessary and ultimately highly destructive aesthetic treatment, where the condition 'is like' the conditioned yet independent of it thanks to some ill-defined 'quasi-cause'. A clear risk of the crudest kind of dogmatism appears in this series. It is one where a scientific concept is taken analogically and inaccurately to support a metaphysical model at odds with the science in approach and in content. This was always a potential pitfall in Deleuze's return to the Stoics, due to their experience-based but to modern minds dogmatic and unscientific approach to nature.

However, Deleuze has complex and concrete arguments that not only deny any accusation of simple dogmatism, but also offer a productive and rich interpretation of the Stoics. Put simply the arguments are, first, that the transcendental condition is not a cause of properties in actual things, but the explanation for changes in their significance. The 'quasi-cause' does not change actual measurable things but their relation to sense. This means that actual measurable changes are incomplete and make no sense independent of this relation. What is a number independent of its relation to the intensity of feelings giving it a series of relations to other bodily effects, meanings and values? How can any number give the full measure of the potential for such relations for any value? Second, even if sense is itself conditioned by its actual expression, this is only as an effect in a special way: the effect is not of the same nature as the cause (the former is ideal whereas the latter is bodily) and it changes only in its expression while remaining neutral in itself. 'Effect' must not be understood in the cause-effect dyad, but as a claim about a parallel process to actual causes and effects whereby actual cause A and actual effect B run asymmetrically to virtual effect A′ and virtual effect B′. So the actual elements do not cause the virtual ones, but rather the Ideal effect accompanies the value or significance that occurs with the actual cause-effect relation. For example, when Romeo takes the poison that causes his death, we are dealing with actual causes and effects, but these have an actual intense value (for instance, death for Juliet as unbearable) and this has an effect on relations of series of neutral infinitives ('to grieve' increases in the intensity of its relation to 'to despair' and 'to love'). Note how this raises another objection to Deleuze – again in line with modern science and philosophical naturalism – through the possibility of a science of the kinds of sense, values and intensities associated with psychological states. Why can't these states also be treated by empirical sciences? Aren't such sciences the only valid source of knowledge about them? We have already looked at this kind of objection and the straightforward version of the answer that it is because there is something incomparable and novel in the actual manifestations of intensity demanding a transcendental explanation rather than a merely causal one. A further development of this could be that the restriction of science, for example to conscious psychological states, fails to explain the connectedness, adaptability and capacity for change of such states, in particular beyond minds and into social, biological and physical processes.

Sense or the Deleuzian surface is an effect but only in a way that can be traced and 'put into effect' in the cause. This does not mean that we cannot describe it. We can, both in terms of their ideal properties, neutrality for instance, and in terms of their actual relations (this actual expression of 'to love' and 'to hate'). So sense is always more than the ways we have represented it and the possible representations we judge it to be open to. It can seem that Deleuze is highly repetitive in returning to the problems raised by his transcendental philosophy in its insistence on interaction with impassibility and neutrality, but each time he is adding different facets to the problem. In the series on double causality, he is emphasising the shift from a single causal law to a double 'quasi-causal' determination (as in asymmetrical or different in two directions). He is also showing the importance of thoroughness in this impassibility, which is where the critique of Husserl comes in. According to Deleuze's reading, Husserl rediscovers the sense of the proposition as transcendental thanks to his method of bracketing or transcendental reduction. This is because the brackets must separate the sense of the proposition from specific actual referents, manifestations and significations, since these too can be open to doubt due to their variations; they can be illusions or dreams, for instance. Yet some kind of sense persists after this bracketing – a sense Husserl calls the 'noema' resulting from a directedness bracketed from the contingent reality of what it is directed to (a 'noetic' process). So, like Deleuze, Husserl deduces a sense – the noema – independent of what it is actually referring to but standing as a condition for it. Here is a passage from *Ideas* showing this reduction or epoché and the sense as essence that is deduced as a transcendental thanks to it:

> The transcendent world receives its 'parenthesis,' we exercise the epoché in relation to its actual being. We now ask what, of essential necessity, is to be discovered in the noetic processes pertaining to perception and in the valuation of liking. With the whole physical and psychical world, the actual existence of the real relation between perceiving and perceived is excluded; and, nonetheless, a relation between perceiving and perceived (and between liking and liked) remains left over, a relation which becomes given essentially in 'pure immanence,' namely purely on the ground of the phenomenologically reduced mental processes of perceiving and liking precisely as they fit into the transcendental stream of mental processes.
>
> (Husserl, 1983: 215)

I have quoted at length here to draw out the range of similarities between the two thinkers. Both stress immanence in the transcendental, that is the condition is not in another independent realm and they belong to the same reality. Both move away from actuality as denoted and away from psychic states associated with a particular mind or perceiver. Both separate sense from meaning or signification as something either meant by a particular mind or as a social manifestation. Therefore they have an immanent objective reality as a condition for actuality. So where is the core difference (notwithstanding the contrasts in method and their consequences discussed earlier in my section on transcendental deductions)?

In the series on double causality Deleuze's account of the differences is complicated and involves many connected points, so I will draw out each of these points, making only a few further references to other series where these add something or refine it. Deleuze's arguments fall under the rubric that Husserl does not go far enough in establishing the neutrality of sense in terms of the way its form is still determined by presuppositions characteristic of images of thought as dependent on identity and on the subject:

1. Though Husserl treats sense as an attribute, that is as the necessary effect of a process and condition for it, he then defines this

attribute as a predicate and, hence, as a well-defined concept rather than as an event variable in its expression. So sense is still determined by identity in a concept.

2. Sense therefore becomes referable to objects that its identity as predicate corresponds to and sense becomes the sense of something that shares the same predicates. When the sense is the infinitive 'to green' nothing actually is 'to green' and things only express it as a singular event in a singular way. When sense is the predicate 'green' defined adequately in terms of concepts then actual things corresponding to them become overdetermined and no longer singular but comparable in their relations to general terms.

3. Husserl avoids paradox and nonsense in his definition of sense, but this imposes logical principles on transcendental ones at the cost of missing the genetic role of paradox, nonsense and problems. We have seen that Deleuze's account of genesis depends on singular and passing responses to eternal problems (which are eternal because they are paradoxical). Husserl's logical principle, or the imposition of a demand for identity and non-contradiction, is set up as a *transcendent* principle that invalidly limits the transcendental ones.

4. This imposition of the transcendent logical principle is the imposition of common sense and good sense, as widely criticised throughout Deleuze's work in this period. The object and sense are subjected to common sense in its capacity to account for the identity of things (*What is this?*) and to good sense as a principle for the distribution of any possible object (*Any possible object can take its place in a classification of objects according to predicates*).

5. This elevates common and good sense even further than usual because they can now be taken as independent of an empirical and historical account (*these are the principles of our tried and tested reasoning*). As transcendental, they become the basis for necessary conditions for any valid form of thought: a *doxa*, or common belief system, becomes an *Urdoxa*, or necessary condition.

6. The identified individual also remains in the transcendental as deduced by Husserl, because the directed consciousness bracketed from contingent aspects retains the form of 'subjective identity'. An individual 'I' is presupposed in the pure directedness, for example, of perception. This is not a given person or a pure subject, but the principle that any directedness presupposes a kernel or 'nucleus' of individual identity: not any particular person, nor a universal subject, but an individual point of view.

The focus on form is important in Deleuze's critique of Husserl, because Deleuze objects more strongly to the illegitimate transfer of forms of identity into the transcendental than to the dogmatic elevation of particular identities into universals. This is because transcendental philosophy is itself contradicted and limited in its processes by this move:

> Thus, not only is everything which must be engendered by the notion of sense given in the notion of sense, but what is even more important, the whole notion is muddied when we confuse the expression with these other dimensions from which we tried to distinguish it. We confuse it 'transcendentally' with the dimensions from which we wanted to distinguish it formally.

(LoS, 98, 120)

This criticism is taken further in the series on the ontological static genesis through the point that if an individual or monadic kernel is maintained in the transcendental, then convergence is imposed and presupposed on all the series of sense, which then becomes a continuum of convergent lines. Once again, the main point is about what is lost in terms of genetic potential if we assume such a convergence and continuity. Creative moments and the openness of the new come from synthetic divergences, where series branch out yet retain relations through series of other processes. In Husserl, Deleuze sees the loss of the productive power of excess and lack in series articulated by singularities, turning points or bifurcations. This point about genesis is reinforced in the series on the logical static genesis through the remark that Husserl imposes the model of the proposition in its identified logical form on problems and on sense. However, here we can start to see a more flexible reading of both thinkers, since Deleuze is giving a dramatic account of their differences (Husserl is not radical enough and betrays sense) but also resting this drama on a reading of analogies which point to other possible interpretations.

4
Morals and events

In order to understand the moral philosophy put forward in *Logic of Sense* it is helpful to remember what it cannot call upon, what it cannot aim to arrive at and what it has to work with. As we have seen in the previous two chapters, Deleuze's philosophy denies a set of familiar grounds for philosophy and for language. The subject, self and individual are replaced by processes of individuation. This is also true for communities or classes of subjects and for any wider collection of elements with a set identity. Furthermore, Deleuze gives priority to sense (relations between infinitives expressed in actual things) over denotation, signification and manifestation (the reference, meaning and situation of utterance of a proposition). His moral philosophy therefore emphasises the significance of events over facts, meanings and subjective intentions. This does not mean that he denies the existence or reality of any of these entities; it is rather that they are never independent and free-standing. Whenever a moral philosophy attempts to ground itself on a free will, consciousness, subject, self, set of facts, meanings or intentions, *Logic of Sense* provides an alternative account where relations between series, sense and events take precedence and explain the emergence of other identities, thereby insisting that we never have a complete reality until we chart underlying processes. These cannot be understood in terms of prior identities or transcendent values and laws. Moral problems for Deleuze are therefore not of the form 'What are the criteria of right and wrong in this situation?' or 'What are the values and laws we can appeal to in this situation?' Instead,

135

the problem is much more thoroughgoing and paradoxical, since it asks how series should be replayed given the events contracting and splitting them according to disjunctive syntheses. Or put more simply, the problem is: how to respond to events that constitute and dismember persons, individuals and worlds?

I have written earlier in this book about the pragmatism and empiricism of Deleuze's philosophy, but pragmatic resources are not available to him in his moral philosophy if these are understood as relying on a wise and practical middle-ground for the resolution of disputes. This is because his empiricism and pragmatism are radical in the sense that they necessarily give priority to creation and to open experimentation, rather than to the best available transient and harmonising basis for action. The pragmatic matter and empirical evidence charted in *Logic of Sense* are differential and transforming movements rather than relative stable values or fixed entities set against a changing background. It can seem that modern moral problems are efforts to impose order or consensus – or both – as bulwarks against change and conflict, for example through laws about scientific or medical interventions in a world dominated by new technologies, or through universal rights in a world formed by new global flows and boundaries, or through a democratically attained and always provisional agreement about the extension of private sensibilities into the public realm. According to Deleuze's philosophy, order or consensus can never be the grounds for moral action. Some order is without doubt necessary, as dictated by the reciprocal determinations at work in his complex systems of processes, but that order is always secondary to and in the service of responses to change that can only be replayed well through further change. A role for consensus can also be found, but it is on the basis of the wider connectedness of reality rather than a consensus between a restricted set of beings. Consensus is neither an end in itself nor a necessary condition; it is rather a secondary position stemming from belonging to a reality connecting many different individuals through multiple series and events.

Deleuze's moral philosophy is therefore not of resistance, of mediation or of conservation – however pragmatically and wisely we allow these to bend and to vary. It is a moral philosophy of creativity in relation to events. There is a novelty in each event calling for a corresponding creativity. A true moral problem is something new connecting all individuals and all worlds, all processes and all fleeting identities. This partly explains his resistance to categorical laws or values, since the novelty of the problem demands their reassessment.

For example, from this point of view, a problem set around the killing of innocents in war is transformed by new events, such as developments in weaponry or a protagonist's adoption of a doctrine of annihilation. The problem is therefore one of immanence with no possible transcendent basis in freedom, laws, objective reality, virtues or values, because its novelty puts all real connections back into play. All is 'within' and nothing 'above'. The creativity called for by the problem should not necessarily be viewed as a conscious inventiveness, but rather as openness to evolution. Moral problems are not specifically human, nor even addressed specifically to humans, because the problem itself occurs primarily within irreducibly diverse series and events (and as an Event drawing them all together in a novel distribution of series and of events). It is not nonsense, in Deleuze's approach, to study an animal or plant evolution as a response to a moral problem. The development of a novel means for capturing a prey, or ensuring better procreation, may not be willed and therefore may not be analysable in terms of praise and blame, but it is a selection in the middle of events and series, with their injuries, ideas and expression of values. This does not commit us to the judgement that animals or plants are involved in better or worse selections than humans. It is to be beyond such judgements because, as we shall see below, moral problems choose us as much as we must then select within them. Neither does it commit us to the view that we are shaped by the problems that select us to the point of being absolved of the burden of the problems gripping others (whether humans, plants or animals). As we shall also see, and as we have seen in the philosophy of language and philosophy of events, problems, series and events are interconnected to the point where any worthy response to our problems is also a response to the problems of others.

So what if we are then asked whether this capacity to know about connection is what sets humans apart from other processes? The answer is that knowledge is but a small part of connectedness. The evolution of a plant species drawing an environment into a rich network of relations and novel developments may not involve consciousness of its role, but the evolution expresses this role nonetheless and arguably pulls it off in a much more successful way than knowledgeable humans have ever done. And what if we are asked whether the capacity to destroy sets humans apart? This too is a potential for other processes, as in the mutation of a virus or too great a success for a predator. What then of changes that cannot be ascribed to living things: the erosion and boiling up of rock formations or the disappearance of seas? These too can be seen as expressions of a moral problem – it again depends on the perspective chosen for the approach to the problematic tensions and pulls. The drying up of a sea is an answer to a problem that can also be studied from a human perspective. Though *Logic of Sense* can seem to be Deleuze's most humanistic book, through its study of the events assailing singular individuals, such as an artist succumbing to alcoholism, the structure of his moral philosophy is anything but humanist, because this would restrict and prejudge the encounter of series of events by misunderstanding the place of the human within these processes.

PRINCIPLES FOR MORAL PROBLEMS

The limitless connectivity of Deleuze's system of processes should not be seen as cause for quietism and despair, nor for a complete repudiation of human moral action. Instead, he is providing us with a series of connections whose processes demand singular creative activity, sensibility and thoughtful selections. We are not presented with a chaotic set of connections. On the contrary, each individual brings a singular determination to the series of processes, for example through the series of singularities converging in a world and through their restriction to define the individual and on to their identification in persons and properties. However, neither are we presented with a system amenable to utilitarian calculation. The ideal or virtual conditions for actual change are immeasurable and incomparable. This is because sense, defined as intensive difference in infinitives and Ideas, cannot be represented within a measuring system without losing its dynamic quality. We can only measure the virtual differentiations as they are expressed in actual differences. So any moral principle cannot have measure and comparison at its heart without missing what gives value and significance to individuals: their singularities. Once again, this does not mean that Deleuze's philosophy cannot engage in utilitarian calculations or commit to human values. It means that these must always be balanced and added to through thoughts and actions worthy of events which cannot be reduced to human values or to comparisons between outcomes of actions, or even to comparisons between different systems of rules governing possible actions. In other words, values set as identities and actions, then compared through measured outcomes, can only ever be part of a wider moral system that works with the damage these comparisons can inflict in hiding the singular, individuated, connected, yet also disjunctive nature of reality. 'We' are the same because we are all essentially different and differentiated right down to the core of our being – of our becoming.

So Deleuze's moral philosophy is determined by a moral problem in the strong Deleuzian sense of problem as a series of tensions demanding transformation but always resisting resolution. As such, there are no good moral questions allowing for final answers. There are only worthy expressions of moral problems. Does this mean that there is no effectiveness and decisiveness in Deleuze's approach? No. Effectiveness is only part of a wider series of principles where actual effects must be taken with ideal ones. Decisiveness is only part of a wider series of selections where any selection is necessarily partial, destined to fail and demanding of reconnections within irreducibly complex moral problems. This complexity is described in great detail, but rather densely, in the twentieth series of *Logic of Sense* 'on the moral problem for the Stoics'. (I am wary of the addition of 'philosophy' to this title in the English translation, since it is not clear that Deleuze is restricting the problem to a philosophical context – quite the contrary.) To counter the opaqueness of the series, I will list its main moral claims in more simple form and then discuss significant aspects in greater depth through a reading of the closing lines of the series. There are at least six principles (different interpretations of the twentieth series may come up with more and further principles appear in other series).

The first principle is that *the moral problem involves a singular response to the challenge of how to mix logical propositions, bodily effects and an ideal sense* (the Ideas and infinitives explained in the two previous chapters of this book – understood, roughly in this moral context, as the intensities that can invest different values). This challenge is the lesson of the stick and the egg example given at the beginning of the twentieth series. The egg draws together the bodily depth of the yoke, the mobile surface of the white and the logical inflexibility of the shell. In showing an egg and a stick to a disciple, the Stoic sage is presenting a task in response to the question 'What is morality?' Morality is the problem of how to break the egg. Unlike a more traditional moral position, where not breaking eggs might seem to be the final goal, Deleuze's approach is resolutely realist, yet also demanding of tact, care and an individual thoughtfulness. So any moral problem mixes physical effects, such as wounds or novel sensual attunement, with established structures of meanings and things (the logical proposition), with changes in intensities in ideas that explain alterations in the value and significance of the meanings and of the physical effects. The moral problem and its

139

replaying must bring wounds, ideas and values together in a new mixture. This can only be done by breaking the egg and making an individual and singular mix. For example, the decision to seek a cure for a disease in a body that may not outlive it must draw on different physical effects, on a critique of established structures of the meaning of health and sickness, and on changes in significance or ideal intensity, from the multiple points of view emerging with an individuation. A logical structure of meaning alone, or a wound, or an overvalued new sensation, or a universal value neither determine nor resolve a moral problem. Deleuze's definition of moral problems provides a context for their replaying which could never be based solely on knowledge, or wounds (and the competitive struggle for their avoidance), or sensations (love or revenge), or universal values (the sanctity of some life-forms).

Second, in accordance with the traditional characterisation of Stoic morality as willing the event as it happens, *the event of the mix or of the breaking must therefore be willed*. This is because the breaking is necessary, not in terms of how it must be taken and pursued, but in terms of the necessity of its happening. A moral problem is therefore posed badly if it starts with the denial of an event, for example in seeking to ignore or to ban a bodily practice or set of ideas, desires and phantasms. So a further lesson of the egg and stick is that the egg is being broken and has to be broken; it is a mistake to seek to retain it as a whole or to deny that it is fractured. The breaking has to be willed or welcomed. However, it is only helpful to think of this as passivity to the event, if we understand passivity as allowing oneself to be set in motion by it rather than simply letting it happen. Deleuze's moral philosophy is progressive rather than acquiescent. It does not turn away from events, for example, in the way a conservative morality may try to turn back the clock on medical advances or on social developments. But neither does it simply accept novel material conditions, new ideas and revolutionary desires – let alone 'natural' disasters. The challenge is always to conduct the intensity of these events and their significance, while resisting their necessary inner compulsion to confirm injuries, ideas and values as final and inevitable. And yet, the following sentence appears to belie this interpretation: 'Stoic morality is about the event; it consists in willing the event as such, that is, in willing that which happens as it happens' (LoS, 143, 168). Everything here turns on the concept of the event and on Deleuze's insistence on willing it as something that is arriving and not as something that has happened. The event is never solely a fact for Deleuze; it is a passage and a process 'as it happens'.

Therefore, in interpreting his moral philosophy, we must remember that to will the event could never simply be to accept a state of affairs, since there is no simple state of affairs to accept, only a complex ongoing multilayered process of transformation. Resignation is therefore a form of replaying and indeed one that may be a poor way of responding to a given event.

This means, third, that one side of the moral problem is 'divination', that is the divining or deducing of the arrival of the event, not in terms of actual effects – things that have happened – but in terms of signs of what is to come. In other words, *moral philosophy is partly about charting series of actual turning points and the ideas they express, in order to divine how they constitute new and connected problematic events*. For example, a dropping birth rate with all its bodily signs (later births, for instance) and meaningful ones (justifications and reasons) calls for a divination not only of what the turn implies for actual futures (reducing populations, immigration and emigration) but also the ideal turning points (different values associated with children, for instance). The thing to stress here is that divination for Deleuze is not the misleading modern caricature of Stoic mysticism, gullibility and resignation, but rather a thought about relations of turning points and their implications and about the selection of different creative responses. This connects to his more overt moral and political positions, as advanced in the essays collected in *Desert Islands and Other Texts* and *Two Regimens of Madness*. Deleuze's positions involve a diagnosis of a situation in terms of its sources, a divination of its legacies (actual and ideal), the creation of words and places opening the situation to its most liberating potential and a focus on what is singular about the situation: 'Against apocalyptic history, there is a sense of history that unites with the possible, the multiplicity of the possible, a swarming of the possible in each moment' ('Les Indiens de Palestine', in *Deux régimes de fous*, p. 184). To will the event is never to be resigned to it, but to seek to release its connections and differentiations (how we connect through variations in ideas and values). It is to stand up to those who would wish to see the event only in terms of barriers, differences in identity and pure outcomes. There are no absolute differences, universal laws or pure ends in any event.

However, another side of the moral problem is how to will or to welcome specific actual events as they actually occur, that is no longer as signs and as expressions of widely connected events, but in a single event occurring to something or to someone in the present. The fourth principle is therefore that, *on the one hand, the moral problem runs through time and across all connections and to will the event is to attempt to divine these connections of turning points and to creatively respond to them by drawing them together. On the other hand, though, the problem is how to will this single actual event as it happens.* To will the event is then not to deny it, nor to divine its position through time, nor to accept its consequences, but to affirm its occurrence in the present. Note the importance, again, of a paradoxical oscillation between two sides or poles characteristic of problems and paradoxes in Deleuze's philosophy. Note also that this paradoxical element is always genetic, in the sense of producing something, rather than a blockage to thought in a simple contradiction. For example, a falling birth rate is on the one hand a widely connected event with many turning points, many physical expressions and ideal effects, and countless shifting intensities or values. It is also, however, expressed in a singular event such as *this* late pregnancy, premature baby, cherished child, *this* joy, *this* loss, *this* grief, *this* love. The moral relation between wide connection and singular expression and the problem of divination explains why Deleuze often treats morals through art, since this creativity expresses communal significance through singularity (for example, in the multiple perspectives yet also shared studies of grief, sexuality, love and illness in Almodóvar's *All About My Mother*, 1999). Deleuze's moral problem registers both the connected ideal event and the singular present one as events to be worthy of and to affirm, but in multiple ways rather than through a single response. The oscillation in events between what could be seen as the personal (but is really the singular) and what could be seen as the universal (but is really the differentially connected) is crucial to Deleuze's moral position. He refuses to conflate the two – in the way some moralisers impose their personal events on others through the artifice of universal values or credos – and instead constructs a system where the singular and the connected are in contact with one another but call for different responses: a difficult balance of what can only belong to individuals and what connects to all things.

Deleuze expands on how to be worthy of the event in these two ways, in his fifth principle, through a surprising discussion of the necessity of representation. Readers of *Difference and Repetition* will be aware that representation is criticised as one of the negative aspects of a detrimental image of thought; we should not assume that thought must work through representation, because representation imposes a set of forms of identity on the represented thing. However, though representation must not be given this prior role, it still plays an essential part in the divination and affirmation of the event. The principle is that *in divination and the willing of the present event, a representation must always be considered with an expression.* A representation designates an object or an event and associates it with a signification or meaning, for example when we describe a situation in response to the question 'Tell me what happened?' But, for Deleuze, this representation is necessarily lacking, with respect to an event, without an expression of its significance – not what it is, or what it means, but how it changes values or infinitives, that is how it alters relations of intense investment (for example, when we try to dramatise the effect of a meeting rather than describe who we met and what was said, *and then everything changed* . . .). The moral problem is then also a problem of how to relate representation and expression so that the object or actual event is not taken in abstraction from the virtual one (the event as sense and surface, in the vocabulary of *Logic of Sense*). In the series on moral problems, Deleuze explains this through the difference between a death and its significance – a discussion he carries through other series in the book and, indeed, throughout his books. We can represent a death and understand its meaning, but in terms of a moral problem this is never enough. We must also express its sense, something that cannot be shown cognitively in a picture of an actual thing as a content to be understood, or explained through a set of predicates, but only dramatised. For example, Jacques-Louis David's painting of the death of the French revolutionary Marat is not only a representation of the death (though it has to be that too), it is also an expression of everything the death entails in terms of ideal effects, which ideas change in relation to others and with which intensities. The meaning or signification of the painting is 'Marat is dead', its denotation is the dead Marat, but its sense is a differentiation in the intensities of infinitely many relations between infinitives ('to hope', 'to despair', 'to revile', 'to impose', 'to love', 'to respect', 'to grieve', 'to kill', 'to die' and so on). The moral problem is conditioned by the challenge of balancing representation and expression in the same way as an artist in the communication of a particular death and its wider significance, for instance in the way a photographer uses the horror of the onlookers to capture the end of hope and love – in Bobby Kennedy's murder – or the line of mourners leading up to a displayed body to capture respect and a power stretching beyond death – John Paul II – or in the idea of death in the lifeless repetition of a once vivid image – Warhol on Marilyn. Moral questions are often presented as demanding a dispassionate setting and assessment. Yet, in his principle on representation and

143

expression, Deleuze affirms that this abstraction misunderstands the nature of the event and of the problem. A problem is moral because it is an occasion for the precise representation of a singular event and an individual passionate engagement with interconnected shifts in values. Note that this individual engagement must not be confused with the response of an individual, since it always involves more than one actor due to the expressive interconnection of individuals and events. This singular expressiveness sets Deleuze's approach at odds with any moral philosophy that approaches moral questions through abstract and sanitised general cases addressed to universal rational judges.

The previous point leads to a sixth principle with respect to moral problems and events. *We have to express the event in its eternal significance and we have to represent it in its present happening.* These are in tension, since as we have seen in Deleuze's work on time, the eternal event is always past and yet to come but never present, whereas the present event is always passing away and opening to the future but never past or future. However, as I shall discuss in a later section on time, concepts of eternity and the present are reversible and relative for Deleuze. From the point of view of the passing present, that which has passed and that which is yet to come are eternal (like an idealised memory or fantasy) whereas from the reverse view the passing present is eternally passing and infinitely subdivided in past and future directions (the tortoise ceaselessly approaching but never reaching the hare). This is an important paradox in *Logic of Sense* which can be summed up in the statement that there are two times (Aiôn and Chronos) which are not reducible to one another, yet which are incomplete without one another and which give different perspectives on their shared relations. It is helpful to keep this in mind when studying the different roles of time in the book, since it can seem that Deleuze is sloppy in his use of 'eternal' and 'present'. He is not. Instead, his work on time is an attempt to explain and enact the absence of a single grounding time or an agreed theory on the relativity of time, replacing them instead with definitions of time consistent with the different processes relating the virtual to the actual or Ideas to actualities or infinitives to their expression (and the reverse). Deleuze's philosophy of time cannot simply be called relativism about time since this would be to miss the paradoxical, structural and genetic quality of the relation between times. The relativism is between different processes in a dual and then ramifying structure. These processes set up paradoxes between the perspectives set up from each process. The paradoxes generate series of creative responses, such as the proliferation of different ways of defining eternity in philosophy and theology.

HOW MORAL PROBLEMS ARE REPLAYED

At this stage of the study of Deleuze's moral philosophy, I want to focus on the view of time where actualisation or the demands of representation hold sway over considerations of the eternal part of any event. According to this view, in the present the event of a death is a dying on the cusp of becoming past and waiting for a future that never comes; it is a waiting for death and waning of life rather than death itself, if this is understood as a final end. There is therefore a distinction drawn by Deleuze between an event that has passed or that is yet to come ('To die' understood as 'Marat has died' or 'Marat will die') and an event that is happening in the present ('Marat is dying'). Once this distinction has been drawn, on the basis of his definition of the event as a process, we can see why he defines the living present as a passing away into the past and a moving towards the future, since, if strictly defined as a simple present instant, the event would lose its movement (at time t, Marat is either alive or dead and not dying). This explains why representation is never enough, since real movement in the present involves changes in values, or more precisely in the intensities of values. Nothing really happens in Marat's dying moments until David invests them with different flows of pathos (growing outrage at his supposedly ignoble murder, burgeoning reverence for his virtues – which was then to wane) and physical flows (loss of blood, draining of colour, muscular release, tilting of the head, parting of the lips as they dry). The pathos and movements raise the set of facts captured in the painting to the level of an event of significance.

In eternity, by contrast, death has always happened or is always about to happen, but never strictly a present dying. This is a very difficult and strange claim. It recurs through *Logic of Sense* and relies on the abstraction of the infinitive (to die, rather than this dying) and on the necessity of expression ('to die' and all its relations to other infinitives require actual expressions which are when death happens). It is helpful, if a little dangerous too, to think of this in Platonic terms: like a Platonic virtue that can be only presented imperfectly in given cases, Deleuzian virtual death can only be accomplished in an actual case. However, the dual key to Deleuze's reversal of Platonism is that Platonic perfection becomes the pure variation of the infinitive ('to care' rather than 'Care'), so the Idea

145

is difference rather than identity, and both sides of reality require one another, but in an asymmetric manner that preserves the neutrality and impassibility of the neutral Idea as differential rather than as sameness. But then how are these differentials interpreted as 'having happened' or 'about to happen'? It is because, even if they are movements rather than identities, as movements they are waiting for different actual expressions which will determine them in the present. Until this actualisation, they are therefore potentials which have happened (in prior actualisations) and will happen (in later ones). By way of analogy, we could think of a colour as a potential to be warm or to be cold, depending on how an artist places it in a representation alongside other colours and in a particular shape. The ideal colour is never warm or cold, though it has been in earlier paintings and will be in later ones.

The many definitions of death demonstrate the complexity but also the precision of Deleuze's thought. On the ideal or virtual plane we have the infinitive 'to die' which can be subdivided into relations to actual things as a potential to 'have died' or 'will die'. On the actual plane we have the process 'dying', which is never a present final death, but infinite stretches of 'to be dying' falling away into the past and projecting into the future. This falling away and projecting is limitless in the present and he claims that all the past and all the future are in the present as passage, because we cannot in principle cut any past event or future one from the present. The present is passing away from all of the past and projecting into all of the future, for example in the way distant events and incongruous events can be brought into a present moment. *If only they had not crossed the ocean before their revolutions! What are we leaving now for our children's children?* The originality of Deleuze's structure comes out strongly, here, when we realise that any individual (mountain, plant, animal or human as extended singular processes) is all of these deaths in series of paradoxical relations of representation and expression. In human terms, this means that you are a potential to have died, a potential to die, a dying as passing away and a dying as projection towards death. All of these are interlinked and none are complete without the others. More shockingly, perhaps, when something has actually died it remains as a virtual trace in the relations of 'has died' and 'will die' that it expressed. This explains something that may strike interpreters as incongruous in Deleuze's writing. He often speaks of shame and nobility, of worthiness and baseness (for example in his essay about shame and T. E. Lawrence in *Essays Critical and Clinical*). Why would a thinker opposed to judgement and to the focus on the particular human person use such terms? Why would a philosophy so dismissive of factual autobiography and person-based psychology apparently ally itself to the narrow judgements that they thrive upon (such as the ignoble search for the 'dirty little secret' rightly reviled by Deleuze, for example in his reading of Lewis Carroll)? It is because it is not Lawrence's particular and actual shame that matters, but the traces of shame and honour his life bequeaths impersonally for others to express anew in the multiple ideal relations of 'to shame' and 'to honour'. There is some judgement at work in selecting how we shall repeat the traces left by others, but it is not in judging the past persons, but finding ways of connecting to their virtual traces by expressing them anew. Though selection can involve judgement it necessarily exceeds it and subsumes it in the chance-driven creativity necessary for real selection.

All of this can seem detached when compared to real moral problems such as how to achieve a just repartition of the earth's resources or how to share limited resources when there are disproportionately large just demands. Deleuze is not simply dealing with practical ethics or morals here, but instead with something that seems close to what is commonly known as metaethics or the philosophical presuppositions of moral philosophy. The kind of presuppositions he is working with are indeed very pure; they are not considerations about goodness or about the worth of different moral positions with respect to different types of knowledge, but about the broad metaphysical concepts and systems his own moral philosophy must build upon. The main questions in the twentieth series of *Logic of Sense* are not about how one should behave morally, but what kind of metaphysical context is at work in events leading to moral problems. However, an abrupt distinction between metaethics and practical moral philosophy does not hold for his work. This is because the presuppositions are practical. They extend from theoretical questions, through ones of principle and up to issues of individual action, to the point where theory and practice distinctions fail. Deleuze's moral philosophy is constructed on his philosophy of language and philosophy of events in such a manner as to situate it within questions such as 'How must I act in order to live with these events?' rather than 'What should I do with this moral dilemma?' The first question appears against a background of turning points, both actual and eternal. The second is faced by two or more apparent oppositions. The first is the problem of how to live with the moral knots that constitute us. The second is a question of weighing up arguments for and against a set of options. The first arrives at an action, which only descends into an opportunity for judgement afterwards and falsely. (*This is what we are doing; that is what they did wrong.*) The second arrives at a judgement, only then to pass on to a justified action. (*This is the just path we should follow; we are following the just path.*) Deleuze's wager is that the second question presupposes and conceals the first, to the point where, if it is taken as the fundamental moral question, it leads to a false image of the moral problem: 'What is truly immoral is every use of the moral notions, just, unjust, praiseworthiness, blame' (175). Does this then mean that Deleuze eschews all principles? Is his philosophy the worst kind of laissez-faire, the culmination of philosophical relativism and cynicism?

No. The closing passages of the series on the moral problem draw together his moral principles in a way that describes and guides moral action, not as judgement or as based on judgement, but as a conjoined acting and representing in response to events. It is common for the later sections of each series to have this condensed and prospective character, not because they lead on to the next series, but because they concentrate the series they belong to – and hence all series – and also because they connect to and question all series through a disarming combination of simplification and complexity. This is not a contradiction. The simplicity concerns the structure relating novel concepts (by drawing many together in simplified form) and the complexity concerns their interpretation within the structure (through an esoteric presentation). This is a deliberate and consistent ploy, since Deleuze is demonstrating his moral approach on one level, which is to donate something which prompts action according to a well-determined structure, but on another level he is refusing to dictate which specific action to take. The closing passages of many series therefore benefit from being read as concentrated summaries *and* as demands for experimental but rigorous interpretation *and* as loose provocations wrapped in enigmas.

So how should we replay moral problems? We should play them as actors playing a character, because the character captures the eternal quality of the Idea or infinitives as always there to be replayed differently, while the singular performance corresponds to the one-off quality of the passing present: 'The actor occupies the instant, while the character portrays hopes or fears in the future and remembers or repents in the past: it is in this sense that the actor "represents"' (LoS, 147, 173). So any 'moral action' must both represent what is singular in its events and connect this to a universal part to be played differently by others. Representation is therefore also to be understood with its French sense as performance, in addition to picturing or identifying again, and Deleuze's concept of dramatisation must be understood as theatrical. There is a precise philosophical understanding of performance in relation to time here, since it combines eternity with the reduction of time to the smallest possible stretch of time. The moral act must insist on its fleeting quality and on the fleeting quality of all its identified components, while also conveying the timelessness of what makes it different through the Ideas and infinitives it expresses: 'To bring about the correspondence of the minimum time which can occur in the instant with the maximum time which can be thought in accordance with the Aiôn' (LoS, 147, 173). So the physical wounds, the meanings and the ideas in the act should be made as individual as possible rather than mixed and confused with others: 'To limit the actualisation of the event in a present without mixture, to make the instant all the more intense, taut and instantaneous since it expresses an unlimited future and the unlimited past' (LoS, 147, 173). As actors or mimes, moral players do not simply will the event, they repeat it differently. They take what is happening and, by representing it to the maximum of its singularity, in a further singular way they have selected, they give it a novel sense and significance, which then remains as material for others to follow and replay:

> This is how the Stoic sage not only comprehends and wills the event, but also *represents the event and by this selects it*, and that an ethics of the mime necessarily prolongs the logic of sense. Beginning with a pure event, the mime directs and doubles the actualisation, measure the mixtures with the aid of an instant without mixture, and prevents them from overflowing.
>
> (LoS, 147, 173)

HOW TO ACT MORALLY (PRINCIPLES)

How is this acting, divining and representing moral? If we understand moral philosophy in its broadest understanding, as providing directions as to how to act, the principles for moral problems outlined in the previous section seem utterly inadequate. This insufficiency covers nearly all questions about action, from the most personal (what should I be?) to the social (how should I treat other persons?) to the global (how can I behave in a just way?) and up to the universal (what is the good?). It is not enough simply to answer that Deleuze has a critique of such questions and, in particular, of

149

their reliance on persons and of their presuppositions with respect to types of moral problem and valid or useful answers. The spirit of such questions captures an understandable and legitimate concern to go beyond wide moral principles and into the detail of how to act. Moreover, it could never be enough to evade that spirit with the claim that we cannot direct what each individual should do when called by singular events, since such an admission would negate the whole exercise of outlining the moral problem in the first place. What is the point of defining the moral problem, unless to construct a series of principles, critical contrasts and models guiding our difficult pathways through events that do indeed mix physical hurt, ideal contradictions and unthinkable emotional intensity?

Two series provide us with answers to these objections and a third addresses the awkward but important question about a possible extremism or lack of 'seriousness' in Deleuze's positions. The twenty-first series 'on the event' and the twenty-second series 'porcelain and volcano' sharpen his principles with respect to questions about how to live with events (with wounds and with alcoholism in particular). The thirteenth series 'of the schizophrenic and the little girl' charts a passage between different extreme interpretations of Deleuze's principles, most notably in terms of a mistaken understanding whereby all actions are seen as relative and essentially the same, except for their 'intensity', which should always be increased by seeking 'becoming' and 'difference'. Finally, the twenty-fourth series 'on the communication of events' and the twenty-fifth series 'on univocity' reflect on the relation between individuals and events to counter the criticism that Deleuze's philosophy is an individualism. Far from defending a philosophy based on individual desires and self-protection, his position stresses the connectedness of individual to world, of worlds to other worlds and of events to all other events. As I explained in the introduction to this book, Deleuze's philosophy is holistic rather than individualistic. As such, its most persistent weakness could be the incapacity to differentiate rather than the modern problem of the reliance on isolated selfish wills and desires.

However, a further difficulty about individualism is raised by these 'moral' series in *Logic of Sense*. It is not the isolation of the individual that may be at fault in his philosophy but its restricted perspective. The moral cases covered by Deleuze can seem narrow, idiosyncratic and overly aesthetic; they do not necessarily have a wide scope in terms of experience, neither do they engage directly with real cases, preferring instead to work through literary accounts.

Shouldn't a moral philosophy seek out the most general moral situations and trace them empirically according to social surveys rather than through artists' fictional and often indirect portrayals of moral struggles shared by few and repudiated by many? The answer to this criticism is that Deleuze is not seeking a general experience, behaviour or set of symptoms from the works of Bousquet, Fitzgerald, Lowry, Artaud or Carroll. Instead, they allow him to trace more detailed principles of the moral struggle with events. So he is not following their work as particular cases with a more general importance but as guides to a practice which reveals features of the individual engagement with the event behind personal struggles. This is once again a transcendental work, where the conditions for a practice are deduced from singular examples. It falls prey to the critique already outlined in the previous chapter: that it is illegitimate to go from a singular case to universal conditions. But it also illustrates the answer to this critique: the singular reveals features of all singularities and explains their interconnection. The singularity of the example explains how all examples are different, yet also how they communicate through the conditions guaranteeing their difference. So Deleuze is not interested in the personal lessons of Fitzgerald's fight with alcoholism, but in the more abstract features this fight reveals for the relation between the illness and the relation between series, events and the replaying of events in a moral context.

Here are some of the principles deduced by Deleuze in the twenty-first series:

1. Moral philosophy is about a concrete and poetic way of living. It is about actual creative lives.
2. This concreteness comes from vital wounds and aphorisms, from the injuries and singular features that define lives.
3. We have to search for the eternal side of our wounds.
4. Events do not only happen to us; they await us, draw us in and signal to us.
5. The eternal side of the event is revealed when we replay an actual event and express its impersonal and pre-individual effects and not what is general, or particular, or collective, or private in it.
6. We must strive to be worthy of the events that happen to us rather than resent them.
7. Resentment has many faces and resignation is one of them.
8. To draw out the eternal truth of an event is to struggle against its physical effects: to wage war on war, to will death upon death.

9. To will the event is to select something from within it that connects to all events.
10. There is not only misery in any event but also splendour.
11. Splendour emerges when the physical wound is diminished to its smallest point.
12. Sense or the significance of the event is its splendour.
13. Sense is what is expressed in the event; we express it when we replay the event in an understanding, a willing and a representing that select within the event.
14. We must become the child of our events and not of our works, since the works are children of the events.
15. The actor selects what is past and future in the event, what has passed away and what is yet to come, against what is happening.
16. The actor selects by diminishing the present to its smallest point through a multiple slicing away of what has passed and what is yet to come.
17. So the paradox of the actor is to select the past and the future in the present.
18. The actor does not play a person but a complex theme of sense or the infinitives expressed in the event.
19. So the actor redoubles the actual physical event with a counter-actualisation: this is what moral selection is and how to be worthy of the event.
20. An abstract line, a contour and splendour must be drawn out in a counter-actualisation.
21. A physical wound and physical mixture is only ever just from the point of view of the whole, which, in its parts, has countless injustices driving our resentment.
22. Humour selects the eternal side of the event.
23. In the present actualisation of the event, life seems too weak for the individual living it, but in its eternal side the individual is too weak for the life.
24. The duality of weaknesses is the essential ambiguity of death as that which is most deeply inscribed in me as finality, but also as that which is the furthest remove from me as impersonal.
25. The event happens as *my* death or *my* wound; it is counter-actualised as *it* dies.
26. 'Everything is singular and thereby collective and private at the same time, particular and general, neither individual nor universal' (LoS, 152, 178).
27. There is ignominy in those who make use of war or who serve it: they are creatures of resentment.

28. There is ignominy in saying that each one of us has his or her particular war or wound, since those who pick at their wounds are creatures of bitterness and resentment.
29. Only the free have their war or their wound, because they counter-actualise them as actors.
30. Only the free then understand all mortal events as one Event free of accident and denouncing all resentment.
31. Tyrants make allies through their resentment as slaves and as servants.
32. The mobile and precise point where all events come together is also the point of transmutation where death turns against death, where I turn against myself; it is the figure where the most singular life substitutes for the self.

Deleuze's moral philosophy is much richer and more precise in its moral guidance than might at first appear in his prior principles on divination, representation and acting. He has positions on war and on tyranny; he gives positive recommendations for the reception of events; there are precise distinctions drawn between different acts and how they can be characterised, for example in terms of resentment or free affirmation through counter-actualisation (which is itself described more fully in the series on events). Yet many doubts remain and I want to respond to two types of further objections over the next two sections. First, how are these principles workable? They still seem abstract and vague when aligned against specific wrongs and ills. Can Deleuze's concept of counter-actualisation work in practice? Second, aren't these principles and concepts still too individualistic? He always seems to be fighting against an inherent bias towards the individual by stressing the connectedness of all events. But shouldn't a just moral philosophy start with relations of self to other, or communal relations, or simply with community or love, rather than with tortured individuals struggling to become free actors replaying the events that torment them and only thereby rising to pre-individual connections? Can Deleuze do justice to the call of others and the way moral life starts with a living together rather than apart?

HOW TO ACT MORALLY (EXAMPLES)

Deleuze's discussion of the French novelist Joë Bousquet's works is one of his most important studies of moral action in relation to the event. Bousquet (1897–1950) belonged to a wealthy bourgeois family in South West France and became a novelist and poet following a devastating injury incurred in the First World War. He was part of the surrealist group of writers and his literary friends included Paul Valéry, André Gide, Paul Éluard, Jean Paulhan and Louis Aragon. Born in Narbonne, he lived nearly all of his life in Carcasonne. He was left paralysed with a severed spinal cord as a result of a bullet wound suffered in the third battle of the Aisne, in May 1918, near the strategically important ridge of the Chemin des Dames – site of horrendous loss of life and dismal tactical decisions, notably in the infamous Nivelle offensive leading to tens of thousands of deaths, widespread mutiny and execution of the mutineers in 1917. Like Deleuze's reading of Charles Péguy's *Clio*, another victim of the war, the work in *Logic of Sense* does not do full justice to the connections between the philosopher and the novelist. It does, however, provide insights into how a full Deleuzian interpretation might develop, as well as indicating why Deleuze selected Bousquet's moral example.

The connections between the two thinkers encompass a shared admiration of Max Ernst (Bousquet collected surrealist art-works and exchanged letters with Ernst) to a surprising common inspiration derived from Duns Scotus as one of the sources of Deleuze's notion of the neutrality of the event and Bousquet's work *Les Capitales ou Jean Duns Scot à Jean Paulhan* (1999), a book cited by Deleuze in *Logic of Sense.* There are further links, in the context of *Logic of Sense*, given the different roles played by Alice for Carroll and by diverse surreal muses for Bousquet, including his long-term friend Germaine, or 'Poisson d'or', whom he loved and wrote to over many years. Bousquet writes of the girl as enabling the passage from his wound to an immaterial and surreal world: 'A shadow would say to other shadows: look at that very blond young girl, look at her in the songs she inhabits forever. Music and wind had to be her eternal domain. An officer shattered by a bullet was all her love' (Bousquet, 1967: 51). Deleuze's discussion of his own concept of surface in relation to girls in the thirteenth series of his book reflects on why the trope of the girl allows for contact with ideal and paradoxical movements rather than ones inscribed deep in the body, but he is careful to avoid privileging this relation and insists on many different figures at work in poetic creation, as well as the violence and actual illusions contained in all of them. Against interpretations that focus on one or other figure associated with creativity, Deleuze denounces the 'grotesque trinity of the child, the poet and the madman' (LoS, 83, 101). Alice and Germaine permit a transition to a virtual surface of sense for Carroll and for Bousquet, and this surface explains their creativity in relation to the girls, but here, as always in Deleuze's work, the transfer is singular and does not allow for the identification of emblems or perfections. The cults of the child, the poet or the madman are not consistent with his thought.

Bousquet's work transforms his wound into an artistic theme where it becomes a shadow of pain and suffering alleviated by morphine, but also a destiny to be affirmed and redoubled in his art. He does not seek to deny the event of the shot and subsequent paraplegia, instead returning to it through his books in surreal ways, mixing times and characters to the point where wartime nurses and contemporary companions merge, as do his former self and his current one. The wounding thereby becomes an artistic event as well as a physical one and the life as an artist of acute sensibility and great passion rises out of, or hovers with, the curtailed life spent bedridden in deep pain and protected behind a heavy curtain from direct light. Perhaps the strongest parallel with Deleuze's work is through the idea of becoming a double or ghost whose acts replay its destiny thereby changing, not the outcome of events, but their tone and significance:

> *Man is a ghost.* It is in his acts that he is closest to the reality his fleshly being is wholly stolen from. *His work is a fragment of the being that his being is only the dream of.* Do not imitate reality, collaborate with it. Put your thoughts and your expressive gifts in the service of the days and facts that make them distinct; enslave yourself to the existence of things; if you are not what they lack, you are nothing; you will enrich that which is with that which was its presentiment in you.
>
> (Bousquet, 1979: 28)

This passage, similar to many others on ghosts and shadows in Bousquet's works, can help us to understand the application of Deleuze's moral principles, since Bousquet neither tries to deny his wound, nor blame it, nor ignore it. Instead, he treats it as a fact or an event calling for a reinvention which will run parallel to the event and alter its sense. This is allowed by the duality in both writers' approaches since Deleuze's counter-actualisation or re-enactment and Bousquet's shadowing and haunting split reality into physical 'facts' or what is happening and acts or the free creation alongside the fact. Creation cannot negate what occurs, but it can put it in touch with a source of values running counter to its suffering and injuries. So the wound becomes four movements forming a complicated intertwining of the wound as it occurs in the present suffering, of the past wound, of the future wound and of the creative act capable of changing the intensity of the relations between these different times of the event. Each of these movements is transformed by one of them. The free act redoubles the happening and thereby changes the past and the future: the potentially tragic curtailment of youth becomes an entry point to poetic invention, sensibility, love and friendship.

Two features of the act of redoubling or counter-actualisation should be drawn out to understand Deleuze's moral approach. First, the act splits everything occurring, everything that has occurred and all that will occur into two parallel, connected but asymmetrical sides. On a physical side the wound has happened, is happening and will have happened in the future – all condensed in the present suffering. This is the event as a fact that must neither be denied nor resented. It is here that we have the first component of the Nietzschean *amor fati*, or love of destiny, traceable back to Deleuze's *Nietzsche and Philosophy* and quoted in his discussion of Bousquet in *Logic of Sense*. Some care must be taken in interpretation though, because there is a lot at stake in different versions of *amor fati* as love of fate, love of destiny or love of the event. Since Deleuze has a precise definition of destiny running counter to the ideas of accepting one's destiny or of fate as always negative, I prefer to use event in its place. *It is never a love of destiny, but always a love of the event.* To love the event is never to accept it in its significance, or to seek to bend to it in its entirety, or even to make it deeper in its wounding. It is not to attempt to negate something that has happened in the body and that therefore has a present, past and future as that happening which no amount of denial can eliminate. Instead, it is to select something to be affirmed within the physical event.

Yet, this affirmation would seem to contradict the love of the event as it occurs, either by simply having to submit to the event in order to affirm it exactly as it happens, or to seek to make it deeper in following its consequences and affirming them. This difficulty is resolved because the event is two-sided. In parallel to its physical side, the event has an ideal side as a surface event where the act can change the ideas and intensities associated with the event *as past and into the future independent of the occurrence in the present*. It is on this side that the event is affirmed. Ideas and the surface intensities or their relations do not have to bend to the causal relations unfolding on the physical side, because they are not themselves physical and subject to causal laws, but rather are expressed in actual states. For example, Bousquet's wound, as a presence in his books, does not have strict causal relation to his actual wound and the writer exploits this side of the wound to draw out some aspects of the physical one (its capacity to generate new ideas, in particular in a surreal and dream-like manner): 'What would have ruined my life as a man has perhaps saved the invalid that I became. I have lived as a woman, wishing to give birth to spirits, to nourish them with my sensations' (Bousquet, 1979: 13). Thus, for instance, the nurse who first treated Bousquet recurs through his books as a dream-like figure merging with other surreal caring companions. Similarly, the soldiers who risked their lives dragging him in a tarpaulin down from the ridge appear at unpredictable and disconcerting moments as signs of a mute and unconditional human generosity. Bousquet draws this care and brotherhood out of the event of his wounding.

The second important feature of the act of redoubling follows in part from the first and qualifies the use of 'free'. It is only free in the relation between the two sides rather than on one or the other. Thus there is no actual free-will that could be free of all actual determinations. Neither is there a virtual or ideal creative freedom unconditioned by unconscious impulses, movements and desires. Instead, freedom emerges with the asymmetry of the sides, since as creators we escape actual cause and effect relations and introduce novel significance, value and intensity in parallel to our actual lives, whereas, in terms of these novel intensities, we are but transformers of flows of intensity into novel flows. *Freedom comes with the generation of sense within determined actual and virtual circuits.* Any selection will have a series of determinations, but these determinations, whether actual or ideal, are selected by our actual acts – experimentally and in ways that can never lead to knowledge. So these determinations will not be causally determined and there is a virtual freedom, but it is a structural one regarding series rather than one of a foundational free-will, since there is no such thing as a free identifiable entity on the virtual line or the actual one. Freedom lies in the openness of an asymmetrical structure we can tap into but never stand independent of as finally free actors. The asymmetry and duality of Deleuze's structure explains the moral capacity to select within events that have nonetheless selected us:

> With every event, there is indeed the present moment of its actualization, the moment in which the event is embodied in a state of affairs, an individual, or a person, the moment we designate by saying '*here*, the moment has come.' [. . .] But on the other hand, there is the future and the past of the event considered in itself, sidestepping each present, being free of the limitations of a state of affairs, impersonal and pre-individual, neutral, neither general nor particular, eventum tantum . . .;

or rather that has no other present than the mobile instant that it represents, always doubled into past-future, forming what we must call the counter-actualization.

(LoS, 151, 171)

The ideas and surface intensities selected in counter-actualisation are never present as such. Instead, they form a reserve, an *eventum tantum* or unique great event, to be expressed in all actualisations in a singular way. Perhaps Deleuze is playing here on Aquinus's verse 'Tantum ergo sacrametum', replacing the great – and unique – sacred Host from the benediction of the blessed sacrament with the great unique Event in which all events come together, receive sense and lose particular injuries and injustices. Such an interpretation is not fanciful, given Deleuze's remarks on the catechism in the appendices to *Logic of Sense*. The above passage must therefore not be understood as implying that we can only counter events in the past and in the future, but is rather claiming that we can only counter or redouble events through the past and the future, *the whole of the past and the future,* since in the present they are already happening. All Deleuze's moral principles outlined in the previous section must be considered against this structural background which underpins their practical power. It is as if we should return to them with the prefix 'when an event strikes select what is to be in the eternal whole within the present passing away and future projection through your free creative acts according to the following principles'.

THE CRACK-UP

Deleuze's moral philosophy is based on free acts redoubling events. But does this put it hopelessly out of touch with a contemporary approach to life, where the finality of future events falls more and more within the grasp of cures and preventions rather than a Stoic replaying of the event? If we can change the path of events, *actually* change them, what point is there in the example of Bousquet, living with a wound that had no cure – only compensation or another life in literary creation? Is Deleuze's philosophy then too time-bound and pessimistic, turning to the latest and most noble forms of consolation in an age where we have come to expect and achieve a twisting of events to our will rather than a willing of events as they happen? His thought works through the transcendental conditions of any event and brings our acts to bear primarily on values and then only indirectly and unreliably back onto actual occurrences. This does not mean that he denies real acts or actual causes and effects; it is rather that these are not enough, requiring an extension that explains the intensity and open or free flow of events beyond any predicted outcomes. Is this but mere diversion, when we seem to be in a world on the brink of a new material determinism, where divining the significance of events turns out to be a waste of energy when compared with the prediction and early cure of effects we do not want to have to live with or affirm? So even if Deleuze in no way commits us to abandoning actual efforts, he still divides our resources unnecessarily with a virtual transcendental realm lacking even a practical worth, given the advances of modern science and knowledge, of our statistical and probabilistic tools and of the political drive to exploit them. And even if he answered that many or most do not have this luxury, and that perhaps the most threatening dangers for our world still elude our power to bend them to our will, would the right response not be to seek to extend that power, rather than dilute it in quasi-mystical poetic consolations? In short, do his opposition to naturalism and his commitment to transcendental philosophy lead to the failure of Deleuze's moral philosophy to adopt a hope grounded in the success of science?

These questions are answered in Deleuze's reading of F. Scott Fitzgerald's late short story 'The crack-up' written in 1936, four years before his death. The story forms the centre piece of the eponymous posthumous collection of essays and letters edited by Fitzgerald's long-time friend Edmund Wilson; it is prefaced by a moving poem as dedication where Wilson speaks of the essay as green and lucid emerald. *The Crack-Up* is a surprisingly pessimistic and exhausted set of essays and reminds us that Deleuze's taste is very often for exhaustion and noble death rather than blithe pleasures, unambiguous victories and guiltless celebration (for example, in his work on Beckett in 'L'épuisé'). Could it be that he did not have the right inclination for glorious modern progress? He did not. However, the reason for this parting does not lie within particular tastes or capacities but with an often good humoured and carefully argued study of the nature of hope, well-being and belief in progress. 'The crack-up' attracts Deleuze because it charts the beginning of cracks within an apparently flawless existence, the gilded 1920s and Fitzgerald's early and great success:

> There is another sort of blow that comes from within – that you don't feel until it is too late to do anything about it, until you realise with finality that in some regard you will never be as good a man again. The first

sort of breakage seems to happen quick – the second happens almost
without your knowing it but is realised suddenly indeed.

(Fitzgerald, 1993: 69)

Like Deleuze, Fitzgerald charts two sides of events, a subterranean
one working in the background and emerging late but powerfully,
and a seemingly more real and tangible side, but one ultimately over-
powered by its more secret twin. The story tells of the way Fitzgerald
falls ill and folds in on himself when told of his illness and of a poor
prognosis by a doctor. But the tale rebounds because he survives,
only then to be brought down by a different sickness, a lack of will
and creative barrenness, triggered by the news of his unexpected
survival: '– And then, surprisingly, I got better. – And cracked like an
old plate as soon as I heard the news' (72).

For Deleuze, 'The crack-up' is then not about Fitzgerald's crack-
up and its early signs, for example in his alcoholism (which
Fitzgerald denies in the story – explaining that he had not touched
a drink for six months around the time of the breakdown). It is
about the way any actual life remains in touch not only with its past
and future events, but all past and future events and the intensities
of significance accompanying them. It is therefore also about the
way any life is stretched by this contact, not necessarily in a negative
way, but in a manner that connects actual physical events to
effects way beyond their immediate actual causes. This does not
mean that we not should pay heed to these causal relations, to cures
and preventions, to needs and pleasures, to poisons and nourish-
ment. Neither does it mean that we should not work in the name of
progress. It means that this work takes place against a wider background testified to, for example, by the silent work of the crack in
Fitzgerald. The porcelain in the title to the twenty-second series of
Logic of Sense is an allusion to the belief that any actual thing is necessarily flawed under its actual surface because its significance and
value put it in touch with paradoxes and tensions that belie any
claim to perfection. Put simply, *there is necessarily a flaw in all things
because they matter – because they have a sense.* So though we are right to
struggle for progress and to cure ills, the drive behind that struggle
and the values directing it are such that it could never claim to free
itself of the return of novel forms of injury and crack-ups, prepared
by the contact of actual events to what they express across times and
places:

> The real difference is not between the inside and the outside. The
> flaw is neither interior nor exterior; it is at the frontier, imperceptible,

160

incorporeal, ideal. It has complex relations of interference and crossover, of skipping junctions, with what occurs on the outside and on the inside, one step for one, one step for the other, but to different rhythms: everything noisy that happens does so at the edge of the flaw and would be nothing without it; conversely, the flaw does not pursue its silent path, does not change direction following lines of least resistance, does not weave its web, without the strike of what happens.

(LoS, 155, 181)

I have alternated translations of *fêlure* by 'flaw' and by 'crack' in this reading of Deleuze's work in order to draw attention to the invisible quality of the crack. We tend to associate a crack with a break or a visible line, but the claim is that breaks are points of contact with a many-branched patina of flaws, many of which remain invisible until the final crack-up.

This is the reciprocal determination of virtual ideas and actual wounds: they owe their vividness to each other, according to processes of mutual determination that resist linear tracking or transcendent rules. His argument is that there is no injury unless it brings together value and actual change, but the rates and rhythms of change are different on both sides. For example, the worth given to a life sometimes runs ahead of and sometimes lags behind the actual events that come to shape it. A different valuation of life was prepared for in the carnage of the Nivelle offensive, or in the still reverberating aftershocks of the murder of those who refused to fight or could not due to illness. For Deleuze, later actions change the value of earlier ones and thereby really change those very actions. When he speaks of worthiness to the event this can apply to action of behalf of others, for example in redeeming an action or a name, no longer with the supposed futility of action for the dead, but with a real effect on them back through time (*real splendour and glory*): 'They were talking about this Bill. Some case Sir William was mentioning, lowering his voice. It had its bearing upon what he was saying about the delayed effects of shell-shock. There must be some provision in the Bill' (Woolf, 1976: 162).

It is shocking to read the claim that a break or wound is incomplete, or not even an injury at all, until it is brought into contact with ideas and their surface intensities. It is even more shocking to think that the idea of the wound is incomplete without its actual occurrence deep in the present. A good way of understanding these unsettling claims is through contrasts of value and idea, of emotional investment and thoughtful reach. Fitzgerald captures this well in the crack-up when he tracks the flaws at work behind his own disintegration to minor slights and no doubt unperceived insults. The perpetrators did not share a value system sensitive enough to pick up on the injury they were laying the ground for – nor did Fitzgerald. Later critics, for example his obituary writers, see 'The crack-up' as morose, but that is not Fitzgerald's point at all. It is rather that nothing is simply of one value or of another, and that therefore the work of 'contradictory' moods and passions underlies any one of them. He is not shaking a pall over all his works but instead explaining how the early ones prepare for the later sparse and gloomier production, and the final despair and death: 'I have spoken in these pages of how an extraordinarily optimistic young man experienced a crack-up of all values, a crack-up that he scarcely knew of until long after it occurred' (Fitzgerald, 1993: 80). The early life and the later one complete one another and call for one another across ideal or 'surface' connections. Moreover, the ideas are incomplete if they are not connected through actual events (and Fitzgerald returns often to the impossibility of understanding his crack-up and the lines running through his career from the outside). But the crucial point for a reading of Deleuze comes at the end of the 'porcelain and volcano' series. *It does not follow from the incompleteness of an idea or an actual event that closing connections or completing circles are the right free course of action*:

> The question of whether the crack can avoid incarnation, effectuation in the body in one form or another, is obviously not justiciable according to general rules. The crack remains but a word so long as the body is not compromised by it and so long as the liver and the brain, the organs, do not present those lines in which we read the future and which themselves prophesise.
>
> (LoS, 160, 188)

The moral problem is rather how to redouble the events occurring to us. These events are signs of the future and the past, but they have no necessary path. Deleuze's moral principles never recommend a particular course of action or align to necessary rules or models. On the contrary, they put forward guidelines and examples for picking our own way through the events that happen to us. His gift is of moral freedom in a complex structure and not compulsion or imperatives.

INDIVIDUALS, SOLIPSISM AND THE COMMUNICATION OF EVENTS

Do the free act and the models of the actor and mime commit Deleuze to a moral solipsism? Does he fall foul of the same objections brought to Sartre's existentialism, a philosophy that formed Deleuze's early years only to be repudiated later (to the point of refusing the reprinting of his earliest student articles on Sartrean themes)? Is the Deleuzian individual essentially alone and thereby misanthropic? If so, does his moral philosophy fail on community and responsibility grounds through an inability to give full moral worth to others?

The key to answering these questions lies in the difference between individuals and individuation. Deleuze's moral philosophy is not based on the individual as an independent foundation and, when he speaks of actors, these are not primarily individual free-standing beings. Instead, the moral actor is understood better as the coming together of series of communicating processes. This means that any individual is only a temporary and illusory entity drawing together much wider processes. Furthermore, there is no contradiction in speaking of moral acts in this context – as if Deleuze were simultaneously repudiating and depending on free-willing subjects – because he has an account of action running counter to those that claim that a free act must have a first and independent cause. Instead, the act is a description of a knot or fold of processes – similar to the description of the movement of a herd or swarm as it is veering one way or another as one (*the bee swarm followed the bear up the tree*). Deleuze's position involves an explicit criticism of the claim that we must be able to identify a self-sufficient actor when we speak of an act, since his position is that behind any such actor we shall find endless converging and diverging series. Actors are then possible but nonetheless incomplete elements in the description of an act and when we say 'they selected this path' we are also saying 'and these series worked through their selections'.

The twenty-fourth series 'of the communication of events' is a long discussion of the problem of communication, not in the sense of verbal communication, but in the sense of contact, harmony and interference (as in communicating vessels where adding water to one tube leads to a levelling out and change in potential energy in the others, for instance). It is a mistake to think that individuals are isolated, because all series and all events communicate. The real problem and possible objection are then not about solipsism but about the coherence and yet resistance to law of these forms of communication. The problem of the non-linear and law-resistant communication of events is the main topic of the twenty-fourth series; it covers the following broad points:

1. the difference between cause and quasi-cause;
2. the role of destiny in the communication of events;
3. how events are compatible and incompatible;
4. whether we should think of events as contradictory and identifiable as such;
5. whether (with Leibniz) we should think of events as incompossible;
6. the distance between events;
7. convergence and divergence;
8. disjunctive synthesis as the communication of all events in one.

We have covered many of these points in more technical areas concerning philosophy and language in earlier chapters. Here, I want to give a short account of them, but a much longer discussion of how they guide Deleuze's answer to questions of community and moral togetherness through the communication of events.

The argument can be summed up as follows. Relations between events are not causal, because they involve different sides of reality where we should speak of expression rather than cause. So in terms of moral problems we cannot think of destiny as involving necessary paths, but as a relation between necessary actual causal relations and expressive relations regarding sense, value or significance, where free actors can intervene. This means that there is neither pure necessity not pure free will, but rather a series of interferences between them; 'we' are partly determined and partly free, in ways that cannot be easily partitioned and organised. This relation of events involves questions of compatibility and incompatibility, where there are no absolutes such as 'this can never be in contact with this' but rather different degrees of potential for expressive contact such as 'this is far removed from this and has a weak potential to be drawn within its ambit'. Events can never be separated according to final identities, nor can they be set up as contradictories, because though we may have contradictions at an actual level – mapped out according to concepts and predicates – when these are seen in complete relations with the sense they express, they come into contact and into relations that cannot be thought in terms of absolute differences. For example, we might say that it is a contradiction to speak of a serene and happy Scott Fitzgerald in 1936 since we know that he was experiencing a deep form of despair. The concept Fitzgerald in 1936 cannot have the predicates 'happy' and 'serene'. However, from Deleuze's point of view, given that any actual thing expresses all potential infinitives (to joy, to despair, and so on) but to lesser or greater degree, it is more a matter of how compatible different views of Fitzgerald are, not in a frozen state 'in 1936', but in relation to novel free acts, including indeed the act of freezing at a given time or ascribing given fixed predicates. Our interpretation of Fitzgerald is one such act, so is Wilson's dedication and so is each obituary or critical notice.

So, against Leibniz, Deleuze does not think that events are inherently incompatible, but rather that we should think of them in terms of their 'distance' from one another. They may be far removed, but this does not mean that they have no contact. Everything connects and can be connected, but this connection is not smooth and well-regulated; it is a matter of series that converge and diverge according to disjunctive syntheses carried by mobile elements running along the two sides of all series. Examples of such mobile elements are the puzzle 'Who was F. Scott Fitzgerald?' connecting each obituary, or the problem of how to convey both his happiness and his despair in a combined reading of *Tender Is the Night* and *The Crack-Up*, for instance. The first example is of a mobile element as actual lack; the second as virtual excess. The two belong together yet cannot be satisfactorily reduced to one another. Thus the moral problem for the critic is how best to achieve a reciprocal determination of both while maintaining the excessive potential of the one within the empty space of the other along parallel actual and virtual series. The concept of disjunctive synthesis is designed to capture the way each act branches series out and yet also assembles them by selecting different actual elements. An act thereby has an effect through different shadings of all expressible infinitives. This explains Deleuze's at first odd comment about love and friendship in the series on univocity: 'My love is an exploration of distance, a long journey which affirms my hate for the friend in another world and with another individual' (LoS, 179, 210). When we act out of love or out of friendship we also connect to and express hate. The moral challenge is how to be worthy of the event of love or of friendship given its wider contacts and communications: how to maximise the intensity of actual friendship while also affirming its other relations and potentials. This does not mean that we have to make them actual. It means that we must not pretend that they do not exist, as if there is a love free of all hate and a friendship without rivalry.

According to this view of the communication of events, questions of community become complicated yet also very precise. There is no primary communication with others as identities, as if we were all the same, or shared the same values, or could understand one another fully. This fails because, behind any identity, there is always a further contradiction and opposed predicate, otherwise the opposites would be indistinguishable. Deleuze rejects Leibniz's work on incompossibility yet often depends on his principle of the identity of indiscernibles – no two distinct things can be exactly the same – and on his principle of reason – every difference has a reason. However, the way Deleuze takes this further is by allowing the extra difference to flow through all the prior identities: *each new difference sets a differential movement through the series it joins.* So the adoption of the principle 'we communicate through our differences' follows Deleuze's definition of humour: it takes them up to the point where they touch on nonsense, but thereby open us on to sense as well – and on to the genetic and creative power of paradox. Against the analytic use of the principles and the way they support the theory of incompossibility, because beings with contradictory predicates such as 'Adam sinner' and 'Adam not sinner' cannot inhabit compossible worlds, Deleuze argues that given a distinction in a predicate we have a difference flowing through all of them through the mediation of sense and ideas. The contradictory predicates change sense and ideas for all the other predicates. And since no predicate is complete without that sense, the argument for incompossibility fails and has to be replaced instead with a thoroughly variegated world. There are not many incompossible worlds, or many possible worlds with no real contact. There is one reality connecting multiple worlds, individuals and persons. All communicate in this world, but never on the basis of a perfect communication, or one with the promise of perfection, even infinitely delayed.

The distinguishing marks between individuals may well be imperceptible, yet they are necessary conditions for the distinction drawn between similar but never absolutely identical interlocutors. In place of a dialogue of perfect equals, there is a contact with others through the way we converge and diverge according to disjunctive syntheses, that is according to the way things we lack and things in excess of us draw us together. We communicate through our differences, our problems, our need for sense and values and the excessive and connected nature of this sense and of those values – the way in which they always go beyond what we want of them. This allows Deleuze to set his concept of counter-actualisation away from solipsism of individuals and away from problems of 'other minds' or 'other subjects' or absolute otherness, because the conditions for counter-actualisation impose a necessary connectedness upon it. This does not mean there is no place for identity and for its capacity to separate us. On the contrary, the actual physical depth of scissions and divisions is a condition for the expression of ideal and

surface connections, but the latter take priority due to their eternal
return in contrast to the constant passing of the identities that
express them. We are eternally connected but provisionally separate:

> But on the surface, where only infinitive events are deployed, it goes
> otherwise: each communicates with the other through the positive char-
> acter of its difference, through the affirmative character of the disjunc-
> tion, so much so that the self merges with that very disjunction that
> liberates outside itself, that liberates the divergent series as so many
> impersonal and pre-individual singularities. Counter-actualisation is
> already thus: infinitive distance instead of infinite identity. Everything is
> done through the resonance of disparates, point of view on point of
> view, displacement of perspective, differenciation of difference, and not
> through the identity of contraries.
>
> (LoS, 175, 205)

In short, when we express infinitives such as 'to love' or 'to hate' we
must do so through what is different in our singular expression
because the infinitive itself is only difference or a potential to be
expressed differently and to connect differently to other infinitives.
So any togetherness is not one that suffers and fails through the infinity of actual identifiable differences, but one that connects because
it resists identity and is the genetic condition for the production of
novel differences. It is because the infinitive can be expressed differently that we connect through the multiple ways we express it. When
we do so we change the distances between infinitives and affirm their
connection across those differences. This is no longer a world where
there can be absolute oppositions or perfect identities. It is one
where we are necessarily part of a community because the reality we
express is one of communication through divergences, through disjunctive syntheses.

The key move is to realise, therefore, that Deleuze's moral philosophy and principles cannot be addressed to lone individuals; on the
contrary, they are only addressed to free actors within communicating series. By convention we can abstract the actor from the series to
speak of the act, but in reality this abstraction is a cut falsely denying
a real completeness of series and events. So each of the Deleuzian
principles outlined here is necessarily about our relation to others,
because the events they turn on are events for all and not events for
one – they are events flowing through all rather than through one. If
we take a principle such as 'we must strive to be worthy of the events
that happen to us rather than resent them' and apply it in a purely
selfish way, we must have misunderstood the principle, because the

events we should strive to be worthy of are communal events, they are occasions of communication rather than isolation. Edmund Wilson grasps this when, in mourning his friend and his own hopes for a truly cosmopolitan literature in *The Crack-Up*, and in collecting Fitzgerald's last works in 1942, he writes a dedication that expands beyond private grief and remembrance and a lone despairing death, through a setting of world war and of his novels within violent historical moods and rhythms – and the way they implicate all of us:

> Tonight, in this long dark Atlantic gale,
> I set in order such a tale,
> While tons of wind that take the world for scope
> Rock blackened waters where marauders grope
> Our blue and bathed-in Massachusetts ocean;
> The Cape shakes with the depth-bomb's dumb concussion;
> And guns can interrupt me in these rooms,
> Where now I seek to breathe again the fumes
> Of iridescent drinking-dens, retrace
> The bright hotels, regain the eager pace
> You tell of . . . Scott, the bright hotels turn bleak

We cannot be worthy of the event unless we strive to express it through others and for others and in response to others' expressions, unless we strive to connect it to others, as far as its potential and our potential can carry it. We cannot be worthy of the event if we pretend that this communication is one of identities or between identities. We cannot be worthy of it, if we claim it to be blocked by final negations, or governed by untouchable and invariant transcendences, values or laws. To be worthy of the event is to redouble it by creating a synthetic communication through disjunction, variation and difference, refusing pure oppositions:

> [. . .] disjunction become synthesis introduced its ramifications everywhere, so that the conjunction was already coordinating in a global way divergent, heterogeneous and disparate series, and that, affecting the detail, the connection contracted a multitude of divergent series in the successive appearance of a single one.

> (LoS, 175, 205)

TIME AND UNIVOCITY

Are there more didactically unambiguous guidelines about how to act in *Logic of Sense* than the many principles regarding events? Is it really necessary for him to turn back the question on the questioner, or more precisely to return the question to its genetic problem, because the event stems from a perspective and only that perspective can be worthy of it? Despite his resistance to the term, Deleuze's moral philosophy seems open to the accusation that it keeps to very general lines due to its resistance to particular rules or laws. This leads to the suspicion, perhaps generated from a much more pessimistic view of actors than Deleuze's, that the Stoical example and deflected principle are useless in practice: too vague and evasive to be of any purpose. Furthermore, the book's wildest but also most important claims on the connection to all events in one Event and on the relation of any present to the whole of time – past and future – raise the objection that the bar is simply set too high for any individual to follow a course of action consistent with Deleuze's structures. Could it be that even if we accept all the negative points put forward by Deleuze, on identity, resentment and opposition for example, we still remain in a whistling sandstorm when asked to move forward in a well-chosen manner? Even if we accept the invitation to move beyond moral judgements, are we in a position to make moral selections in the knowledge that they are closer to Deleuze's model and examples, or does he leave us on the brink of the special discouragement of those led by a thinker who refuses to provide tangible guidance yet also demands the highest standards of behaviour?

Two series raise and attempt to answer versions of these questions: the twenty-third series 'of the Aiôn' and the twenty-fifth series 'of univocity'. They are both highly technical. The first is about time and the paradoxes of Chronos and Aiôn. The second is about univocity, or Deleuze's ontological thesis that being is said in the same way of all things, rather than differently depending on their types or kinds, or attributes, or differences as substances. For example, an ontology constructed around the belief that God and His creations have different ways of being would be at least 'bivocal'. Against such ontologies and the way they ground transcendent metaphysics (where one form of being stands independent of and above the other, yet also commands it) Deleuze's univocal approach claims not only that being is said of all things in the same way, but that 'all beings are, as becomings, the same' or being is in reality an interconnected process for all things – in contrast to definitions of being as a stasis disturbed by external movements and changes. This returns us to the objection we started with, since univocity as becoming seems to commit us to an endless morass when we need to make moral selections. If a form of being is superior or radically different from others, then moral actions can follow more easily, for example in banning blasphemy of God or gods on the basis of their inviolability. Similarly, if identities are fixed, then it becomes simpler to define injury and wrong; for instance, if the essence of a being is to be free, then taking away that freedom can be defined as wrong. Deleuze does not have recourse to such certainties; indeed, he thinks they are ill-founded and tries to demonstrate this throughout *Logic of Sense* in the deduction of dualities of connected series related through disjunctive syntheses. Disjunctive synthesis is a process of univocity since series are ramified by it but at the same time connected through shared elements (the empty place running along all series and the surface of sense as varying intensities from his philosophy of language, for instance).

The series on univocity responds to the objection that it is impossible for a limited individual to select within infinite and connected series that exceed any principle for making that selection: 'The problem is therefore one of knowing how the individual would be able to overcome his form and his syntactical link with a world in order to attain to the universal communication of events, that is to the affirmation of a disjunctive synthesis beyond logical contradictions [. . .]' (LoS, 178, 208). For example, in conclusion to the previous section I pointed to Wilson's historical, artistic and emotional extension of Fitzgerald's work and of his own grief. Yet this extension is still limited; despite Wilson's cosmopolitanism it still adopts a standpoint and limited perspective from two sides of the Atlantic, a friendship born of privilege in Princeton and the loss of an equally rare and gilded 'eternal Carnival by the Sea' (Fitzgerald, 1993: 90). How can it be possible to connect with everything? If it is not, what is even the point of placing ourselves within this horizon, if not to trigger a terrible nihilism – a loss of values for having aimed too high? Deleuze's answer depends in part on his reading of Nietzsche's eternal return (only difference returns and never sameness) but perhaps more so on what he sees as returning and on how it returns (as sense rather than as things that can be denoted or meanings that can be understood). The first step in his argument is to insist that if we are connected it is not as identities or through identities. *So we do not connect through who we are or what we do, but through how we express the ideas and sense connecting us.* This means that we can differentiate moral selections, not on the ground of how many actual things they draw on or draw together, but on the contrary, on how we express the conditions for our actual differences.

Actual differences are important as part of the moral problem, but not as the ground for free selection. Instead, as genetic conditions for actual variations, sense and ideas must be expressed through changes: by becoming something other than what one is. This leads to the principle that we should select away the forms of identity that prevent us from expressing the ideal intensities and differential variations that constitute what Deleuze calls 'the pure event': 'Counter-actualising each event, the actor dancer extracts the pure event which communicates with all the others and returns to itself through all the others; making of disjunction a synthesis affirming the disjuncture as such and making each series resonate inside the other' (LoS, 178, 209). It is called a pure event because it cannot be mapped onto any particular actual identity, but instead is only expressed in the creative move away from them and towards something novel. So it does not matter that Wilson cannot include 'everything' in his cosmopolitanism, because according to Deleuze's moral philosophy, we connect with all potential sense and ideas by creatively expressing some in novel actualities. However, this connection is not the same for every act, some leave more relations obscure and in the background than others; some bring more into distinct focus. The challenge is therefore to connect with as many infinitives as we can, by expressing them as distinctly as we can. The use of 'can' here, as in Deleuze's version of a question derived from Spinoza 'What can a body can do?' (Deleuze, 'Ontologie-Ethique'), is not the basis for a calculation about possibilities, but rather an occasion for open experimentation, where the criteria for the experiment are extension at the level of sense and intensity at the level of singular infinitives. We have to express as many infinitives as distinctly as we can, yet also express those infinitives at the highest intensity that we can. A balancing act is asked of us, rather than a one-way destructiveness or inclusiveness. This is why he points out the resonance of series with one another and the moral task could be seen as maximising resonance while avoiding a descent into chaos or the temptation of static but secure identities. This resonance can only come from setting ourselves in movement.

None of these moral principles, however, should be taken without an accompanying study of Deleuze's philosophy of time. Perhaps the most enduring factor of the modern experience of moral action is its dependence on the arrow of time, in its passage from a past losing significance to a future as source of utopian value through a present loaded with the responsibility of action and decision. We act to redirect the past for a better future in a present loaded with past contradictions and future dreams:

> Life is the creation of a present, but this creation is continued creation, as is the world in God's eyes according to Descartes. The cohesion of an anteriorily impossible cohesion of a body is constituted around the trace, around the anonymous burst of birth into the world of being-there. To be the contemporary of the present given support by the body, it is not enough to accept this body, to declare it. We must enter into its composition; we must become an active element of that body. The only real relation to the present is incorporation.
>
> (Badiou, 2006: 530)

Thus, for Alain Badiou, the trace issuing from the past must be assumed in the present through an act of continued creation. This act brings eternal truth into appearance and projects a novel incorporation, new bodies created with the truth, into the future. According to this model, past and future do not have the genetic roles assigned to them by Deleuze. Instead, the former feeds into the present act as trace and the latter is constituted by the present it must be true to, in its creative revelation of a truth. This provides an inspiring frame for heroic modern acts as decisive and novel choices testifying to eternal truths and calling for continued choices for these truths, for instance in the birth of justice movements bringing an eternal truth about a wrong into present activities through the creation of new political bodies and thereby also creating a movement for other creative acts to be loyal to (in their present and thus only ever creatively rather than conservatively).

From the arguments of *Logic of Sense*, this moral 'presentism' misses the paradoxical relations of time, replacing them instead with a single structure (which can itself be internally multiple – as it is for Badiou). The present becomes the focus for time. It is determined in two ways: first, as a moment of continued choice, though punctual in the sense of plural and disconnected and not as a single choice left unchanged thereafter; and second, as a direction from past to future. The choice and the necessity of its continuation are what allow time to be focused on the present by organising multiple past, present and future ramifications into the present creation of a body (*now begins the movement for justice*). The past is drawn together in the new body it was already a preparation for. The future is beholden to the choice and to the eternal truths it calls us to choose again in future presents (*I choose again this truth in this new way*). It could be claimed that there are two sides of time in this approach through the present, just as there are for Deleuze. This is not the case, though, because in the 'presentist' model the eternal truth is wholly dependent on the present choice bringing it into appearance. So, unlike Deleuze's ideas and infinitives, these eternal truths have no function outside the continual decisions to make them appear, whereas for Deleuze, infinitives and ideas are neutral and impassive and only thereby are they at work in any present. This reduces the present to a necessary but secondary partnership in an asymmetrical process. But is this then to sacrifice present acts for their conditions? Is it then an ethical and political loss of nerve or bad faith, since, though the role of the present is accepted, for example in the necessity of representation and selection, the full responsibility of the present act is abrogated in favour of the Stoic worthiness of the event? Why does Deleuze extend such rights to times outside the present, at the apparent cost of the loss of worlds of truth and choice? At stake is the loss of worlds where, in Badiou's powerful words '[. . .] each human animal is accorded several times the chance to incorporate into the subjective present of a truth. The grace of living for an Idea is distributed to all and for many types of procedure – the grace of living, tout court' (Badiou, 2006: 536).

The answer to these severe criticisms can be found in the twenty-third series of *Logic of Sense*. In 'of the Aiôn', Deleuze demonstrates the incompleteness of a time organised around the actual present. Thereby he also refutes the point that ethical action stands primarily on action in the present, even if this is in relation to eternal truths. The following lines finish the twenty-third series and are striking in directly turning against the vocabulary and ordering set out in Badiou's work in *Logiques des mondes*, despite forerunning that book by thirty-eight years. Deleuze turns to the present and to incorporation in order to separate them through the definition of a present as counter-actualisation, that is a present selecting, not eternal truths, but which infinitives to express with the present as wounding and actualisation:

> The present of the instant, representing the Aiôn, is not at all like the vast and deep present of Chronos: it is the present without thickness, the present of the actor, dancer or mime, a pure perverse moment [. . .] It is not the present of subversion or actualisation, but that of counter-actualisation, which keeps the former from overturning the latter, and the latter from being confused with the former, and which comes to redouble the double.

> (LoS, 168, 197)

The passage ends with the French expression *redoubler la doublure*. On the one hand, this can mean to double the lining, as in a cloth, which would play well with the idea of the Deleuzian surface doubling the actual and the virtual and calling for a redoubling in the act that counter-actualises the event. On the other, it can mean doubling the double or understudy, which fits much better with the references to actors and mimes. Doubling the double would then draw attention to the way any act is played by an actor and responds to a double rather than to an original. An act must then not look to capture an eternal origin or truth, but draw out the intensity and breadth of the event by selecting its underlying movements in a new way, and by playing these through a new acting out, replay or counter-actualisation.

What is at stake in these apparently hair-splitting distinctions? There is no denial of the call of the present for moral action in Deleuze's philosophy. There are instead two presents: the present where the call to action and the event are inscribed on the body and where past and future concertina into the present. This is a moment of urgency, but also of delusion and error, unless the relation of this future to the past and to the future as open reserves of pure potential is also expressed and replayed in a singular manner. Here comes the other present, then, the one Deleuze calls the present of Aiôn. It is a present where the act becomes one of an actor in a series of other parts and actors, all redoubling what came before and hence refusing to depend on a belief in a final subversion of the series or a final realisation of its internal truth. Instead, the present must be returned to the way every present is in touch with every other through the pure past, as record of all their variations, and the pure future, as the reserve for all openness or freedom. The test of the difference between philosophies of the present as urgency for eternal truths and final acts and the present that doubles these with another present as redoubling is in their power to survive the return of failures and positive difference (it is always both). This is the heart of Deleuze's moral philosophy: only by affirming our singular place along series that also consume it can we live well with the ever present danger of resentment and discouragement. *Only acts that redouble the event can express all its most intense potentials while avoiding the fatal beliefs in eternal beings or values, for these can never outlive the certainty of future waste and collapse that stand as a condition for any action.*

5

Thought and the unconscious

Gilles Deleuze deposes the human thinker as the basis for thinking. I would say more precisely: any kind of thinker is deposed as a basis of thinking. There are, however, two ways of misunderstanding these claims; both are prevalent mistakes when a claim is made about deposed rulers. First, the fact that thinkers are removed from a position of unchallenged power does not mean that they leave the scene completely. On the contrary, for Deleuze, familiar kinds of candidates such as human subjects, animals, machines and iterative procedures retain much of their functions but they are shorn of claims to priority, control and precedence. Thinking becomes something that works through and with familiar thinkers, rather than simply without them or straightforwardly from them. So we are thinkers, but only insofar as we take our place within wider processes. When we use our familiar tactics to force our minds and bodies to think – ritualistic walks, structured methods, heuristics, showers at exactly the right temperature, stimulants and arguments on the edge of defeat or sordid victory – we insert ourselves into these processes and, without understanding them fully, we take our necessary places within something called thinking.

Second, just because one ruler has been removed does not mean that another similar unitary source of power comes to reign. It is wrong to surmise that Deleuze simply shifts from thinking as conscious exercise to thinking as unconscious process, or to thinking as a bodily practice or biochemical reaction. It is equally wrong to insist that, even if final rulers disappear, the laws governing the exercise of power remain and can be charted as the real authority, either standing within any right thinking, or operating within all thought, relegating other processes to its opposites in feelings, affects, instincts or material interaction. For Deleuze, such rules emerge after thinking and have no legitimate final arbitration over it. *This is because thinking is not a fixed process. On the contrary, it is one that introduces creation into series by re-enacting itself in relation to different events.* We are very far from thinking, in this sense, when we repeat a procedure or apply a rule; we are much closer when, in sensing the limits of rules and procedures, we create new approaches and transform problems. As we have seen in Deleuze's approach to questions in morality, learning as a response to problems is at the heart of thinking rather than any following of set plans or rules. This does not mean that thinking is unstructured. On the contrary, creativity requires structure and emerges from it, but as we have seen in previous chapters on philosophy and language, structure is itself open and transforming in Deleuze's work.

The role of thought in the transformation of structures explains its importance in *Logic of Sense.* Thinking relates lack in some series of a structure to excess in others; thereby it allows a space demanding to be filled to be put in touch with a source of intense potentials. For instance, a doctor might work along a series of symptoms looking for the known illness that will draw them all together. The question 'What is the common factor?' is a sign of the lack. It calls for assistance from a series of potentials, the combinations of symptoms found in different illnesses, say, or the indications that allow likely candidates to be eliminated. From Deleuze's point of view, it makes more sense to speak of these series of lack and excess than of the doctor's thought at a given time; a serial process over time replaces the content of a mind. Thought is therefore an empty place and an overflowing potential running along series in structures. Is this not then to follow a set procedure? No. There is an experimental element in the enquiry, not only with respect to each new patient, but also with respect to much wider patterns, for instance in the way doctors continue to learn from new cases and question assumptions, but also in the way new forms of understanding and practice emerge over time.

Thought does not therefore have a fixed and independent identity of its own, or proper site, or even a fixed set of properties or predicates: it is strictly what it does as process. Measuring thinking power as an independent capacity, in an IQ test, say, is therefore mistaken, since this power depends strictly on the processes where it appears.

176

It does not have the extractable and transferable qualities implied by the concept of independent capacity. Thinking varies with its problems, events, series and individuals. When we measure it or identify it empirically in psychological tests, we correctly identify a capacity to do those tests (though not necessarily over time and certainly not objectively since external series will always be at work in the background). *We never identify thinking capacity as such, which is not an object of measurement but one for discrete descriptions in the context of individual but shared problems and creative attempts to unblock those problems.* Thus, to return to the example of doctors seeking diagnoses, there certainly are skills that transfer between specialist areas, but from Deleuze's point of view this is not through the transfer of a measurable fixed capacity but through the overlaps and contacts between different series. This allows for better explanations of errors, for example when a particular series clashes with another and a sign is therefore misread despite great diagnostic skill. When compared with the way you learn from past experiences in the round by transforming yourself, your IQ or measured skill-set is but a narrow, restrictive illusion of comparability. It owes more to the normalising demands of bureaucracy, to the comparative demands of capital and a repressive need for ranking than to an objective assessment. Thought appears when it functions to bring series and events together, without having to impose an external identity upon them. Thinking, for example through a fantasy or project coursing through a life and giving it a new direction while connecting to its physical and emotive prompts, brings together the series constituting the life, not as a full answer or a conscious and free effort, but as a transformer with minimal and often nonsensical substance. How then can structures alter if there is no external catalyst or actor independent of them? What allows bodies, inscribed by events, wounded by them, led by them through unconscious drives, to strive to be worthy of events and counter-actualise them in novel creations, thereby diminishing the wound and extracting an eternal truth from it? It is thought as an immanent power to assemble, redirect and renew the relation between multiple series and their events.

Is this too abstract and mysterious? Here is a concrete example. In his short story about sibling relations 'Farewell, my brother' (1990), John Cheever describes a family meeting as a growing schism where two tendencies draw apart from one another because one is affirmative and joyful and the other draws its energy from assessing this joy negatively through pious and bitter judgements. The event is the meeting in all its physical and ideal ramifications. It is inscribed in bodies, for example in the way joy is exhausted as it becomes the object for judgement. This exhaustion is itself manifested in increasing alcohol consumption as a failed solution – as it often is in Cheever and in Deleuze. The event is also the expression of ideal connections, the idea of the family loses intensity in its relation to love through the middle part of the story. One of the main characters, the narrator of the story, feels and reflects on this event, sees its growing negative ideal and bodily energy, and is himself subject to unconscious effects and phantasms (the simply crafted yet uncanny dream sequences of Cheever's work are particularly effective). Then, at the turning point of the story, a thought emerges. In truth, it was emerging before that point and is also a complex shockwave after it. The point is merely where the thought is expressed most intensely for the reader. According to Deleuze's definition, *the thinking process of emergence is when an act in relation to ideas, physical prompts, unconscious drives and phantasms on the edge of wakefulness and sleep, draws all series together and yet breaks them into a new pattern*:

> Then I picked up a root and, coming at his back – although I have never hit a man from the back before – I swung the root, heavy with sea water, behind me, and the momentum sped my arm and I gave him, my brother, a blow on the head that forced him to his knees on the sand, and I saw the blood come out and begin to darken his head.
>
> (Cheever, 1990: 32)

The act itself is not the thought for Deleuze. It is only its expression. To arrive at the thought we also have to look for the phantasm, a semi-conscious, semi-unconscious imagination, not fully willed, since it occurs to the thinker, yet not fully unconscious either, since the thinker has access to it and a chancy degree of control over it:

> Then I wished that he was dead, dead and about to be buried, not buried but about to be buried, because I did not want to be denied ceremony and decorum in putting him away, in putting him out of my consciousness, and I saw the rest of us – Chaddy and Mother and Diana and Helen – in mourning in the house on Belvedere Street that was torn down twenty years ago, greeting our guests and our relatives at the door and answering their mannerly condolences with mannerly grief.
>
> (Cheever, 1990: 32)

Thinking for Deleuze is in the relation between the phantasm series, the act series and, most importantly, the surface of intensities investing different infinitives or values expressed in all series. It is therefore in the relation between bodily series, ideal series and their intensities. But it is also in the way phantasms draw sense out of the act as the act actualises them. Phantasms run along series in a way an act or a fixed mental content never could. They have plasticity and a multiple character permitting them to haunt and generate different elements of series while drawing them together. Perhaps a good way to get in touch with this complex approach to thought is through our own thought processes in the rhythms of a tenacious and damaging crisis, not at a point where we have to make a thoughtful decision, but rather in the tangle of thoughts, hauntings, nightmares, calculations, discussions, arguments and partial essays constituting a struggle with an enduring problem. Thinking is in the tangled web and not in the decision with its false claim to calculating neutrality. (*We've failed again. Another phantasm of peaceful victory dies. What do we have the strength for next?*)

THOUGHT AND PROBLEMS

All of this is very far removed from what we ordinarily associate with thinking, for example with ideas or representations as contents of a mind, or with chains of reasoning, either in a mind, or a machine, or as disembodied formal symbolic chains, or as biological or artificial neural networks. We might say that the thought in Cheever's story is something like 'To hit my brother' or 'To wish him dead' or 'The pain will stop if its cause is eliminated' or 'Pain-ended if and only if Brother-ended' or 'Necessarily pain ended if brother ended' or 'transition from scan state A to scan state B'. But none of these options could satisfy the problem of thought in relation to serial context as presented by Deleuze. This is for quite technical reasons within his philosophy, but it is also for a traditional reason. First, technically, *anything* in Deleuze's model must be a two-sided process of series and events. Things will be differentiated in terms of how they are such processes and to what degrees, but not in terms of independence or externality from them. Moreover, things can be described as limited in one way or another, but in reality such a description will always be incomplete. In principle, any thing is without limit and it will be differentiated by how it selects within multiple infinite series, rather than how it imposes finite boundaries on them. So thought, as an identified content, idea or representation (however sophisticated the imaging), is a non-starter for him. Of course, that is not to say that he is right about these claims, but merely to insist on the consistency of his philosophical model. Neither is it to say that Deleuze's philosophy does not allow for descriptions of mental content, or syllogisms, or representations. It is rather to claim that any such restriction of the processes standing for thinking is an incomplete and, at least according to the arguments of *Logic of Sense*, a misleading model for thought.

Second, in terms of traditional philosophical problems, Deleuze challenges the association of right thinking with good outcomes. Instead of assuming that if we think correctly we shall arrive at practically or morally good outcomes, he alters the focus to a more equivocal relation between thought and events. Thinking is in the relation of actual occurrences to ideal or virtual conditions (usually expressed as infinitives in *Logic of Sense*). These conditions include relations of infinitives, problems, events, series and their expression in an actual situation. Thought must bring all of these together and, since the relation of problems to actualisations and counteractualisations is not one of solutions or necessarily good outcomes, thought is itself not in any necessary relation to such outcomes. This does not mean that Deleuze denies that correct and careful thinking can influence the end of an action; it is rather that he does not view this relation as a key grounding problem for thought. Instead, he is concerned with the way thinking is a response to problems that cannot allow for clear-cut moral or practical solutions. This includes the problem of the relation of thought to goodness itself as it appears in the multiple failures of well-intentioned thought.

In the twenty-ninth series 'good intentions are inevitably [or perforce] punished', Deleuze investigates this relation of thought to bad outcomes, or to unwilled outcomes. He draws on his work on the cracks or fault lines of a life, as discussed in the previous chapter, to describe thoughtful actions and well-intentioned actions as having fault lines of their own. This is not because the thought is limited by what it does not know or control, as that which is as yet unexplored, but rather because it is immanently flawed. His reading of Zola in the fifth appendix to *Logic of Sense* is a study of this relation between fault lines and intentions, showing how unconscious faults interfere with and engulf conscious intentions, denying them the independence they require to be certain of good outcomes. The originality of the work on Zola lies in the idea that the faults can be understood as a kind of heredity which not only transfers through genes, but also through environments and inherited phantasms. The flaw running through lives is imperceptible to those who will suffer from it as an event, it is part of the death drive that gives determinacy and energy but also destruction. Thought cannot shake off such inherited fractures, but only divine, represent and replay them differently. There is then a joust between acts and our conscious representations of them, and unconscious conditions for those acts, which explain why they are ours and how they acquire significance:

> [. . .] if it is true that the instincts are formed and find their object only at the edge of the crack, the crack conversely pursues its course, spreads out its web, changes direction, and is actualised in each body in relation to the instincts that open a way for it, sometimes mending it a little, sometimes widening it, up to the final shattering – which is always assured by the work of the instincts.
>
> (LoS, 325, 378)

It would be a mistake then to confuse actual instincts and causal determination with Deleuze's use of the fault-line as the transcendental condition for significant determination. Your instincts are yours because of the singular way you express and work with them. This working itself has a mobile and pure condition which will eventually engulf it, because it is in tension with a necessary search for identity in actual bodies.

Again, examples are helpful in understanding these points. Deleuze is not claiming that thinking cannot solve a puzzle such as how to cross a country in the shortest time possible using as many different forms of transport as possible. There is often a single right answer to such a puzzle and indeed it may have a good outcome such as arriving on time – *for once*. However, it is when the motivation and significance of arriving on time is introduced that we move closer to Deleuze's understanding of a problem. Timeliness could then be a sign of growing mania ('The first step to knowing who we are . . . is knowing where we are and . . . WHEN we are') or imminent breakdown ('It's not the despair, Laura. I can take the despair. It's the hope I can't stand' (Morahan, 1986)). The solution to the first puzzle is then not a solution to the underlying problem which itself cannot be solved in that straightforward a manner. Moreover, that which appears to be a good solution before we take account of the underlying problem can turn out to be a false solution, or even a worsening, after we fold in the problem. This does not mean it cannot be alleviated, or that all approaches to the problem are equally valid. It is rather a commentary on the nature of problems in relation to thought and to solutions. The simplest version of this commentary is that problems do not simply disappear – in the way the puzzle does – they remain latent and capable of morphing into new and unexpected forms. This is because their components are not concrete or ideal 'boxes' such as the different routes one can take across a city, but rather interconnecting variations in intensities that will invest ideas and actual things differently. For instance, there are many modern puzzles connected to saving or gaining time, but these take their place within problems concerning the value of speed and its social and moral ramifications. Each solution to a problem can be an intensification of values running counter to the direction of solution (for example, in the tensions associated with quicker global movement, yet flattening of global diversity – in all its advantages and damage). Taken to the limit this view also therefore implicates puzzles and solutions, because they too have a value-horizon which leaves a legacy that belies the idea of once and for all resolutions.

For Deleuze, thought is necessarily accompanied by physical wounds, ideal changes and surface or value effects, all of which return in ways beyond its control. It is therefore not something outside thought that destines it to failure. It is something deep inside and something on its surface or envelope. More precisely, it is in the inevitable passage from the physical to ideal, and from the ideal to the physical, in chance-driven asymmetrical relations of reciprocal determination, that thought fails its own good intentions. The wound outdoes the idea, or the idea outlives the wound (which it necessarily always does), or surface intensities shift imperceptibly, making ideas redundant or repugnant, or magnifying wounds that once were shrugged off: 'The famous mechanism of "denegation" (that's not what I wanted . . .), with all its importance for the formation of *thought*, must be interpreted as expressing the passage from one surface to another' (LoS, 208, 242). It is because things return differently, or because Chronos, as the time of action, is in a paradoxical relation to Aiôn, the time of infinitives and intensities, that any intended outcome will be punished. When we think speculatively, that is with plans and projected ends, we connect to what Deleuze calls the speculative form of the Freudian death drive: an inevitable fault within thought in its relation to time and to events. It is because they matter, because they have sense, that thoughts also have a death drive through the changes in sense driven by novel actual and ideal events. The problem of thought is therefore not how to arrive at a given end. It is rather, how to live with the unforeseeable yet structured legacies of thought and the desires accompanying it. For example, in his *The Picture of Dorian Gray*, Oscar Wilde tells of a futile attempt to escape death and ageing, but the book goes much further through an investigation of the relation between good and bad intended thoughts and their outcomes. Wilde's conclusions are Deleuzian in the impossibility of intended good outcomes, where these try to outdo the layered and repeated legacies of earlier intensions, desires and events: 'A new life! That was what he wanted. That was what he was waiting for. Surely he had begun it already. He had spared one innocent thing, at any rate. He would never again tempt innocence. He would be good' (Wilde, 1949: 261). Eternal youth is unattainable, not only physically, but also because an invariant body would still fail due to its necessary surface contact with shifting ideal intensities: 'Lying on the floor was a dead man, in evening dress, with a knife in his heart' (Wilde, 1949: 264). It is not only 'impossible' intended outcomes that fall foul of this death drive, but any outcome. Some will succeed and some will fail, not in measure of their goodness and the validity of the deductions they stand on, but through a chance-driven interaction with eternally shifting values, ideas and future bodies.

The questions motivating Deleuze's work on thought are therefore unfamiliar. He is not asking 'What is a thought?' or 'How do we think right (in relation to specified outcomes)?' or 'What is the general form of right thinking?' Instead, if we turn to the titles of the series from *Logic of Sense* where thought is discussed, we find a very different and at first glance very surprising set of topics: the phantasm, the inevitable punishment of good intentions, sexuality, serialisation and 'orality'. The titles reflect a psychoanalytical approach to thought, an angle which will seem odd or even downright wrong to many philosophers, but also right to others, who will point out that the study of thought without the unconscious is poor in the extreme, perhaps one of the few truly wrongheaded enterprises. The selection of psychoanalysis is apt and accurate and should not be confused with a work of clinical psychoanalysis. Work by Freud, Lacan and Melanie Klein allows Deleuze to study the relation between conscious acts and unconscious processes, and between phantasms and different cognitive processes. He is not primarily concerned with notions of cure or diagnosis, or with psychoanalytic theories of the unconscious *per se*, or specific cases and illnesses in themselves. His notion of cure and health is more specifically philosophical and artistic (as developed, later, in his *Essays Critical and Clinical*). Rather, psychoanalytical work allows for an entry into the complex relations of language, phantasm, body and event; this work is a philosophy of thought at the surface between conscious and unconscious processes. In turn this allows Deleuze to connect his philosophy of language and moral philosophy to questions about how thinking relates to efforts to replay events through language.

A question such as 'What is called thinking?' is not at the heart of Deleuze's enquiry, because for him thought is a process among many rather than the foundation for reflection on any possible process. We need to think because we are caught in a web of series and events – we are caught in this web because we think, feel, dream and fantasise.

SERIATION AND THE PHANTASM

The sixth series of *Logic of Sense* 'on seriation' is a good place to develop an understanding of the relation between thought and Deleuze's structure. The current translation for the title uses 'serialisation' for *mise en séries*. I prefer 'seriation' as a more accurate term given Deleuze's reference to Lacan's use of seriation as a putting into series, or more accurately as the necessary occurrence within a series of any given thing. Moreover, the term is in common usage in aesthetics (after Panofsky, 1983), as well as by Sartre on Jean Genet in a more negative sense of insertion into series, and fits the content of Deleuze's work very well, though with significant contrasts. He is discussing the way things are put into series and the necessity of that inclusion. Nothing can stand independent of the series it takes place in, or more radically, nothing actually 'is' at all unless it is within series that give it its denotation, signification, manifestation and sense. This opposition to abstraction, in the sense of a claim to independence in the separation from a context, is important in Deleuze's work; it should not be understood as the denial of abstraction as method, but rather as a critique of positions that associate a completeness or higher truth in the abstracted thing. Thought therefore comes within and must bend to seriation, in terms of what the thought is, what it is about, what it means, who utters it and its sense, value or significance. The broad points of the sixth series, however, do not so much concern this structural positioning as its implications for the things positioned. Deleuze shows how seriation generates novelty and paradoxical terms within a strict formal structure. He also shows how it implies necessary paradoxes and slippage between terms – neither of which must be viewed simply in a positive or negative manner. The sixth series therefore supports the claim that thought (viewed as the generation of novelty and the manipulation of the genetic potential of paradox) can arise independent of well-defined sources (the thinker or mystical founts such as genius or any type of formal state or identified content).

Deleuze begins the sixth series with a further study of the paradox of indefinite regression which states that the definition of a term requires additional terms which also require supplementary definition, and so on indefinitely. His interest in the paradox lies in the way it sets up series as double. This is because we have a series of terms-defining and terms-defined exchanging across names: D defines C defines B defines A; and A is defined by B is defined by C is defined by D. It could be claimed that these are the same series and that 'defines' and 'defined by' are interchangeable, but the counter-argument is that in the first series each term designates the sense of another, whereas in the second it is its sense that is designated. Relations in Deleuze are neither commutative nor transitive because they take place in asymmetric structures. By the time you arrive at the second term of a relation, the first has been changed by the movement. For example, when we say that 'growl' means 'anger', 'anger' designates the meaning of 'growl', but when we go on to say that 'anger' means 'rage', 'rage' designates the meaning of 'anger' which is no longer that which designates the meaning of 'growl' but a meaning in its own right designated by 'rage'. A good way of feeling this difference is to put yourself in a series of people commentating in turn on a group they all belong to. Is there a shift in impressions when you change from being the describer to the described, from saying 'What C meant by a' to being the designated of 'What D meant by a'? From a Deleuzian angle, the difference in feelings are signs that designated and designating are not interchangeable – assuming, of course, that you do feel a difference. His broad point is therefore not only that meaning and sense are always open to further definition (and expression) but that any definition or designation divides a series: 'The serial form is thus essentially multi-serial' (LoS, 37, 50). This explains why he uses 'indefinite' rather than 'infinite' to describe the paradox. The deep problem is not that the regression goes on infinitely, but that at each name it divides indefinitely, that is without firm principle as to which path to follow. His argument is then that, in the absence of such firm principles, different more mobile and singular principles must come to guide a creative form of selection.

The multiplication of disjunctions in series applies to all aspects of the proposition: its designation, its signification, its manifestation and its sense. They are all dual and then subdivided into series around each aspect. Moreover, with respect to thought, there is a deep irreducibility to this multiplicity because the series any event or concept belongs to cannot be mapped symmetrically onto another. So it is not as if we have a series of signifiers pointing to a series of signified with a neat one-to-one correspondence. On the contrary, each association of signifier to signified disrupts all the others. Deleuze's commitment to asymmetries is therefore also an opposition to injective functions (and indeed to the stability of any function); one-to-one relations do not hold across series. When the meaning of a term is 'clarified' by a further definition, this does not only concern that pairing but runs through all the series and all their divisions. It is as if each move within a labyrinth changes it each time, so any past record of a path would be redundant or at least transformed and requiring interpretation and unravelling anew. Seriation should therefore not be understood simply as a situation within a fixed series, but rather as an interaction of multiple series with no overall formal logic or limits. Thinking takes place within all these series as reverberations of events through language, bodies and sense (understood as fluctuation of the intensity of significance or value). It takes that place with no stable properties of mirroring, or symmetry, or even reliable functions which could serve as a basis for restricting thought to a given zone or process. Any such restriction would be an invalid cut in thought rather than an accurate picture of its location or mechanism. Under the scrutiny of language, thought does not admit to limits circumscribing the function of representation: it is never a question of 'Where?' but always one of 'How?'

Now this is not cause for despair. It is not that we cannot act or that there is not a formal structure to act within and understand. It is rather that we shall never have a final order of relations or logic to work on. Every thought and every act is experimental and has an experimental bodily and ideal matter to work within. Moreover, this experiment is with a necessarily unconscious element, in the sense of beyond conscious knowledge and reflection. Instead of searching for regularities, we search for changes by seeking to create new ones. For instance, in a reading of Lacan's seminar on Poe's 'The purloined letter', Deleuze stresses the trail of small and big differences, and lack of determinacy over continuity and resemblance: '[. . .] the essential appears when small or great differences appear and predominate over resemblances, when they become primary, thus when two completely distinct stories develop simultaneously, when characters have a vacillating and ill-determined identity' (LoS, 38, 52). This reference is interesting because, very much in accord with Deleuze, Lacan is examining the relation of repetition to thought and the unconscious in Freud and across a wide range of literary sources. The two philosophers make similar points with respect to thought, in particular with respect to the displacement and transformation of rules, though Lacan resists summing up the relations between series and stays much closer to literary and psychoanalytical analysis, whereas Deleuze describes a more fixed structure that he then subverts. On the other hand, Lacan provides illuminating schema showing the cycle of conscious efforts and the return of unconscious effects subverting them – this is absent in Deleuze's treatment, perhaps because he covers this cycle in his philosophy of time. Nonetheless, the three main characteristics of seriation drawn out by Deleuze are shared: first, the displacement of terms of two series with respect to one another is essential as a condition for sense; second, the signifying series is in excess over the signified; and, third, a paradoxical term runs along series on both the signifying and signified side, thereby bringing them together, as an empty place on the one and as occupant without a place on the other.

When asked for an example of this combination of unconscious and conscious processes, of bodily and ideal series, and of event and sense, the surprising answer dominating many of the closing series of *Logic of Sense* is 'the phantasm'. The word has at least two roots useful for following its role within Deleuze's philosophy. First, derived from Plato and then appearing regularly in the philosophical tradition, a phantasm is a mental image or belief derived from the senses. In Platonic philosophy, the phantasm is negative, in the sense of illusory and as leading to lesser or false knowledge when compared to the Idea; it is a lesser copy of an original because it is acquired through the senses. Thereafter, the concept varies in value, from a necessary if potentially misleading aspect of thought in some branches of empiricism to a downright false one that we should strive to avoid in the Platonic heritage. In line with his reversal of Platonism, Deleuze's position is with those who hold the phantasm not only to be necessary, but also productive and valuable. He develops this idea of overturning in relation to the phantasm in the first appendix to *Logic of Sense*. In psychoanalysis, the phantasm is a fantasy, a set of scenes and beliefs, which is produced by the imagination, by the unconscious and consciously to differing degrees. At one end of the scale, we simply produce phantasms and can release ourselves from them. At the other end, phantasms occur to us unconsciously, in dreams and awake; we can entertain them and flex them, but essentially we are in their grip. In the thirtieth series 'of the phantasm', Deleuze gives his version of the phantasm according to the following main characteristics:

1. The phantasm is the result of actions and passions.
2. It is the chance-driven movement where the ego opens onto novel impersonal and pre-individual intensities.
3. The phantasm is a pure event that expresses infinitives (for example, to murder, to save, to witness).

So Deleuze's version of the phantasm (also developed at much greater length in the important appendices I, II and III to *Logic of Sense*) is that it combines actions and passions, not as an image or representation, but as something that expresses them. The phantasm is not a conscious or unconscious picture that we can give rise to or that happens to us; it is a process resulting from passive situations and active ones. It is therefore not 'in the mind' but rather party to thinking processes.

The meaning of result in the above points should not be associated with strict causes, but rather with the sense of the phantasm as a transformer positioned within asymmetrical expressive relations, where the phantasm expresses the actions and passions it results from by transforming them in such a way as the 'cause' is sundered in its 'result' (hence the asymmetry). Lacan is particularly strong in describing these in his work on 'The purloined letter', for instance, where he demonstrates the independence of a symbolic order from consciousness and its capacity to restructure itself and to return differently:

> The matter that [the structure of determination of a symbolic order] displaces through its effects moves far in scope beyond that of cerebral organisation; though some of those effects remain party to its vicissitudes, others remain nonetheless active and structured as symbolic, capable of materialising in other ways.
>
> (Lacan, '*Séminaire*' p. 5 [my translation])

We can use some symbols generated by our actions and passions, yet others are reworked independent of consciousness and return differently, changing not only our relation to the chains of symbols, but also our relation to the ones we selected for conscious manipulation. It is worth noting that, in a discussion of Mallarmé on chance, Lacan makes use of one of Deleuze's favourite references in his discussion of the open or 'dice-throw' characteristics of this symbolic interaction. Both thinkers situate thought within a wider game of chance whose rules we cannot control but merely grasp intermittently and partially. Where Lacan speaks of the matter of the symbolic order (in the symbols we use in early speech), Deleuze goes beyond symbols and into pre-individual singularities, or series of virtual turning points. This then leads him to a different view of language where these turning points are the intensities or values that can invest relations of infinitives.

For instance, if we return to the example from Cheever cited at the beginning of this chapter, the infinitives 'to kill', 'to bury' and 'to mourn' operate in the background of different dreams, phantasms and acts. Thinking becomes an activity incorporating those infinitives through each of those media at different degrees of activity and passivity. When we fantasise a murder, begin to plan it, or even when we arrive at the semi-autonomous physical accomplishment of what began with a phantasm, our thoughts take their place in a series of processes underway consciously and unconsciously long before any accomplishment. Indeed, Cheever's stories often connect to the deep Deleuzian truth that there is never a final accomplishment: the act is a turning point among others and launches series of events as much as it reacts to others. Again, Deleuze's work on the phantasm should in no way be seen as orthodox psychoanalysis (nor should Lacan's work on 'The purloined letter'). He is investigating a set of processes which can be accurately tracked according to psychoanalytical concepts such as the phantasm, but like the later work with Guattari in *Anti-Oedipus*, the point is to separate the powerful model of how consciousness and the unconscious work together from the imposition of a set of restrictive images governing this form. In short, we must learn from the phantasm, both in terms of the structure of thought and within the individual process of a given series in which a thought takes place, or more precisely runs through. But there is no final form of the phantasm itself, for instance as types or contents, allowing for a restriction of thought in terms of its openness or series and events in terms of their kinds. The key to understanding this point lies in the infinitives as singularities or turning points with open and multiple relations. There is no general pattern governing those relations and were they interpreted in terms of childhood trauma, or familial sexual phantasms, or underlying images, metaphors or even physical restrictions, this would run counter to the Deleuzian enterprise and its insistence on the multiplicity and neutrality of sense, as expressed in his work on infinitives. A phantasm expresses a series of infinitives in a certain way, but there is no determination of the universal form of singularities by any general form attached to the phantasm.

THOUGHT AND SEXUALITY

Against the previous claim, on the exemplary rather than theoretical importance of psychoanalytic work for Deleuze, it could be
objected that psychoanalytic forms around the phantasm are central
to *Logic of Sense*. After all, many of its series take familiar psychoanalytic concepts such as castration or orality and incorporate them into
Deleuze's wider concepts. That is completely correct. The point
is rather that this relation allows for a description of Deleuze's
processes in terms of thought and the unconscious, rather than a
formal and necessary restriction of those processes in terms of psychoanalytical theories. In order to show this, I will work through the
main arguments of the thirty-first series 'on thought' showing the
primary claim about thought and Deleuze's series alongside the discussion of the phantasm. These arguments are designed to demonstrate the openness and necessary creativity of thought against views
of thinking as hermetic and contained in limited and reliable chains
of reasoning and representation:

1. Any intentional thought is separated from its outcomes (cas-
   trated) because actions are cut off from their unconscious results
   in terms of intentions; the origin of the phantasm is transported
   by it, in the same way as an act expressing a series of infinitives is
   overtaken by them and by subsequent actions. For example, a
   well-intended lie (to lie, to repair) is necessarily overtaken by subsequent views of the sense of the lie, or how it is valued in terms
   of intense relations to other infinitives (*I was only trying to protect
   you!* – to lie/to protect – *Yes, but now I cannot trust you* – to lie/to
   deceive).
2. Castration, taken in the strict psychoanalytical account of a relation towards the mother, is then only a partial and bound account
   of a particular physical effect (where the unconscious wound
   must also be seen as physical). The beginning of the thought or
   of the phantasm is more than this castration; it is a pure openness, in the sense of a non-physical beginning on the surface
   between ideas and bodies. Deleuze describes this as a neutral
   energy; it is a limit both to physical causal explanations and to
   explanations in terms of ideas. It is an energy or source that can
   only be replayed rather than traced.
3. The two previous points on the origin and finality of the phantasm illustrate the independence of Deleuze's model from any
   given phantasm or account of their forms. He reinforces this by

drawing a distinction, based on a reading of Klossowski, between the energy of sexual difference and the difference in energy constitutive of thought (for a long discussion of Klossowski on the phantasm, see the third appendix to *Logic of Sense*). This difference follows from the structure of series and events, from disjunctions and paradoxes, and not from any image of the unconscious. Serial processes swallow any given phantasm and have the power to transform it while they work through it (which is why the content of any phantasm, castration, say, should not be confused with the process it describes).

4. Thought is a matter of geography and topology, that is it alters things through movements between bodies, ideas and surface intensities (rather than causes and effects governed by laws). These movements operate metamorphoses, for example on sexuality or on human relations. The phantasm, as thought, goes from the figurative (the loving couple or sexual relation) to something abstract (an abstract line indicating a direction). So, here, abstraction is not in the sense of an abstract concept, as dismissed earlier, but in the sense of a plan or diagram, as developed in Deleuze's later books. Thought connects by changing things along abstract lines, altering relations across wounds, ideas and values. It is the source of novelty underwritten by Deleuze's notion of eternal return, as eternal return of an energising differential potential. The phantasm facilitates these movements by separating the actual figure from its ideas and from connections that an actual situation 'does not permit'. Castration is the process of separation in the phantasm; sublimation is the process of reconnection along different abstract lines. It is helpful, in understanding this power of thought and of the phantasm, to return to Deleuze's work on paradox and nonsense. In entertaining nonsense, irregularity and paradox in the phantasm, we do not draw that nonsense or paradox into actuality, but instead we draw the actualities determining things as nonsense, or transgression, or perversion into a realm which connects them differently and makes space for new potentials. *How dare you take me that way? You are always taken thus.*

5. Thought then is an artistically creative endeavour risking phantasms in order to connect to what he calls pure events, that is to infinitives shorn of their contact to actualities and left only with their mobile relations to all other infinitives. Deleuze gives the example of the Proustian phantasm 'Will I marry Albertine?' The pure event is the 'to marry' as a potential for different kinds

of relations to 'to desire', 'to love', 'to commit', 'to enjoy', 'to betray', 'to sacrifice' and so on. The progressive nature of this creativity comes out well here and is reminiscent of Deleuze's use of splendour and glory from his work on moral philosophy and on Péguy, discussed earlier in this book. There is a glory and freedom in the refusal to tie an infinitive, such as 'to love', to given rules or actualities, which perhaps explains Deleuze's rare moments of vicious attack in his disdain for base commandments such as 'True love can only happen between an X and Y' or 'True desire can only occur where there are blessed outcomes' or 'True love has been captured once and for all in Raphael's *Madonna of the Pinks*'.

These points allow for answers to a number of critical questions. First, when asked how it is possible to adopt psychoanalytical examples, theories and approaches and yet also claim not to be limited by specific forms such as the Freudian Oedipal complex, the answer is that Deleuze goes beyond the particular content through his insistence of the role of the pure event and infinitives:

> It is only there [in metamorphosis, sublimation and symbolisation] that dying and killing, to castrate and to be castrated, to repair and to bring on, to wound and to withdraw, to devour and to be devoured, to introject and to project, become pure events on the metaphysical surface that transforms them, where their infinitive is extracted.
>
> (LoS, 221, 257)

Second, when asked why it is necessary to go beyond familiar conceptions of thought as instrumental and end-driven, the answer is that it is because the capacity for novelty in thought and the moral and metaphysical importance of that novelty demand a more radical account of the nature of thought and its special connection to openness free of prior determinations. Third, when asked whether there is actually anything radically new in thought, the answer is that it is through their relations to infinitives or values that actual things acquire significance. Things matter because they are open to change and because they connect to the conditions for that change (as released by the power of the phantasm). Finally, when asked what is the moral significance of thought. It is not in the moments where it struggles for sameness and identity, but where it takes the chance to imagine things differently, not by promising a different identity, utopia, perfect world, blessed realm, but by separating verbs and actions from the actual injuries and wounds they inflict, to open them up to a dual awareness of the inevitability of wounds and of the potential for them to happen differently and better: 'For the event is only well inscribed in the flesh, in bodies, with the will and freedom which befit the patient thinker and only in virtue of the incorporeal part containing their secret, that is, their principle, their truth and their finality: the quasi-cause' (LoS, 221, 258).

The principle associating thought to transformations in response to events, intensities and ideas inscribes thought within the important concept of counter-actualisation – also rendered as re-enactment or replaying, here. Thought has to replay physical events in order to draw out their potential to be minimised in the present as passions, that is as negativity, but maximised in the past and future as activities, as novel and intense connections to multiple turning points and infinitives. Thinking must enrich ideal and intense relations while diminishing the actual injuries that prevent such relations taking place, for instance in the way pain or fear prevent thinking and turning to others' pain. However, there can never be such a thing as the perfect thought, one not requiring embodiment and hence further passions or negativity for its expression. The art of thought is to move towards the pure event, but necessarily through the body and without a perfect close. This allows for an answer to another possible objection to Deleuze: that he leaves thinking rudderless and without point. This is true: in the sense that he cannot provide universal actual goals, but it is also false, since he provides guiding directions, one of which teaches us to seek the actual paths and goals leading along those directions.

The seriation of thought processes, their insertion in series, not as untouched units, but as transformed actors in a shared drama, explains Deleuze's remarks on the brain at the close of the thirty-first series: '[. . .] the brain, not only as corporeal organ, but as inductor on another invisible, metaphysical, surface where all events are inscribed and symbolised [. . .]' (LoS, 223, 259). The organic brain is part of processes determining it as an operator where it is the condition for novelty and counter-actualisation through language. It is not that the organic brain is extended into a metaphysical one; it is rather that the layers of mutually conditioning series are multiple processes running asymmetrically. Brains are not 'part' of these processes, but reverberations through them (the notion of part would reintroduce a dominant identity). These early remarks on the brain are developed much later with Félix Guattari in the concluding chapter to *What Is Philosophy?*, 'From chaos to the brain'. Multiply-connected and manifold brains allow thinkers to become free, by releasing them from the reductive time Deleuze calls Chronos, where a passive present engulfs the past and the future – the present of suffering. This requires the metaphysical unfolding and folding of the brain outside any given receptacle or location, so that thinking is ascribed to the processes of 'perplication', to use the beautiful neologism from *Difference and Repetition* capturing senses of folding but also complication, paradox and puzzlement; these are topological movements rather than the content at a location or a given iterative function. For Deleuze, the brain is not so much extended, as metamorphosed in multiple ways, each suited in passing manner to different series and events, connecting them by changing them. It could never be enough to give an empirical or naturalistic account of these processes as different practical extensions, since this could not account for the metaphysical basis for the multiplicity, for its relation to the unconscious, to language and to sense. Perhaps one of the most important aspects of these remarks is a response to the accusation that Deleuze's work on thought is still too humanistic, almost romantically so. This is not the case. Thought could never be human thought, or the brain a human brain, if by this we mean something contained in a human body or associated with human consciousness, souls or values. Animals, plants, people are all implicated in thought and are thinkers, in the same way as all events are linguistic, because thought is the description of the operation of ubiquitous processes explaining and standing as a condition for novelty. Thought is not a capacity solely embodied in things for which thought is possible – however much we then extend this outwards. It is a process changing the relations between different layers of series in a creative manner that responds and initiates events running forward and back through those series.

DYNAMIC GENESIS

The concept of dynamic genesis is important for understanding why Deleuze accords a central role to thought, language and the phantasm. It responds to the somewhat technical question: how are thought and the brain inductors of the surface of values and infinitives? In more simple terms: how can thought alter sense and values, if these are defined as 'pure' and 'neutral'? What allows thought not only to express infinitives, but change their relations? Deleuze's answer is developed in the twenty-seventh series 'on orality' and the thirty-fourth series 'on primary order and secondary organisation'. This latter title captures one of the keys to Deleuze's philosophy: its different sides, realms, series and processes admit to distinctions with respect to process. The genetic process from actual things to infinitives is primary. The genetic process from infinitives to actual differences is secondary. We have to be very careful here. This does not mean that actual things are primary, but the exact opposite: *pure events are primary because of the nature of their role in the genesis of actual things when compared to the role of actual things in the genesis of pure events.* Neither does it mean that the processes are independent of one another; it means that despite their interdependence, a type of process is primary and another secondary. Here, primary and secondary are distinguished through their imperviousness to passing away. Secondary organisation, though necessary, has no form of permanence and is engulfed by the primary order, whereas primary processes retain an aspect of neutrality with respect to secondary ones. In other words, an aspect of the virtual component returns eternally in primary process. More precisely, the elements of surface, the infinitives, are unchanging, but their relations are altered. No aspect of actual series, or of the actual side of series, is free of a transforming genesis through the surface and its relation to ideas. Thus the twenty-seventh and thirty-fourth series develop ideas also found in Deleuze's work on the neutrality and impassibility of sense (as worked on in his philosophy of language). More importantly, they explain a counter-movement to the static ontological and logical geneses supporting the necessity of actual identified things as expressions of pure differences. These go from the virtual to the actual, whereas the dynamic genesis goes from the actual to the virtual. As such, the former corresponds to the process of actualisation described in *Difference and Repetition,* while the latter corresponds to differentiation. The different approaches underline one of the most important principles of Deleuze's philosophy: all actual things and all ideas have two inseparable but distinct sides in relation to processes relating them to pure events or pure infinitives; the nature of that distinctness is what gives his philosophy direction. However, it would be a mistake to conflate the different treatments of this principle. There are connections between the two books, but differences remain and matter. The study of the processes is more sensitive and subtle in *Logic of Sense,* less metaphysical machinery and more practical and inventive experimentation with paradox, series and event.

Deleuze demonstrates these points in the twenty-seventh series by tracing the priority of a dynamic genesis going from bodies to pure events in the context of orality, that is from the role of the mouth for speech and for language back to the necessary role of pure sounds, or infinitives, for that orality:

But then we are faced by a final task: to retrace the history that liberates sounds, making them independent of bodies. This is no longer a static genesis that would go from the supposed event to its actualisation in states of things and to its expression in propositions. It is rather a dynamic genesis that goes directly from states of things to events, from mixtures to pure lines, from depth to the production of surfaces, and which must implicate nothing of the other genesis.

(LoS, 186, 217)

Static genesis is about the emergence of static states, in the sense of an identifiable equilibrium – and hence a basis for judgement and comparison, but also a necessary expression. These aren't finally stable but allow for temporary distinctions, which in turn allow for actual things and their limits and boundaries as part of processes that then sunder them and overcome those boundaries. This counter-process is the dynamic genesis where we do not move towards temporary stasis but towards permanent movement and difference, hence its title as dynamic. This is rendered possible because dynamic genesis changes the relations of pure differences, pure variations or pure events – which can all be rendered as infinitives – and this change then feeds back into what it generated. This circle corresponds to Deleuze's version of eternal return and to his account of the circle of the proposition. The surface referred to so often during *Logic of Sense* is the surface of intensities in their dual and circular investment in the relations of actual things and the relations of infinitives through the processes of static and dynamic genesis. The reason Deleuze insists on the direct contact from things to events and on the purity of lines is that actual things and infinitives or pure events must not belong to the same domain and be subject to the same laws, for this would conflate his philosophy into materialism with no need for a neutral and impassive realm. Similarly, static genesis cannot be implicated in dynamic genesis without compromising the priority of the latter. The reason we cannot forget the virtual plane of pure events is that it guarantees the productive return of pure differences and openness against a filling of the actual world with the sameness of things and laws – irrespective of how relatively open these prove to be. *Otherwise your empiricism is but a matter of faith denying the historical desire and attainment of law and identity.* The Deleuzian question put back to those who would conflate the virtual back onto the actual is 'How then do you explain novelty against the filling in of the world with identities, whether these be laws, things or ideas?'

But what is the relation of these arguments to thought? It is thought, defined as a creative relation between events, intensities and actual things, that can experiment with novel contacts with infinitives. Thought therefore combines actual things and their pure virtual conditions, for example in the way composers take the pure sound – free of its associations with known bodies, instruments and scores – and release its transforming power, its dynamism, into new instrumentations and compositions. The same is true for painting and colour, but also for mathematics and relations (not pure numbers – for that would return us to Platonism). Orality then is something that can be moved by processes escaping physical wounds and fixations that Deleuze traces following Melanie Klein. The physical world around the mouth is one of wounding mixtures, of dangerous substances, terrifying separations and longings. Klein charts a route from these mixtures via partial objects (separated from functions and allowed to float freely) to novel and perverse orientations (both liberating and potentially dangerously blocked), to a body without organs free of orientation. Deleuze reads this in a detailed manner foregrounding his work on schizoanalysis with Guattari in *Anti-Oedipus*. Kleinian psychoanalysis allows Deleuze to describe dynamic genesis as a passage through a series of stages which begin with separation, of mouth and mother's breast for example, but that at the same time depend on free flows, underpinning a novel orientation of mouth to anus. The point is not to judge the passages and to set their stages and parts within an account of fixed values but rather to show their two-sidedness. There is destructiveness but also productivity in dynamic genesis moving from depth to surface:

> And then the first stage of dynamic genesis appears. The depth is clamorous: clappings, crackings, gnashings, cracklings, explosions, the shattered sounds of internal objects, and also the inarticulate howl-breaths of the body without organs which responds to them – all of this forms a sonorous system bearing witness to the oral anal voracity.
>
> (LoS, 193, 225)

It would be a mistake either to use this dependence on Klein and Freud to dismiss Deleuze's work or to fold simply onto their analyses. He is following their studies as descriptions of the kinds of processes that lead from an actual world of physical mixtures to an unconscious one that stands as a condition for it and brings genesis as pure change within it. But it is not the case that this is the only possible description, or that it is the true final one. This would contradict his point about the neutrality of sense, which cannot be subject to law, psychoanalytic or otherwise. Klein and Freud, and

Deleuze's work on schizophrenia, offer us an expression of the process of dynamic genesis.

The work on dynamic genesis and psychoanalysis is developed further and connected to all aspects of Deleuze's philosophy in the final and thorny thirty-fourth series. I want to draw out points from this series as responses to a difficult question for any process philosophy. Why do processes not tend to entropy? How can life and thought renew themselves and generate new forms, connect to novel intensities, give energy to novel ideas and highlight new events rather than exhaust themselves or spin off into chaos and confusion? These may seem odd questions for philosophy, better suited to physics rather than metaphysics, but they turn on important explanations for Deleuze because they focus on the twin extremes of chaos and stasis that threaten his structures from within (and from without when they are taken up by thinkers of 'common sense'). He offers us an experimental construction which seems to have implicit flaws in its situation between pure events and necessary actual identities. The response to these questions brings together the study of structures, for example in language, and his work on sexuality and thought, for instance in the relation between the phantasm and Freudian death drive. Thought and the phantasm are described as introducing a forced movement into series, that is the twin empty places and placeless occupants running through series set off a resonance of growing amplitude through them. This growth counters the entropy implicit in the requirement to express infinitives in identified actual things. For example, in concerns about the future of humanity, the phantasm of the end of the world resonates through bodies and ideas thanks to the empty places 'when?', 'where?', 'how?' as they course along series of ideas and physical places on the globe. In parallel excessive series, placeless occupants accompany those questions – 'war', 'global warming', 'end of oil', 'capitalist collapse' and so on. But these negative movements are also accompanied by positive creative ones resisting the notion of end and feelings of despair with counter ideas 'to renew', 'to seek peace', 'to love', 'to hope' and acts affirming them. The event is a two-way resonance with its occurrence in series and its counter-actualisation (hence the principle of worthiness to the event described in Deleuze's moral philosophy). On a different but connected diagram, an example could be of the phantasms and reflections associated with the sensations and affects leading to a decision to renounce animal flesh. From a Deleuzian point of view the decision is not a sudden break, but an interaction with extended series.

As an accommodation with the demands of static genesis, a choice responds to increases in resonance along those series as the empty place. For instance, the question 'Where to draw the line in killing other living beings?' moves through the different series constituting our lives until we perceive that a line has been crossed. In asymmetric process though, a placeless occupant, perhaps the desire to affirm all living beings ('to love', 'to respect'), carries the demands of dynamic genesis into the choice preserving it from finality thanks to a restless and life-affirming experimentation. *When it stops, so do you, or rather, only the part that was not worth preserving for eternal re-enactment.*

These structures and their resonance explain why the phantasm is described as requiring four series and two movements. The actual series splits into one of excess and one of lack, as does the ideal series. Each has its resonance, in contact with the other's, and open onto the surface of intensities energising all resonance. This is a view of life as struggle between inertia and dynamism, only saved from entropy through the creative power of thought, and from chaos through the requirement of a pendulum-like movement between the series. Language plays a crucial role in this movement and in a counter-actualisation of the event in its requirement for actualisation. Language emerges along the stages of Deleuze's account of dynamic genesis as physical mixtures or wounds. The stages are given expression through the mouth, then designated, given meaning and manifested in speech, and only thereafter given sense when an infinitive is expressed. Life moves from the wound (bleeding), to the cry (where the bleeding is doubled by another vocal series), to its description and communication (my wound), to its association with a universal potential ('to bleed' expressed in this singular way). Deleuze approaches this movement through psychoanalytical accounts of sexuality in order to emphasise the importance of perversion for thought and creativity: thought must break with notions of propriety in order to create. But he also shows how sexuality is the key to the passage to language and to sense from physical mixtures, because sexuality is the limit case for those mixtures. This is because sexuality is the limit of equivocity. It can be connected analogically to all other things in a cycle of denotations and meanings to the point where that cycle must be broken in the passage to a pure event and infinitives that are expressible in all things, yet limited to none of them: 'This is why, at the same time that sexuality is deployed over the physical surface, it makes us go from voice to speech and gathers together every word into an esoteric whole and in a sexual history which will not be designated, manifested, or signified by these words, but which rather will be coextensive and co-substantial with them' (LoS, 246, 288).

In response to the claim that objects and their meaning are all we need to explain life, Deleuze follows psychoanalytic studies of sexuality to show that objects and meaning arrive at an unsatisfactory ground in sexuality unless we move to another level of language which introduces pure significance or value alongside chains of denotations, meanings and manifestations. This can seem highly speculative until we realise that Deleuze's point is that cycles of explanations work through analogies until they reach the ground analogy (sexuality, in the case of psychoanalysis). However, this ground itself requires an explanation for its function as ground, that is how it sets the explanations and analogies in movement, how it explains novelty in everything it supports. For example, in biological explanations this ground could be the struggle for survival (which would be very close to Deleuze's point about sexuality). In Spinoza's metaphysics it would be the conatus. In Nietzsche's it would be will to power. Even in common-sense accounts, such a limit point could be defined in common sense itself and its infinite adaptability and resistance to positive definition. Deleuze's further point is then that all these limits must share a form explaining their resistance to identification and sameness, since once they are identified in this way, they lose the flexibility required to explain new differences in the chain of analogies. This then leads to notions of pure events as conditions for openness and genetic potentials explaining change and novelty.

Is not all this too far removed from thought in its relation to everyday things and questions? Does not Deleuze lose his way in the thickets of psychoanalysis? Is his work not fatally dated by it? Such objections miss the point of Deleuze's philosophy as constructed in *Logic of Sense*. His work is a study of the attraction but also necessary failure of thought based on common sense and the everyday. It therefore looks for the unconscious series conditioning the everyday even in its desire for – sense of, satisfaction in – the falsely simplified quotidian *irrespective of how much 'natural' complexity is layered over it.* His counter-questions determine a problem for philosophy:

1. What do common sense and the everyday presuppose?
2. What is the cost of associating thought with technical practical problems rather than the deep motivations and desires behind any thinking?

3. Which accounts of thought allow us to understand its pervasiveness and potential, but also its terrible capacity to go wrong and end in pain, violence and despair?

The study of phantasms and of sexuality allows for an entry into the genesis and potential of thought in its relation to language and to bodily mixtures, without pretending that thought can work as an external calculator or possibility capable of resolving problems rather than working within them. It shows how thought is a process within other series, but more importantly, how thought is essential to the potential for novelty and for drawing the most pure, that is the least wounding, side of events out of their actual occurrence in damaging mixtures of bodies: 'This something else is that which comes from the *other* desexualised surface, from the metaphysical surface, when we finally pass from speech to the verb, when we compose a unique verb in the pure infinitive with all assembled words' (LoS, 248, 289).

6

Conclusion: on method and metaphysics

> As in this example the word 'solidity' was used wrongly and it seemed
> that we had shown that nothing really was solid, just in this way, in stating
> our puzzles about the *general vagueness* of sense-experience, and about
> the flux of all phenomena, we are using the words 'flux' and 'vagueness'
> wrongly, in a typically metaphysical way, namely without an antithesis;
> whereas in their correct and everyday use vagueness is opposed to clear-
> ness, flux to stability, inaccuracy to accuracy, and *problem* to *solution*. The
> very word 'problem', one might say, is misapplied when used for our
> philosophical troubles. These difficulties, as long as they are seen as
> problems, are tantalizing, and appear insoluble.
>
> (Wittgenstein, 1972: 45–6)

So what of Deleuze's baroque and ever-shifting metaphysical structures, built not on firm foundations, but on problems without
solutions, on untamed paradox? The above passage, taken from
Wittgenstein's preliminary studies for his *Philosophical Investigations*,
captures one of the most powerful external objections to Deleuze's
work in *Logic of Sense*. Is it not embarked on an impossible and
misleading enterprise? Aren't its metaphysical constructions self-
defeating, or at least poor aesthetic creations rather than philosophy,
not only through their desire to place reality 'against the background
of the eternal', but also in language without a stable grammar and set
of rules (Wittgenstein, 1980: 75)? Aren't the concepts of pure difference and pure events words broaching no antithesis and hence use-
lessly detached from 'everyday use'? In selecting insoluble problems
and paradoxes as the genetic core for his philosophy, does not
Deleuze choose insolubility? Had he simply not made such a choice,
wouldn't his philosophy have found a reliable ground in everyday

experience? Given this ground, what then would be the purpose and value of the extraordinary and complex constructions described throughout this book? In short, in *Logic of Sense* does Deleuze not show his true colours as the constructor of the latest and perhaps most obscure metaphysics: 'the foundations of an abstruse philosophy, which seems to have hitherto served only as a shelter to superstition, and a cover to absurdity and error!' (Hume, 1975: 16)?

Deleuze was well aware of these objections, not only in the format laid out by Hume in his critique of abstruse philosophy, but also as part of an inheritance from Wittgenstein and ordinary language philosophy. In his first book, on Hume, he inverts the priority given to epistemology and to scepticism in many interpretations of Hume's work in favour of the moral relation of passions to principles, where the human subject is constituted by these principles and grounded on imagination (*Empirisme et subjectivité*, pp. 143–4). This is a constant quality of Deleuze's readings of other philosophers: he is not solely concerned to counter or disprove, but rather to divine how a philosophy crosses the ages and offers new potential despite its time-bound aspects. Divination is accompanied by re-enactment and the hidden resources of an earlier work are dramatised in a different way in order to release them. Together, divination and theatrical representation – for this is what is meant by replaying and counter-actualisation – form Deleuze's moral position. He teaches us to sense, represent, express and thereby donate, by experimenting with events as they occur in series, in order to be worthy of them. He could have chosen a foe in Hume, in his commitment to common utility and in the conservatism of his historical experimental method, but instead a different but consistent Hume was uncovered, one that was already there, not in historically identified forms, but rather in the conditions for novelty and change in his thought.

Logic of Sense can be read as a continuation of this transfer from knowledge and understanding of nature constituted by given facts to nature as constituted by changing relations. This does not imply a concession to abstract and non-empirical thought. Deleuze's method is wholly experimental, but where the boundaries of the experiment are loosened in the extreme in order to exploit its creative side: experimentation as novel and open creativity rather than as repetitive confirmation or particular disproof. This method implies a change in the approach to the given, reflecting its alteration from a source of solid and identifiable evidence, to an inherent fluidity and change. Deleuze's higher empiricism is therefore a form of experimentation with the conditions for changing relations, when series (such as habits) encounter events (such as shocks to a system). The nature of these events and relations calls for kinds of philosophical structures that do not prejudge becoming out of existence at the outset. This is why Deleuze is so profoundly antipathetic to common sense and to appeals to physical and psychological concreteness, because such apparently innocent and reasonable gestures carry the doom of any primary differences within them. If there is a promise to strike fear in Deleuzian creators it is 'Seek, and you will find' (Matthew 7: 7), for his empiricism must not carry the objective of a search for a desired identity over to its result. Instead, if anything is to be confirmed at all, it is that no fixed objective can reflect the necessarily changing nature of reality. (*Always seek difference and, with luck, ye shall not find it*). The deep meanings of search, creation and experiment must therefore change from verification or falsification to innovation; neither the establishment of truths nor their rejection, but rather an affirmation of new transitory ones. This is not to be foolhardy or to reject structure and continuity: both are necessary conditions for Deleuze's empiricism. It is to be radically critical with respect to intellectual and emotional obstacles to creativity in order to be worthy of the novelty of events.

Deleuze's philosophy of language, constructed by deploying literary insights on philosophical and linguistic theories, is an example of this empiricism. It could be argued that language should be discovered in its everyday use, or through experiments mimicking those of the natural sciences or through a dialectical search for repeated patterns and counterfactuals, where theories stand and fall alongside research in the fields of anthropology, psychology and now neuroscience. None of these methods could alone answer the problem Deleuze is tackling, as defined by knots of different kinds of questions. What explains the capacity of language to mutate beyond fixed grammar? How can language carry emotional significance to the point of expressing and generating novel significance and sense? What would this language have to be like in order to stand as a condition for all events, not as a necessary condition for their occurrence, but rather as a condition after the event where all events are said to be expressible in language? How can paradoxes be generated in language? And how is it that these paradoxes produce value or sense and play powerful roles in the generation of new words and ideal structures? The right experimental fields for such questions are also literary, rather than strictly the sanitised everyday of a self-selecting sect, or the narrow strangled and aspic-preserved relics of language laboratories, or the desperate search for sameness across cultures and individuals. The right experimental method is to take as comprehensive a view as possible of established structures and theories and to test them experimentally and dialectically against problems also produced in literature and played out in lives, not defined with an eye on generality, but with all senses tuned to the singular. The right justification for such experimental constructions is pragmatic. (*How to donate better next time? How can the experiment remain an event for others?*) Thus Deleuze expresses a new experience of the sign in language from Proust. (*Do you feel it?*) He develops a different definition of sense to fit these signs. (*But what does it imply for definitions of denotation, signification and manifestation?*) He then experiments with the many paradoxes and problems the new structure releases through other systems and ossifying common sense. (*How can these be made different and better?*) This may not look like experiments according to popular images of them, or in logically consistent philosophical approximations of them, or in the legal frameworks necessary for the regulation of professions. They are experimental though, if that is to be opposed to abstract reflection and detached speculation. They are experiments coming after the realisation of the dangers of restricted claims to empirical method, particularly where there is already a presumption of identical form. To give this method a simple formulation: seek conditions for change through adjunctions that bring difference into systems approaching stasis. Or even more simply: 'and, differently . . .'

Against Wittgenstein's wariness of the use of problems in philosophy, Deleuze responds that it is only through problems and paradoxes that we retain and develop our ways of thinking about the profoundly changeable nature of reality. Problems are then not obstacles to thinking accurately and clearly about what we encounter in the world, or more precisely about how serial processes are altered by events. They are the resource and the guide for that thinking as something experimental and bound to renew and adapt as its mobile topic slips, cracks, rends, divides and assembles in new ways. Solutions become the real obstacle because they encourage a divide between thought and the dynamic processes within and around it. They entice us into a comfortable world of concrete fictions and resolutions imposed upon a reality of perpetually shifting relations. They impoverish the world without reflecting its reality. Wittgenstein worries about the spread of general uncertainty through the philosophical taste for problems, but he overstresses the negative connotations of uncertainty in a desire to protect the everyday from perplexity and sceptical doubt. Uncertainty, in the multiplication of perspectives on a reality itself multiple and always changing, is far from negative if accompanied by a constant and generous experimentation – as in the uncertainty of a child in the presence of an unfamiliar object and perceptions. What ought we to prefer: accurate, complicated and manifold enquiries or the banishment of the best tools for such enquiries because they do not favour the passing and already faded certainties of restricted groups?

One of the rare references to Wittgenstein – in truth, to his disciples – makes these points explicit in the context of events. It occurs in one of Deleuze's later books, The *Fold: Leibniz and the Baroque,* where he discusses Whitehead's philosophy of events:

> [Whitehead's philosophy] is provisionally the last great Anglo-American philosophy, just before the disciples of Wittgenstein spread their mists, their sufficiency and their terror. An event is not only 'a man is crushed': the great pyramid is an event, and its duration for an hour, 30 minutes, 5 minutes . . ., a passage of Nature, a view of God. What are the conditions for an event so that all is event? The event produces itself in a chaos, in a chaotic multiplicity, under the condition that a sort of sieve intervenes.
>
> (*Le pli*, p. 103)

Everything from *Logic of Sense* on the event is recapped and taken up anew here. There is the critique of the illusion of semblance and sameness: mists carried by the complacent sufficiency of common sense rolling out over an essentially changeable reality. There is the ever-present belief in the priority of passions: in this case, the powerful terror carried through appeals to an apparently easily accessed everyday, against careful but arduous and only fleetingly and obliquely accessible constructions. All is event, rather than the restriction of events to 'happenings-to'. Ubiquitous infinitives must be deployed against occasional gerunds. It is how you express an infinitive such as 'to love' and thereby how you change its multiple relations for all rather than the occurrence of the same loving to everyone. Yet if all is multiple, this is only on condition that this primary multiplicity works through and with a secondary but necessary series of transient identities. You can have your everyday, but others must have their different ones. The everyday is part of the event, but we must not make false claims either for its sufficiency, or for its metaphysical innocence, or for its commonality.

Deleuze returns to these questions on metaphysics and method in Appendix II of *Logic of Sense*, on Lucretius. He draws a series of proposals for a philosophical naturalism resistant to presuppositions of identity: 'The products of nature cannot be separated from a diversity that is essential to them' (LoS, 267, 307). Is this to set up a straightforward opposition between two metaphysical positions: one settled on sameness, the other on difference? No. The lesson of *Logic of Sense* is that diversity is experienced and encountered in language, thought, bodies and ideas. It appears in creative experiments when we consider events as they occur in series. So it is not that the next event is guaranteed to be different, it is rather that the current one is multiple and calls for explanation as differential movement through many-faceted series. Deleuze's metaphysics is then not drawn from outside nature but rather deduced from within it. It is no metaphysics at all, if this is to be a philosophical insult or a reason to flee complexity for the reassurance of illusory identity. Life is diverse and calls for philosophical structures adequate to its potential for change, novelty and renewal:

> There is no world which is not manifest in the variety of its parts, places, rivers and the species that inhabit it. There is no individual absolutely identical to another individual; no calf which is not recognisable to its mother; no two shellfish or grains of wheat which are indiscernible. There is no body composed of homogeneous parts – neither plant nor stream which does not imply a diversity of matter or heterogeneity of elements, where each animal species, in turn, may find the nourishment appropriate to it. From these three points of view we deduce the diversity of worlds themselves: worlds are innumerable, often of different species, sometimes similar, and always composed of heterogeneous elements.
>
> (LoS, 266, 308)

Bibliography

NOTES

1. The excellent research source, webdeleuze.com, has a superb Deleuze bibliography by Timothy S. Murphy, 'Revised Bibliography of the Works of Gilles Deleuze', at: http://www.webdeleuze.com.
2. This book has given a broad approach to Deleuze's thought which risks underplaying aspects of Deleuze's thought due to a desire to enter in debates with many different traditions, some of which do not share the comprehensiveness of Deleuze's intellectual background. I want to draw readers' attention to Lecercle (2002), Kerslake (2007), DeLanda (2002) and Smith (2003, 2006 and 2007) for excellent contrasting studies of Deleuze and, respectively, language, the unconscious, science and mathematics – see also Duffy (2006) for the most up-to-date research on this topic. Research on Deleuze is now served by a new international journal *Deleuze Studies*, edited by Ian Buchanan.

WORKS BY GILLES DELEUZE

Empirisme et subjectivité: Essai sur la Nature humaine selon Hume (Paris: Presses universitaires de France, 1953). Boundas, C., *Empiricism and Subjectivity: An Essay on Hume's Theory of Human Nature* (New York: Columbia University Press, 1991).

Nietzsche et la philosophie (Paris: Presses universitaires de France, 1962). Trans. Tomlinson, H., *Nietzsche and Philosophy* (New York: Columbia University Press, 1983).

La Philosophie critique de Kant: Doctrine des facultés (Paris: Presses universitaires de France, 1963). Trans. Tomlinson, H. and Habberjam, B., *Kant's Critical Philosophy: The Doctrine of the Faculties* (Minneapolis, MN: University of Minnesota Press, 1984).

Bibliography

Le Bergsonisme (Paris: Presses universitaires de France, 1966). Trans. Tomlinson, H. and Habberjam, B., *Bergsonism* (New York: Zone Books, 1990).

'Gilbert Simondon. – *L'Individu et sa genèse physico-biologique*' (book review), in *Revue philosophique de la France et de l'étranger*, CLVI: 1–3 (janvier–mars 1966), pp. 115–18. Trans. Ramirez, I., 'Review of Gilbert Simondon's *L'Individu et sa genèse physico-biologique* (1966)', *Pli, The Warwick Journal of Philosophy*, Vol. 12 (2001), pp. 43–9.

Présentation de Sacher-Masoch (Paris: Éditions de Minuit, 1967). Trans. McNeil, J., *Masochism* (New York: Zone Books, 1989).

Différence et répétition (Paris: Presses universitaires de France, 1968). Trans. Patton, P., *Difference and Repetition* (New York: Columbia University Press, 1994).

Spinoza et le problème de l'expression (Paris: Éditions de Minuit, 1968). Trans. Joughin, M., *Expressionism in Philosophy: Spinoza* (New York: Zone Books, 1990).

Logique du sens (Paris: Éditions de Minuit, 1969). Trans. Lester, M. and Stivale, C., *The Logic of Sense* (New York: Columbia University Press, 1990).

Proust et les signes (Paris: Presses universitaires de France, 1970). Trans. Howard, R., *Proust and Signs* (New York: George Braziller, 1972).

and Félix Guattari, *Capitalisme et schizophrénie tome 1: l'Anti-Oedipe* (Paris: Éditions de Minuit, 1972). Trans. Hurley, R., Seem, M. and Lane, H., *Anti-Oedipus: Capitalism and Schizophrenia* (New York: Viking Press, 1977).

and Félix Guattari, *Kafka: Pour une litterature mineure* (Paris: Éditions de Minuit, 1975). Trans. Polan, D., *Kafka: Toward a Minor Literature* (Minneapolis, MN: University of Minnesota Press, 1986).

and Claire Parnet, *Dialogues* (Paris: Flammarion, 1977). Trans. Tomlinson, H. and Habberjam, B., *Dialogues* (New York: Columbia University Press, 1987).

and Félix Guattari, *Capitalisme et schizophrénie tome 2: Mille plateaux* (Paris: Éditions de Minuit, 1980). Trans. Massumi, B., *A Thousand Plateaus: Capitalism and Schizophrenia* (Minneapolis, MN: University of Minnesota Press, 1987).

'Ontologie-Ethique', Cours Vincennes (21/12/1980), at: http://www.webdeleuze.com/php/texte.php?cle=190&groupe=Spinoza&langue=2 (accessed 2 July 2007).

Spinoza: Philosophie pratique (Paris: Éditions de Minuit, 1981). Trans. Hurley, R., *Spinoza: Practical Philosophy* (San Francisco: City Lights, 1988).

Francis Bacon: Logique de la Sensation (Paris: Éditions de la Différence, 1981). Trans. Smith, D., *Francis Bacon: the Logic of Sensation* (Minneapolis, MN: University of Minnesota Press, 2003).

Cinéma-1: L'Image-mouvement (Paris: Éditions de Minuit, 1983). Trans. Tomlinson, H. and Habberjam, B., *Cinema-1: The Movement-Image* (Minneapolis, MN: University of Minnesota Press, 1986).

Cinéma-2: L'Image-temps (Paris: Éditions de Minuit, 1985). Trans. Tomlinson, H. and Galeta, R., *Cinema-2: The Time-Image* (Minneapolis, MN: University of Minnesota Press, 1989).

Foucault (Paris: Éditions de Minuit, 1986). Trans. Hand, S., *Foucault* (Minneapolis, MN: University of Minnesota Press, 1988).

Le Pli: Leibniz et le Baroque (Paris: Éditions de Minuit, 1988). Trans. Conley, T., *The Fold: Leibniz and the Baroque* (Minneapolis, MN: University of Minnesota Press, 1993).

Pourparlers 1972–1990 (Paris: Éditions de Minuit, 1990). Trans. Joughin, M., *Negotiations 1972–1990* (New York: Columbia University Press, 1995).

and Félix Guattari, *Qu'est-ce que la philosophie?* (Paris: Éditions de Minuit, 1991). Trans. Tomlinson, H. and Burchell, G., *What Is Philosophy?* (New York: Columbia University Press, 1994).

'L'épuisé', in Beckett (1992: 57–106).

Boundas, Constantin V. (ed.), *The Deleuze Reader* (New York: Columbia University Press, 1993).

Critique et clinique (Paris: Éditions de Minuit, 1993). Trans. Smith, D. and Greco, A., *Essays Critical and Clinical* (Minneapolis, MN: University of Minnesota Press, 1997).

Et al. 'Gilles Deleuze', *Philosophie*, no. 47 (1995) (includes the important last essay by Deleuze, 'L'Immanence: une vie . . .')

L'Île déserte et autres textes, textes et entretiens 1953–1974 (Paris: Minuit, 2002). Trans. Taormina, M., *Desert Islands and Other Texts* (New York: Semiotext(e), 2003).

Deux régimes de fous, textes et entretiens 1975–1995 (Paris: Éditions de Minuit, 2003).

'Comment est-ce que je vais sortir de ma sphère des possibles?', Cours Vincennes (17/05/1983), at: http://webdeleuze.com (accessed 28 June 2007).

'Review of Hyppolite's Logique et existence' http://www.generation-online.org/p/fpdeleuze6.htm (accessed 28 June 2007).

SELECTED WORKS ON GILLES DELEUZE

Alliez, Éric (ed.), *Gilles Deleuze: une vie philosophique* (Paris: Presses universitaires de France, 1998).

Alliez, Éric, *The Signature of the World: What Is Deleuze and Guattari's Philosophy?* (London: Athlone, 2004).

Ansell Pearson, Keith (ed.), *Deleuze and Philosophy: The Difference Engineer* (London: Routledge, 1977).

Ansell Pearson, Keith, *Germinal Life: The Difference and Repetition of Gilles Deleuze* (London: Routledge, 1999).

Badiou, Alain, *Deleuze: La Clameur de l'Être* (Paris: Hachette, 1997). Trans. Burchill, L., *Deleuze: The Clamour of Being* (Minneapolis, MN: University of Minnesota Press, 2000).

Beistegui, Miguel de, *Truth and Genesis: Philosophy as Differential Ontology* (Bloomington, IN: Indiana University Press, 2004).

Bell, Jeffrey, *Philosophy at the Edge of Chaos: Gilles Deleuze and the Philosophy of Difference* (Toronto: University of Toronto Press, 2006).

Bogue, Ronald, *Deleuze and Guattari* (London: Routledge, 1989).

Boundas, Constantin (ed.), *Deleuze and Philosophy* (Edinburgh University Press, 2006).

Boundas, Constantin and Olkowski, D. (eds), *Deleuze and the Theatre of Philosophy* (London: Routledge, 1994).

Buchanan, Ian, *Deleuzism: A Metacommentary* (Durham, NC: Duke University Press).

Buchanan, Ian and Colebrook, Claire, *Deleuze and Feminist Theory* (Edinburgh: Edinburgh University Press, 2000).

Buchanan, Ian and Marks, John, *Deleuze and Literature* (Edinburgh: Edinburgh University Press, 2001).

Colebrook, Claire, *Gilles Deleuze* (London: Routledge, 2002).

Colebrook, Claire, *Understanding Deleuze* (London: Allen & Unwin, 2003).

Colebrook, Claire, *Deleuze: A Guide for the Perplexed* (London: Continuum, 2006).

DeLanda, Manuel, *Intensive Science and Virtual Philosophy* (London: Continuum, 2002).

Due, Reidar Andreas, *Deleuze* (Cambridge: Polity, 2007).

Duffy, Simon (ed.), *Virtual Mathematics* (Manchester: Clinamen, 2006).

Goodchild, Philip, *Gilles Deleuze and the Question of Philosophy* (London: Associated University Press, 1994).

Goodchild, Philip, *Deleuze and Guatarri: An Introduction to the Politics of Desire* (London: Sage, 1996).

Hardt, Michael, *Gilles Deleuze: An Apprenticeship in Philosophy* (London: UCL, 1993).

Holland Eugene, *Deleuze and Guattari's Anti-Oedipus: An Introduction to Schizoanalysis* (London: Routledge, 1999).

Howie, Gillian, *Deleuze and Spinoza* (Basingstoke: Palgrave, 2002).

Kennedy, Barbara, *Deleuze and Cinema* (Edinburgh: Edinburgh University Press, 2001).

Kerslake, Christian, *Deleuze and the Unconscious* (London: Continuum, 2007).

Lambert, Gregg, *Who's Afraid of Deleuze and Guattari* (New York: Continuum, 2006).

Lecercle, Jean-Jacques, *Deleuze and Language* (Basingstoke: Palgrave Macmillan, 2002).

Marks, John, *Gilles Deleuze: Vitalism and Multiplicity* (London: Pluto Press, 1998).

May, Todd, *Gilles Deleuze: A General Introduction* (Cambridge: Cambridge University Press, 2005).

Massumi, Brian, *A User's Guide to Capitalism and Schizophrenia* (Cambridge, MA: MIT Press, 1992).

Olkowski, Dorothea, *The Universal (in the Realm of the Sensible)* (Edinburgh: Edinburgh University Press, 2007).

O'Sullivan, Simon, *Art Encounters Deleuze and Guattari: Thought Beyond Representation* (Basingstoke: Palgrave Macmillan, 2005).

Parr, Adrian, *The Deleuze Dictionary* (Edinburgh: Edinburgh University Press, 2005).

Patton, Paul (ed.), *Deleuze: A Critical Reader* (Oxford: Blackwell, 1996).

Patton, Paul, *Deleuze and the Political* (London: Routledge, 2000).

Patton, Paul and Protevi, John (eds), *Between Deleuze and Derrida* (London: Continuum, 2003).

Powell, Anna, *Deleuze and Horror Film* (Edinburgh: Edinburgh University Press, 2005).

Protevi, John, *Political Physics: Deleuze, Derrida and the Body Politic* (London: Continuum, 2002).

Rajchman, John, *The Deleuze Connections* (Cambridge, MA: MIT Press, 2000).

Rodowick, D. N., *Gilles Deleuze's Time Machine* (Durham, NC: Duke University Press, 1997).

Smith, Daniel W., 'Mathematics and the theory of multiplicities: Badiou and Deleuze revisited', *Southern Journal of Philosophy*, Vol. XLI (2003), pp. 411–49.

Smith, Daniel W., 'Axiomatics and problematics as two modes of formalisation: Deleuze's epistemology of mathematics', in Duffy (2006 145–68).

Smith, Daniel W., 'The conditions of the new', *Deleuze Studies*, Vol. 1, no. 1 (2007), pp. 1–21.

Spinoza, Baruch, *The Ethics and Other Works* (Princeton, NJ: Princeton University Press, 1994).

Stivale, Charles J. (ed.), *Gilles Deleuze: Key Concepts* (Stocksfield: Acumen, 2005).

Toscano, Alberto, *The Theatre of Production: Philosophy and Individuation between Kant and Deleuze* (Basingstoke: Palgrave Macmillan, 2006).

Williams, James, *Gilles Deleuze's Difference and Repetition: A Critical Introduction and Guide* (Edinburgh: Edinburgh University Press, 2003).

Williams, James, *The Transversal Thought of Gilles Deleuze: Encounters and Influences* (Manchester: Clinamen, 2005a).

Williams, James, *Understanding Poststructuralism* (Stocksfield: Acumen, 2005b).

Žižek, Slavoj, *Organs without Bodies: Deleuze and Consequences* (London: Routledge, 2003).

Zourabichvili, François, *Gilles Deleuze: une philosophie de l'événement* (Paris: Presses universitaires de France, 1996).

OTHER WORKS

Allen, Woody, *Annie Hall* (1977).

Almodóvar, Pedro, *Todo Sobre mi Madre* (*All About My Mother*) (1999).

Aquinas, Thomas, 'Tantum ergo sacramentum' (hymn), in *Thesaurus Precum Latinarum*, at http://www.preces-latinae.org/thesaurus/Euch/Tantum.html (accessed 1 July 2007).

Armstrong, David, *Universals: An Opinionated Introduction* (London: HarperCollins, 1989).

Ashes since 1877, The, 334notout.com, at: http://www.334notout.com/bodyline/main.htm (accessed 29 June 2007).

Badiou, Alain, *Logiques des mondes* (Paris: Seuil, 2006).

Beckett, Samuel, *Quad et trio du fantôme*, trans. E. Fournier (Paris: Éditions de Minuit, 1992).

Beevor, Antony, *Stalingrad* (London: Penguin, 1999).

Bennett, Jonathan, *Events and Their Names* (Oxford: Clarendon, 1988).

Bible (New King James Version) (Nashville, TN: Nelson, 1993).

Bousquet, Joë, *Lettres à Poisson d'Or* (Paris: Gallimard, 1967).

Bousquet, Joë, *Le meneur de lune* (Paris: Albin Michel, 1979).

Bousquet, Joë, *Les Capitales ou Jean Duns Scot à Jean Paulhan* (Paris: Deyrolle, 1999).

Camus, Albert, *The Myth of Sisyphus* (London: Penguin, 2005).

Carroll, Lewis, *Alice's Adventures in Wonderland* (London: Penguin, 2003a).

Carroll, Lewis, *Through the Looking Glass* (London: Penguin, 2003b).

Casati, Roberto and Varzi, Achille, *Events* (Aldershot: Dartmouth, 1996).

Cheever, John, 'Goodbye, my brother', in *The Stories of John Cheever* (New York: Vintage, 1990), pp. 11–34.

Coen, Joel and Coen, Ethan, *The Hudsucker Proxy* (1994).

Conan Doyle, Arthur, *A Study in Scarlet* (London: Penguin, 2001).

cummings, e e, *Complete Poems: 1904–1962* (New York: Liveright Books, 1994).

Davidson, Donald, *Essays on Actions and Events* (Oxford: Clarendon, 1980).

Dennett, Daniel, *Freedom Evolves* (London: Penguin, 2004).

Dumas, Alexandre, *The Count of Monte Cristo* (Ware: Wordsworth, 1997).

Fitzgerald, F. Scott, *The Crack-Up* (New York: New Directions, 1993).

Fitzgerald, F. Scott, *Tender is the Night* (London: Penguin, 2001).

Hegel, G. W. F., *Phenomenology of Spirit*, trans. A. V. Miller (Oxford: University Press, 1977).

Hugo Victor, *Les Misérables* (London: Penguin, 1982).

Hull, David and Van Regenmortel, Marc, *Promises and Limits of Reductionism in the Biomedical Sciences* (Hoboken, NJ: Wiley, 2002).

Hume, David, *Enquiries Concerning Human Understanding and Concerning the Principles of Morals* (Oxford: Oxford University Press, 1975).

Husserl, Edmund, *Ideas Pertaining to a Pure Phenomenology and to Phenomenological Philosophy: First Book* (Dordrecht: Kluwer, 1983).

Husserl, Edmund, *Cartesian Meditations* (Dordrecht: Kluwer, 1999).

Husserl, Edmund, *Logical Investigations (Vols 1 and 2)* (London: Routledge, 2001).

Hyppolite, Jean, *Logique et existence* (Paris: Presses universitaires de France, 1952).

Kant, Immanuel, *Prolegomena to Any Future Metaphysics* (Manchester: Manchester University Press, 1953).

Kant, Immanuel, *Critique of Pure Reason* (Cambridge: Cambridge University Press, 1999).

Keegan, John, *The First World War* (New York: Vintage, 2000).

Kim, Jaegwon, 'Events as property exemplifications', in Casati and Varzi (1996: 117–35).

Kubrick, Stanley and Herr, Michael, *Full Metal Jacket* (1987).

Lacan, Jacques, 'Séminaire' (15/08/1956), at: http://www.ecole-lacanienne.net/documents/1956-08-15.doc (accessed 3 July 2007).

Lautman, Albert, '*Essai sur les notions de structure et d'existence en mathématiques*', in *Les mathématiques, les idées et le réel physique* (Paris: Vrin, 2006).

Leibniz, G. W. *Monadology*, in R. S. Woolhouse and R. Franks (eds), *Philosophical Texts* (Oxford: Oxford University Press, 1998).

Lévi-Strauss, Claude, *Tristes tropiques* (Paris: Pocket, 2001).

Littré, Paul-Émile, *Dictionnaire de la langue française, en sept tomes* (Paris: Hachette, 1872).

Melville, Herman, *Bartleby and the Lightening Rod Man* (London: Penguin, 1995).

Monty Python, *Monty Python and the Holy Grail* (1975).

Morahan, Christopher, *Clockwise* (1986).

Panofsky, Erwin, *Meaning in the Visual Arts* (Chicago: University of Chicago Press, 1983).

Péguy, Charles, *Clio* (Paris: Gallimard, 1932).

Price, Lucien, *Dialogues of Alfred North Whitehead* (Jaffrey, NH: Nonpareil, 2001).

Proust, Marcel, *In Search of Lost Time* (6 vols) (New York: Modern Library, 1998).

Quine, W. V. O. 'Events and reification', in Casati and Varzi (1996: 107–16).

Sartre, Jean Paul, *Saint Genet: Actor and Martyr* (New York: Pantheon Books, 1983).

Shakespeare, William, *Romeo and Juliet* (London: Penguin, 2007).

Spinoza, Baruch, *A Spinoza Reader: The Ethics and Other Works*, ed. E. M. Curley (Princeton, NJ: Princeton University Press, 1994).

Stanton, Andrew and Unkrich, Lee, *Finding Nemo* (2003).

Steinbeck, John, 'The harvest gypsies: squatters camps', in S. Shillinglaw and J. J. Benson (eds), *Of Men and Their Making: The Selected Nonfiction of John Steinbeck* (London: Allen Lane, 2002: 78–82).

Thompson, J. Lee, *Ice-Cold in Alex* (1958).

Thomson, Judith Jarvis, 'The time of a killing', in Casati and Varzi (1996: 285–302).

Tournier, Michel, *Vendredi ou les limbes du pacifique* (Paris· Gallimard, 1972).

Verne, Jules, *Twenty Thousand Leagues Under the Sea* (London: Penguin, 1994).

Wilde, Oscar, *The Picture of Dorian Gray* (Harmondsworth: Penguin, 1949).

Williams, Donald Carey, 'The elements of being', shortened version of 'On the elements of being', *Review of Metaphysics*, Vol. 7 (1953), pp. 3–18, 171–92; reprinted at: http://www.hist-analytic.org/WILLIAMS3.htm (accessed 29 June 2007).

Williamson, Timothy and Graff, Delia, *Vagueness* (Aldershot: Dartmouth, 2002).

Wittgenstein, Ludwig, *Philosophical Investigations*, trans. G. E. M. Anscombe (Oxford: Blackwell, 1969).

Wittgenstein, Ludwig, *The Blue and Brown Books* (Oxford: Blackwell, 1972).

Wittgenstein, Ludwig, *Culture and Value*, trans. P. Winch (Oxford: Blackwell, 1980).

Woolf, Virginia, *Mrs Dalloway* (London: Grafton Books, 1976).

Woolf, Virginia, *To the Lighthouse* (London: Grafton Books, 1977).

Index

216